The Rough Guide to

Internet
Radio

www.roughguides.com

Rough Guide Credits

Text editors: Peter Shapiro, Jonathan Buckley
Series editor: Mark Ellingham
Production: Helen Prior, Julia Bovis

Publishing Information

This edition published June 2002 by Rough Guides Ltd,
62–70 Shorts Gardens, London WC2H 9AH

Distributed by the Penguin Group

Penguin Books Ltd, 80 Strand, London WC2R ORL
Penguin Putnam Inc., 375 Hudson Street, New York 10014, USA
Penguin Books Australia Ltd, 487 Maroondah Highway,
PO Box 257, Ringwood, Victoria 3134, Australia
Penguin Books Canada Ltd, 10 Alcorn Avenue,
Toronto, Ontario, Canada M4V 1E4
Penguin Books (NZ) Ltd, 182–190 Wairau Road,
Auckland 10, New Zealand

Printed in Spain by GraphyCems

© L.A. Heberlein, 2002
400pp, includes index
A catalogue record for this book is available from the British Library.

ISBN 1-85828-961-0

The Rough Guide to

Internet Radio

by
L.A. Heberlein

ROUGH GUIDES

Contents

Part I Tuning in to Internet Radio

Part II The Directory

contents

contents

contents

contents

Part III Becoming a Broadcaster

Introduction

This book is a guide to the most interesting radio programs in the world. Such a guide was never necessary before, because you couldn't *get* all the radio stations in the world, only the dozen or so in your town. Now the Internet, as it has changed so much else, is changing that. If you are one of the millions of people who have already checked out Internet radio, you know what an astonishing variety of great radio is out there. You could get lost forever exploring it all. This book is designed to help you find radio you love, and reduce the time you spend stumbling around looking for it. If you have never tried Internet radio, this book is also a getting-started guide, showing you, step by step, how to get connected.

The potential of Internet radio is amazing. Every day more stations come onto the Net, every day their streams improve, every day they figure out how to make their web sites more helpful to listeners. Every day you can find some great new radio program you never knew was out there, and fall in love with radio all over again. Radio is changing into something completely new, more powerful, more various, and more useful. The change is not complete. Those of us lucky to live in high-bandwidth neighborhoods feel it first, while computer users in the United Kingdom, for example, not only have limited bandwidth, but mostly still pay for it by the minute, holding back the day when it becomes practical for use as radio. But if the timing of the change is yet to be seen, its shape is already clear.

The one great limitation constraining radio throughout its history has been geography. Except for a few hobbyist "DXers," trying to catch skipping signals in the night, listeners have been mostly limited to radio stations in their own neighborhoods. You may remember a great radio station in the town where you used to live, or one you heard on vacation, but you could never listen to them from where you are now. Well now you can. That is exactly what Internet radio allows.

So it is no wonder that both the number of listeners and the number of stations on Internet radio is exploding. *Every day*, 200,000 new listeners tune in. Most broadcast stations have found their way to the Internet by now, so if you remember a program you once heard in Paris, it is probably on the Net. Far more exciting than the sheer numbers is the breadth and depth of the programming. Freed from the economic and legal restraints that limit what is on the airwaves, Internet radio offers something for nearly everyone. A few examples:

▸▸ An all-Beatles radio stream

▸▸ A program devoted to Frank Zappa

▸▸ Talk radio from Israel, in Hebrew and English

▸▸ Experimental music derived from signals received by radio telescopes

▸▸ A jukebox stuffed with every kind of Indian music you could imagine

▸▸ A station devoted to classic radio programs of the 1930s and '40s

▸▸ The latest news from the world of science fiction

▸▸ A great student station from France

▸▸ Dance music from Belgium, Colombia, the Caribbean, and Asia

Whether you're interested in learning Portuguese, scoping out the latest in African music before it hits the stores, or getting first-hand news from the latest flash point of confrontation, there is a radio station broadcasting live right now to bring you just what you're looking for. And in addition to broadcast stations that extend their signal over the Internet, the ease of Internet radio has also led to a boom of Net-only stations, such as the poetry-intensive station a professor hosts from his office in an English department.

Net-only stations avoid the government regulations that have governed broadcast stations. The broadcast spectrum is limited. It is parceled out by government agencies to a limited number of applicants. In many areas of the world, the Internet provides the only uncensored information. People who would stand very little chance of sustaining an airwave radio station – Zapatistas in Chiapas, Tamil rebels in Sri Lanka – have been able to establish a presence on the Internet. The Yugoslavia wars saw a battle for control of station B-92. B-92 began as a low-watt radio station for young people, but by the time the conflict flashed into world attention, it had become the center of opposition within Serbia, nearly the only public outlet not directly controlled by Serbian President Slobodan Milosevic. Milosevic's troops took over the station by force in April of 1999. When a government-sanitized version of B-92 went back on the air, the true B-92 went to the Internet, broadcasting its news and opinions at **www.b92.net**.

Besides requiring government permission, broadcasting a radio signal over the airwaves is technically and economically demanding. Putting out an Internet radio stream, on the other hand, is something anyone can do. So Internet radio, besides allowing you to hear your favorite radio stations even though you're not physically near them, and allowing repressed information to surface, also improves the producer/consumer ratio. Instead of a mass market consuming a radio product controlled by a few giant corporations, the Internet allows the very distinction between broadcaster and listener to disappear. Tens of thousands of people have put their own streams up. It's easy, and this book will show you how. Anyone who has ever harbored a desire to play DJ can now host their own radio show. And while it is true that not all amateur radio shows will be of lasting interest, much of the volunteer material is excellent, and it's all the result of some individual's passion.

One difficulty posed by the richness of the Internet is finding one's way. There is simply so much out there that it is easy to get overwhelmed by the flood of things you're not interested in, and give up before finding what you would appreciate. That's where this book will help. This is an annotated guide to the stations that are most dependable (so you don't waste your time trying to attach to a station with no bandwidth), most original, more individual, and most interesting, categorized by topic.

Before the guide is a section of the book explaining how to get started. It contains an overview of Internet radio software and step-by-step explanations of how to get the software working: where to download it, how to install it, how to configure it, and how to use it.

Following the guide is a section for those interested in becoming Internet radio broadcasters. Doing so is actually surprisingly easy.

The Changing Face of Radio

The morphing of radio into Internet radio is merely the latest stage in a history of continuing technological change that has led each radio generation to forge new, different, personal relationships with radio. In the beginning were amateur tinkers hunkered over crystal sets they had built themselves, scratching a wire whisker over a rock to bring in signals bouncing off the ionosphere in the night. The first commercial radio station, KDKA, in Pittsburgh, Pennsylvania, broadcast its first program November 6, 1920, announcing the returns in the Presidential election. (Warren G. Harding won). The amazingly rapid growth of radio was a phenomenon faster and bigger than anything seen before. The economic boom around radio was faster and relatively bigger than even the Internet boom of the late 1990s, creating giant corporations such as RCA out of thin air (so to speak) in no time at all. By 1933, 63 percent of U.S. households had radios, and families were sitting together in the living room to hear radio dramas, musical specials, and personal chats from the President of the United States. Radio stitched America together as it never had been before, everyone listening to the President's words for themselves, direct from his voice to their ears, live as he spoke them.

Boys growing up in small towns dreamed of becoming radio announcers. Ronald Reagan was one of them. He began his public career as a radio announcer, on Des Moines station WHO, broadcasting Chicago Cubs baseball games "by recreation." Because of the limited connectivity of the day, unless a baseball game was played locally, the radio announcer had to invent the story of the game from the scanty outline of a wire report: to imagine the pitcher shaking off the catcher's signal from the mound, the long wind-up, where the pitch came in, and how the batter swung at it. Forty years later, as President of the United States, Reagan was still telling tales of the night the wire went dead in the middle of the game and he had to wing it completely.

The transistor transformed radio, and transistor radios changed behavior as obviously as cell phones did later. Radios were formerly big things sitting on a table, plugged into an electrical socket. The transistor allowed people, particularly young people, to pick their music up and carry it with them – to listen to it by the *pool*. So rather than being a collective experience in the living room with the whole family, radio could become a private, very personal experience. You could take the transistor radio into your bedroom and listen to it, under the covers, after you were supposed to be asleep. Broadcasters soon found this new audience. Nowadays everyone is familiar with marketing demographics. People think of themselves as belonging to generations. This was not always so. Where did marketers first start slicing up the audience into age brackets, creating programming just for one slice, so they could market products just to them? It happened with teen radio in the 1950s. That was the first time a demographic was carved out and served. Business found the post-war baby boom, the largest age cohort ever seen, with unprecedented disposable income, free time, and a burning desire for something more than school, church, and small-town life. And they struck a deal. If you will only purchase enough pimple cream and soft drinks to keep us in business, you can have all the Elvis Presley you want.

For the post-war generation, the picture of freedom was the experience of driving down the road with friends in a convertible, the top down and the radio on. The friends, the summer day, the convertible, yes, but all the *life* of the scene came from the radio. The radio provided the beat, the tune, the *energy*. And later still, when this generation began to see themselves as strangers in their own land, outsiders, a *counter-culture*, it was free-form FM "underground" radio that connected them.

At each stage, the technology changed, the audience shifted, but radio retained – or increased – its power to connect people, to create communities, to link individuals to something larger. For the shift worker with his radio strapped to a factory machine, for the cross-country driver trying to stay awake, for the farm wife who will not speak with another person until her husband comes home from the fields, for children imprisoned in their parents' houses, for third-world people who have never left their native village, radio is a lifeline. It connects them to a larger world.

Radio technology is changing again today. The changes allow greater connection than ever before. And they promise to alter the very definition of radio.

the changing face of radio

How Internet Radio Works

From a user's perspective, Internet radio is simple to explain. Using your web browser, you go to the site of a favorite radio station. You click on a button that says "Listen Live." Music starts rolling out of your PC's speakers. This may be all we really need to know about how Internet radio works. But a bit of knowledge of the underlying technology never hurts.

Begin by considering the difference between *analog* and *digital* recording. Sound, we remember from grade school, is waves, just like the waves on a pond. The simplest model of the analog recording process is to imagine a very thin diaphragm inside a microphone (think of a small piece of foil or cellophane) suspended in the air before a singer's lips, trembling as the waves of the singer's voice strike it. The foil is connected to a stylus, which jiggles on a wax surface. Left on the surface is a representation – an analog – of the sound waves. To reproduce the sound, we simply do the reverse. We let a stylus ride over the analog on the recording. Its vibration causes a diaphragm (inside a speaker) to vibrate. This vibration reproduces the singer's voice. This is *analog* recording. It has been much extended over the years. The major advance was converting the sound waves into electrical signals. Employing patterns of magnetism (for example, on tape) provided denser storage. But for all the advancements and refinements, the essential model never changes: storing a picture – an analog – of the sound waves themselves.

Digital recording is a different matter. Rather than storing the shape of the waves, digital recording merely samples how high the waves are at any given instant. If, rather than a picture of a wave passing by, you were given a series of readings of the wave's height over time, you could draw a rough picture of the wave yourself from the data. This is exactly what digital recording does. Many times per second, it samples the waves and records their amplitude (their height). The list of wave heights is just data, a string of numbers, so it is easy to store in a computer file like any other data – like a word processing file, or a digitized picture.

The main problem with digitized sound is that the file is very big. Recording all those thousands of instants produces a huge list of numbers. So computer scientists have created various schemes for *compressing* the data. The easiest way to think of this is pictorially. Imagine that you scan a picture into your computer. Just as digital recording samples the sound wave many times a second, the scanner samples the picture at thousands of places. Think of a grid over the picture, with 10,000 cells – 100 across by 100 down. You could copy the picture by recording 10,000 values, one for each cell. To simplify, leave out the possibility of gray, and consider that you will paint the cell only black or white. In your file, then, you only need to record one bit of information for each cell – 1 for black, 0 for white. You can then save the picture in a computer file as a string of 10,000 *bits* (binary digits). But this wastes a lot of bits. Look at that whole section at the top of the picture, representing the sky. It is represented in your file by over a thousand zeroes in a row. You could make the file smaller by putting in some shorthand to say, "a thousand zeroes here" rather than plodding along putting in every zero. This is what compression algorithms do. They essentially consist of clever schemes to save space by using shorthand representations of patterns found in the string of values. The other half of the process is decompression, expanding the file back to its proper size. If the rules for the shorthand are agreed on in advance, the decompression algorithm can put back the bits exactly the way they were before the compression took place. This is so, except that sometimes, in the interests of more compression, the shorthand leaves out some detail. In that string of a thousand zeroes, there might actually have been a few ones scattered about, which were left out, figuring that you'd never notice the loss. Computer scientists call any compression technique that takes these liberties *lossy* compression, as opposed to *lossless* compression, which is scrupulous to ensure that the decompressed file exactly matches the file as it existed before compression. The software that handles the compression and decompression is called a *codec* (from *co*mpression-*dec*ompression).

If you have any files on your computer representing sounds, this is how they work. For example, on a Windows system, the various sounds the computer makes, say, to alert you to an error, are stored on disk as files with the suffix .wav (for "wave"). Using the Control Panel, you can change which .wav file is played, so that, for example, instead of going "boing" when you make an error, the computer says "uh-oh." Wav files have very poor compression, so that representing a whole song would produce a huge .wav. A major improvement was the MP3 format, which preserved listenable quality (although it does impose some loss), while greatly reducing file size. This convenient file format created a huge explosion of interest as millions of people turned to programs such as Napster to swap MP3 files over the Internet.

MP3 files on disk are not Internet radio, but they're close. In fact, one format for Internet radio is *streaming* MP3, which illustrates the difference. To use a program such as Napster, you first have to *download* a song to your disk. Depending on the speed of your connection to the Internet, it can take a long time for the song to download. While the song is in the process of downloading, you can't listen to the part of it that has already arrived. You have to wait for the whole file to arrive. But then, when it gets to your disk, you can play it over and over, without ever having to download it again. *Streaming* media differs in that it brings to your computer a continuous flow of sound, which you can listen to *at the same time* as it is coming in. And it is never stored on your disk, so you cannot go back and listen to it again. The difference between *streaming* MP3 and MP3 is exactly analogous to the difference between listening to radio and going out to the store to buy a CD.

The technological challenge in creating streaming media is to deliver and decompress the information quickly enough to keep from breaking the stream of music. To this is added the challenge of handling errors in transmission, including packet loss. Unlike, say, a traditional telephone line, the Internet does not work by creating a continuous connection between you and the entity on the other end of the line. Internet protocols work by breaking your message up into small chunks called *packets*, and dispatching each packet individually. If you are in London and your friend is in Singapore, some of the packets in your message may be routed through Sydney while others go through Amsterdam. Packets may arrive out of order, and the receiving software has to sort them properly. Worst of all, a few packets sent through San Francisco may never make it at all, the software will have to ask for those packets to be resent. The challenge of keeping a continuous stream of music going while having to ask for a piece of it again is partially addressed by the technique of *buffering*. A smart codec will build up a few seconds of head start in a buffer, so that if a problem occurs, the music won't stop while the codec is scrambling around to fix the problem. This is why, when you click on an Internet radio station, the sound won't begin immediately, and a status bar at the bottom of your Internet radio player will tell you it is *buffering*. (This is also why, in spite of the precautions, the sound does sometimes just stop.)

Standards for Internet Radio

It would be very convenient for listeners, and help the adoption of Internet radio, if there were a single standard for streaming audio. Unfortunately, there is not. Instead there are several different, conflicting standards. Streaming audio was first popularized by a Seattle company now called RealNetworks, and the format was called *RealAudio*. Apple Computer was already in the market with a format called *QuickTime*. Not wanting to allow a competitor to establish a standard, Microsoft leapt in with a format called *Windows Media*. And there is also streaming MP3, mentioned above. These formats are all mutually incompatible. You can't listen to a Windows Media stream with a codec from Real Networks, and vice versa. (If you think back to the explanation above you can see one reason why: each would use a different shorthand to represent the thousand zeroes.) This is not a stable situation. A single standard is more convenient for everyone, so as soon as one player establishes clear dominance, competing formats tend to wither away. Currently Microsoft and RealNetworks are competing vigorously in an attempt to establish their format as the standard. Part 1 of this book explains what software you need on your computer to be able to listen to Internet radio and be as oblivious as possible to these battles over format.

How Internet Radio Differs from MP3

The words "Internet" and "music" have been coupled in countless news stories over the past year. Yet most of the stories have not been about radio. They have instead been about the use of the Internet to find and acquire MP3 files. The MP3 story has been dramatic, but it has primarily been about vast numbers of teenagers finding (probably temporarily) ways to circumvent paying for music. Internet radio offers much more:

❶ New music Radio remains the primary channel through which people encounter new music they have never heard before. The CD collection (or the MP3 collection) is the archives, the museum of past explorations. What's on the radio is the nodal growth edge, the intersection with the unexplored, the edge of the future, the meniscus of the now.

❷ Interesting arrangements Radio is an art form. A great radio host can put together two songs you've heard before in a way that makes you hear something new about both of them. A radio host can tell you a story without saying a word, creating a narrative by stringing together song selections. Tens of thousands of Los Angelenos get up early Sunday morning to hear Tom Nixon. On his KPFK program *The Nixon Tapes*, Tom usually takes a single theme – "Rain," for example – and walks through explorations of the theme that would never have occurred to you, no matter how big your record collection was and no matter how long you spent thinking about the topic. Though Nixon plays no musical instrument, his achievement is as creative as those of the musicians he brings to us – in the same way that a museum curator selecting and arranging an art exhibition is doing original creative work.

❸ Education In addition to putting songs together, a good radio host can tell you things you didn't know about the artists, the songs, and the times. Karl Haas has taught millions of listeners about classical music. A good world music show illuminates the folk traditions behind today's hit music.

In short, radio is an ideal vehicle for explorers. Radio takes us out of ourselves, into the mind of the host who arranges a journey for us, into other lands, into other times, deep into imagination.

how internet radio differs from MP3

Other New Radio Technology

The Internet is not the only new technology over which radio is expanding its reach. For years, many cable systems have carried digital music subscription services such as DTX. These services offer many channels of commercial-free music, and can be a huge improvement over what is found on the local airwaves. Similarly, two huge satellite systems are just rolling out now: XM Radio and Sirius Radio. These services make hundreds of channels widely available. Satellite services have one strong advantage over Internet radio: you can get them in your car. Much of the time people spend listening to radio, they spend in their cars, and very few cars yet have Internet connections. On the other hand, Internet radio also has several advantages over these services. The first is price. These services all carry a fairly hefty monthly fee, while Internet radio is free. A second is coverage. These services are targeted at major U.S. markets. The Internet is everywhere. But the biggest difference is content. These services are still essentially quite limited. A hundred channels of radio may seem like a lot until you remember that your TV now gets a hundred channels, too, and there's still nothing on it you want to watch. These services follow essentially the same tired model of a few broadcasters and a mass audience. What makes Internet radio so exciting by contrast is the thousands upon thousands of broadcasters, the almost *infinite* amount of choice. It is the very *openness* of the Internet that is its strength. Rather than picking among the selections someone else has chosen for you, the Internet opens up the whole world.

Whenever Internet protocols (IP) compete with a closed system, the Internet wins. One reason is the Internet

Engineering Task Force way for agreeing on protocols, emphasizing "rough consensus and working code," a model for human beings working together, not exactly democracy, but a more pragmatic kind of cooperative human behavior than anything else that has come before. But more importantly, behind the Internet is the power of millions of individual innovators. It's a set of protocols for cooperating and innovating, and those protocols tend to be adopted by people who are interested in cooperation and innovation. The business standard is about control, about proprietary trade secrets, about protecting turf. The Internet standard is about letting a million flowers blossom. This is why IP wins, and will keep winning. That is why, although other things are happening in radio, this book is focused exclusively on the Internet. It's where the most interesting things are happening now, and it is where the most interesting things will happen in the future.

The Future of Radio

As this future unfolds, we will see it altering our very conception of what radio is. A pioneer in wireless phones once remarked, "Some day we'll be telling children about the days when people *stood* by a certain place in the *wall* to have a conversation, because a *wire* came out there." The changes sweeping radio will similarly alter our very conception of the medium so that future listeners will find it difficult to imagine the limitations of days gone by. You can see the basic definition of radio changing right now, starting to blur until you're no longer sure what radio even *is*.

For example, there is no doubt that KEXP is a radio station. It broadcasts over the airwaves. You can see its antenna; you can get it on your FM receiver. When KEXP streams its signal over the Internet, it's still the same KEXP, and there is no doubt that it's still radio. But KEXP on the Internet has features that KEXP on the FM receiver does not. One is real-time playlists. When you're listening to KEXP on the web, you don't have to wait for the DJ to tell you later what you heard, you can see at a glance what you're listening to right now. After a few months of listening to KEXP on the web, real-time playlists can become part of the *definition* of radio for you. So when stuck listening to KEXP in the car, it no longer seems you're really getting the whole radio station. Your definition of KEXP has grown so that what you formerly thought of as KEXP no longer satisfies it.

And consider WREK. On WREK (the real WREK, the one on the Internet), you can listen to *any* of its shows at *any* time. Once you get used to that, the idea that you can't hear a certain radio show because you're not free at 4am on a particular Tuesday starts to seem ludicrous. You can imagine telling children about those days. But the fact that certain shows came on at certain times was formerly a very essential characteristic of radio. When that characteristic disappears, radio is something new and different. Is it still even radio?

But both KEXP and WREK are traditional *radio* stations, with airwave broadcasts. There are also lots of sites on the Internet streaming audio that has never been broadcast. Are they radio? Well, some of them are *just* like radio programs. Others are quite different than anything you've ever heard broadcast. Live365, for example, has nearly forty *thousand* different programs available for listening any time. If this is radio, the definition of radio is changing. And little bits of radio are flaking off and showing up in other places, on web pages that have nothing to do with radio, yet still have an audio portion you can play. For example, if you go to the online stock brokerage E★Trade's site, you'll find a button to click for audio stock-market news. Is that radio? The answer to all these questions is that the definition of radio is broadening and blurring. We will look back from the vantage of a few years, and see that our conception has changed bit by bit until the sum of the changes is radical.

These changes are happening right now. The purpose of this book is to get you out there being a part of them. The next section will get you started.

Acknowledgements

Thanks to all the thousands of volunteers who produce radio programs out of love. Particular thanks to Joni Decker-Wright and Jerry Houck, who created a wide-open radio space called *The Floating World* at KSER and then encouraged me to play in it. My friend Phil Kramer, who does so much to keep my intellect alive, first got me interested in Internet radio, persistently emailing me links until I got hooked and started emailing them back. Jodie Rhodes, my agent, supported this idea and helped make it happen. Jonathan Buckley at Rough Guides is the editor every writer should have. Thanks also to Helen Prior at Rough Guides, for designing and typesetting the book, and to Amanda Jones for proofreading. Highest thanks, of course, to my wife Gillian Theobald for her remarkable forbearance. You the reader owe thanks to my daughter Elaine Heberlein, who revisited every website listed in this book to verify the address.

part one

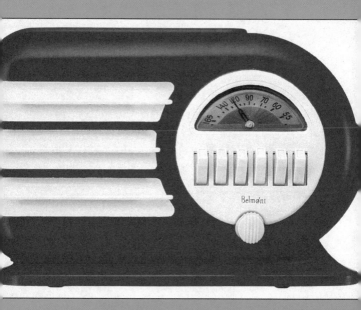

tuning into
internet radio

Tuning in to Internet Radio

About Your Computer

Almost any computer purchased in the last three years is adequate to the task of playing Internet radio. Specific requirements are listed below for the major media players. As a baseline, you will be fine if your PC is at least a Pentium 166 with 64 megabytes of memory (you can scrape by with 32), running Windows 98 or something newer. You also need a sound card and an Internet connection. Most material below applies to Windows systems, as they predominate; Linux and Macintosh systems are dealt with in separate sections below.

Bandwidth

Once upon a time, you improved your cyber-situation by purchasing a faster computer. Today, you make things better by getting more *bandwidth*. Bandwidth refers to the speed of your network connection. It is usually expressed in the straightforward measure of bits per second. A dial-up modem will give you a connection speed of 28.8 or 56 Kbps (thousands of bits per second). You *can* listen to Internet radio with this connection speed. You may experience more frequent drops of the sound and reduced sound quality. (RealSystem Server will detect your slower connection speed and feed you a lower-quality stream, whereas Windows Media Services instead drops out more frequently.) A dial-up modem Internet radio experience is better than no Internet radio experience, but if DSL or cable modem connections are available in your area, they will improve not only your Internet radio life, but also your entire Internet experience. Speeds range from 256 megabits per second to a gigabit per second, that is, at least five times faster than a modem. The biggest difference you may notice is not the speed, but the fact that the connection is always available. When accessing the Internet means waiting for a dial-up connection to be established, one is less likely to use it as a source of quick reference information or entertainment. When it is always on, using the Internet soon becomes one's first impulse.

If you are establishing an account with an Internet Service Provider, which may not necessarily be the same company that supplies your DSL or cable connection, ask about two things. One is the charge for the bandwidth used. Usually the provider will offer a certain number of gigabytes per month for a basic fee, and tack on added charges above this number. It is unlikely that a single person listening to Internet radio in your house, even all day, will hit these limits. But if several people are listening to different stations, as well as downloading large files and watching streaming video, you could get to the limit more

bandwidth

quickly than you would think. And if later you want to start your own streaming radio station, the cost could get prohibitive. The limits vary widely from ISP to ISP, and since it's not a charge that immediately registers, it is easy to attend insufficiently to it up front when choosing a provider, and later wish you had chosen differently. The other consideration is the provider's connection to the Internet. It does you no good to have a megabit connection to your ISP if your ISP is bogged down. Ask your ISP about this in advance. The concern is usually called Quality of Service (QOS). Does the ISP offer any QOS guarantees? As there are no standard metrics that will authoritatively address this concern in advance, one tactic is to ask other users of the ISP what they experience.

Internet Radio Software

When videotapes first entered the lives of home consumers, there were two kinds: VHS and BetaMax. If you wanted to buy a VCR, you had to decide which kind to get. Then, when you went to the video store, you could only bring home tapes in the same format as the VCR you had chosen. This was awkward all around. Video stores had to stock twice as many tapes, without broadening their selection or increasing their market. Eventually one format won out – not necessarily through technical superiority, but more as a result of more successful marketing efforts. This same history has been often repeated as new technologies are introduced, for example, in incompatible Apple and IBM personal computer systems.

The same sort of battle over formats is under way today in Internet radio. Streaming media technology was really launched by Apple, with its *QuickTime* software. QuickTime made little impact outside a small community, however. The first technology to spread widely was RealNetworks' (then Progressive Networks) *RealAudio*. RealAudio was innovative. It made it truly possible to hear sound effectively over the Internet, with listenable quality and not a great deal of dropping out. RealAudio was instantly popular. Microsoft, eager to be part of this important new computer technology, stepped in with a product intended to directly compete with RealAudio: Windows Media Player. Microsoft has poured enormous marketing resources into promoting WMP, and into encouraging its use. Once nearly 100 percent of Internet radio was in RealAudio format. Nearly 88 percent still is. But with Microsoft's aggressive promotion of its technology, more and more of the major radio stations stream in the Windows Media format. (Quite a few stations offer both formats.)

As a listener, you are left in the position a little bit like that of the early videotape viewer, with your Windows Media Player unable to decode RealAudio streams, and vice versa. The difference is that it's easy to acquire both players, and they're both free. Both Windows Media Player from Microsoft and RealPlayer from RealNetworks are available for free download. Unless you're a Linux user, you can install them both on the same computer. The following sections explain in step-by-step detail how to do so. And then you can listen to any radio station, no matter which format it uses.

Both RealNetworks and Microsoft are engaged in public relations efforts to prove their technology is superior. Blindfolded, most listeners cannot tell the difference.

At least, this is true under normal conditions. When bandwidth is poor or the network particularly congested, their behavior varies. RealAudio uses a technology called SureStream, which drops back to lower-quality sound when a better stream cannot get through. Under these conditions, RealAudio can sound tinny. Windows Media lacks the equivalent of SureStream, so under similar circumstances, the stream becomes chopped up with interruptions of silence.

Windows Media Player is supported on fewer platforms than

RealAudio. If you want to use a Linux system to listen to radio, you will not be listening in Windows Media format. On the producers' side, Windows Media servers are only available on Windows computers. So if you want to host a radio station on Apple, Linux, or, say, Solaris systems, RealAudio is your choice.

There is a non-proprietary alternative: streaming MP3. MP3 is an open standard, and it is possible to use it for Internet radio. Various free servers, particularly Shoutcast, stream in the MP3 format, and various free MP3 players, the most popular of which is WinAmp, play MP3 streams. However, the percentage of radio stations streaming MP3 declines each day, and there is little likelihood that this technology will become the standard.

Open standards for streaming media are under development. The MPEG4 standard, in particular, is a solid technological platform that could unify the industry. Apple has committed to making its next version of QuickTime MPEG4-compliant. Unsurprisingly, neither Microsoft nor RealNetworks has agreed to adopt the standard. So we are left with Internet radio coming to us via two utterly incompatible proprietary technologies, neither of which will acknowledge the other. Until this situation clears, the sensible listener will install all the necessary software to listen to *everything*. The following sections explain how to do so.

Installing and Using Windows Media Player

Windows Media Player is widely available, and if your Windows computer is recently purchased or recently upgraded, WMP is probably already installed. If you do need to install it, here is how.

Although it's not crucial, there are reasons for installing

Windows Media Player before RealPlayer. The two programs each want to take responsibility for playing as many different media types as possible, and this contention is resolved most swiftly if RealPlayer goes last.

System requirements for using Windows Media Player are as follows:

➤➤ Microsoft Windows 98, Windows Millennium Edition, or Windows 2000

➤➤ Pentium or Athlon K6 166 megahertz processor, 266 MHz recommended

➤➤ 32 MB RAM, 64 MB strongly recommended

➤➤ 28.8 kilobits per second (Kbps) modem, 56 Kbps recommended

➤➤ 16-bit sound card

➤➤ 256-color video card

There are also versions of Windows Media Player for Macintosh, PalmPC, and Solaris. (No Linux.)

The home of WMP is **www.microsoft.com/windows/windowsmedia**. This page offers a great deal of information about Windows Media Player, including news on new options and platforms. You can subscribe to an email newsletter on the latest Windows Media technologies. You can also download the newest version of WMP, at no charge. The current version is 9.1 megabytes in size, which takes around a minute to download over most broadband lines such as DSL (46 minutes, on the other hand, at 28.8 Kbps). The process of installing WMP is straightforward, but it does pre-

Download Options (Figure 1)

sent a few options and issues which merit discussion. Before beginning the installation process, it is a good idea to close all other programs running on your computer.

When you begin the process of downloading Windows Media Player, you will see the dialog box illustrated in Figure 1.

The default option is to *Save the program to disk*. Unless you plan to install the program on multiple computers, there is no particular reason to do this. If you ever need to re-install the program, you will probably want to go get the latest version anyway, so it makes sense to click the option *Run the program from its current location*. In either case, the program is downloaded to your hard drive, but in this case it is stored in a temporary folder and deleted when the installation is done. If you do choose *Save the program to disk*, remember where you saved it, so that you can delete it manually at some point when you might be in need of disk space.

The Authenticity Notice illustrated in Figure 2 is worth studying if you do not know what it means or why you should care.

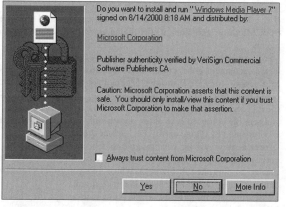

Do you want to install and run "Windows Media Player 7" signed on 8/14/2000 8:18 AM and distributed by:

Microsoft Corporation

Publisher authenticity verified by VeriSign Commercial Software Publishers CA

Caution: Microsoft Corporation asserts that this content is safe. You should only install/view this content if you trust Microsoft Corporation to make that assertion.

☐ Always trust content from Microsoft Corporation

| Yes | No | More Info |

Authenticity Notice (Figure 2)

installing and using Windows media player

Although one hates to be paranoid, the number and intensity of ugly viruses circulating on the Internet is growing at an increasing rate, and the more recent ones don't just print funny messages, they do things like wipe out all your files. The most dangerous kind of file to take onto your computer is an *executable* file – that is, a program. (On Windows systems, most executable files have the three-letter suffix .EXE.) An executable takes control of your computer, and, essentially, it can do anything it wants, up to and including deleting every file. So some security experts advise you never to execute software that has been downloaded from the Internet. However, the whole reason you have a computer is to run programs on it, and the Internet is where the best and most current software can be found. What is a prudent person to do?

This is where certificates of authenticity come in. Trusted third-party sources issue digital certificates. (The best known is VeriSign, mentioned in Figure 2.) The digital certificates verify two things: 1) That the software you're about to execute really does come from Microsoft, and not from some thirteen-year-old sociopath in Bulgaria; and 2) That it has not been tampered with. If the Bulgarian 13-year-old takes a good copy of real software from Microsoft and alters it, the digital certificate will no longer match.

So, although this screen says "Security Warning" at the top of it, it is actually a good thing. It tells you that you really are getting a true copy of Windows Media Player, which really did come from Microsoft. You should decide for yourself what a reasonable security policy should be for your system; one common and sensible approach is to allow onto it only executable software accompanied by digital certificates such as this one.

After a screen asking you to agree to a license agreement, you enter the setup proper, with a larger welcome, and then come to the screen illustrated in Figure 3, which asks you to select which components of Windows Media Player to install.

The only safe thing to do at this point is to accept the choices Microsoft has made for you, and press *Next*. Turning off any

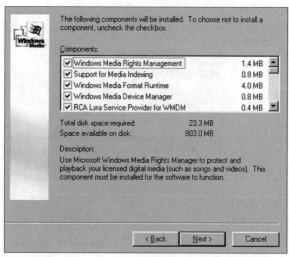

The following components will be installed. To choose not to install a component, uncheck the checkbox.

Components:

☑ Windows Media Rights Management	1.4 MB	
☑ Support for Media Indexing	0.8 MB	
☑ Windows Media Format Runtime	4.0 MB	
☑ Windows Media Device Manager	0.8 MB	
☑ RCA Lyra Service Provider for WMDM	0.4 MB	

Total disk space required: 23.3 MB
Space available on disk: 803.0 MB

Description:
Use Microsoft Windows Media Rights Manager to protect and playback your licensed digital media (such as songs and videos). This component must be installed for the software to function.

‹ Back   Next ›   Cancel

Component Selection (Figure 3)

options may have unpredictable consequences that do not show up immediately, but that will prove difficult to diagnose problems later. For example, believing yourself perfectly capable of managing the digital rights on your PC, and preferring *not* to have Microsoft trying to do it for you, you might think you can do without the "Windows Media Rights Manager." But the description of the Media Rights Manager carries the warning, "This component must be installed for the software to function."

Someone of a critical bent might call this a classic example of bloatware. The previous version of WMP was much smaller and had none of these options. The total disk space requirement for WMP is now 23.3 megabytes, of which only 5.8 is for the media player itself. That is to say, WMP takes up a quarter of the space, and these other mandatory options take up four times as much. If you're interested in seeing what the other mandatory options are,

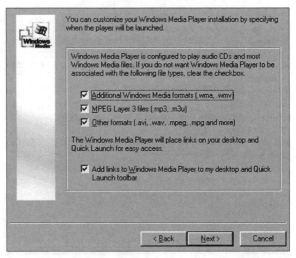

File Format Choices (Figure 4)

highlight each one, and a brief description will appear below explaining what it is for. To repeat, though, exercising any options at this point, even though they are offered, will leave you with a media player that Microsoft says might not work.

The next screen shows you the Windows Media Player privacy policies. This is a good thing to read. Privacy is obviously an increasingly thorny issue in the Internet age. Reading through these policies is educational. They illustrate that the major concern of Windows Media Player is that services be able to charge you for media you play and control your access to it. Nothing that has been added in the latest version of WMP appears for the convenience of the user; all the complexity seems to be designed only for those who would charge the user a fee. In any event, none of this is applicable to Internet radio.

The final installation choice you are given is some discretion over what file types Windows Media Player will command (see Figure 4).

Unless WMP is the only media player on your system, you will almost certainly want to uncheck *MPEG Layer 3 files* at this point. Of course, you can change file type associations later, for example, in Windows Explorer. And other applications will happily try to wrest control of these file types back if they think they should have it. After a bit of dueling back and forth, your applications will hash this out and stop pestering you to take sides. This screen gives you the opportunity to decide which player to use more often. Don't worry about making the wrong choice; you can easily change these preferences later.

After you have made this choice, the installation wizard will declare that you are done and ask you to click "Finish" to finish up. That doesn't mean that installation is done. It means that you're done making choices, and the installation is ready to begin. This installation will run by itself for around five minutes, and then ask you to click "Finish" to restart the computer. This is one good reason to have closed all your other programs. If you haven't done so already, do so now before clicking "Finish."

If you bring up Windows Media Player now, by clicking on the icon installed on your desktop, or by choosing it from the Start menu, you will see a screen like that illustrated in Figure 5.

This screen is a mêlée of commercial appeals you will probably

Windows Media Player Main Screen (Figure 5)

installing and using Windows media player

WMP Radio Tuner (Figure 6)

never want to see again. It's worth a moment, though, to look it
over the first time you bring up WMP. In the main part of the
screen is the *Media Guide*: some entertainment news and various
popular programs Microsoft has selected to bring to your attention. The bar along the left lists various functions you can access
via the Player. *CD Audio* is for playing CDs on your computer.
Media Library is for playing media files (such as MP3s) from your
hard drive. *Portable Device* is for transferring files to a handheld
player (such as an MP3 player). *Skin Chooser* allows you to choose
what you would like to appear on your screen while WMP plays.
(Skins are discussed below.) The important main tab for our purposes is *Radio Tuner*. If you click on this tab, you will see a screen
like that illustrated in Figure 6.

Notice that WMP comes with numerous stations "pre-set."
You can click on these stations in the tuner to try listening to
them. And this is the way the product was designed to be used.
You bring it up, have it open on your screen, and use it as your
radio navigator.

There are several reasons not to use it this way. The most obvious problem with doing so is that only stations in Windows

installing and using RealPlayer

Media format are listed, which leaves out most of the radio stations in the world. But beyond that, the stations seem selected on some basis such as how good a partner they are to Microsoft, rather than how interested you might be in listening to them. But while you have the list of stations up on your screen, it is a good time to get acquainted with it and do a little exploring.

Installing and Using RealPlayer

The system requirements for RealPlayer on Windows are:

» 120 MHz Intel Pentium processor or equivalent

» 16 MB of RAM

» 28.8 Kpbs modem

» 16-bit sound card and speakers

» Windows* 95, Windows 98, Windows 2000, Windows 2000 ME or Windows NT 4.0 with Service Pack 4

» IE 4.0.1 or Netscape 4.0 or later

RealPlayer comes pre-installed on some systems, and RealNetworks has recently been landing many new bundling agreements, but chances are you will need to install it for yourself. It is freely available from the RealNetworks website **www.real.com.** When you go to this site, you will be offered the chance to buy a premium version. Currently, the premium version, called RealPlayer Plus, sells for $29.99. Admittedly, this is not very much money. On the other hand, the $29.99 version does nothing you need, and you should save your money.

Scroll down the page until you see this button on the right of the screen. Click on it. This takes you to a page with half a dozen well-marked chances to download the

RealPlayer
Download Button
(Figure 7)

Looking for "RealPlayer Basic"
on a Page Full of "RealPlayer Plus" (Figure 8)

$29.99 version, as well as a couple of pop-up windows trying to sell you other things. Keep looking until you find the Basic version. If you look at Figure 8, you can find at least seven very obvious ways to download the $29.99 version. The one way to get the free version is on the left, down a ways, in the gray bar. It says "RealPlayer8 Basic is our free player." Click that.

You will be taken to a form you must fill out in order to be allowed to download the software.

You must give an email address. Fill in the country, operating system you are using, language, connection speed,

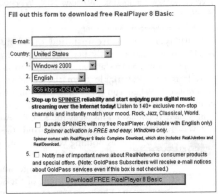

RealPlayer Download Form (Figure 9)

installing and using RealPlayer

16

and then decide your preferences about options 4 and 5. Spinner is an unnecessary bit of complication in your life that only adds to the download time, so the box is shown here unchecked. RealNetworks is a very active and persistent marketing organization, capable of generating a great deal of email, so option 5 is shown unchecked as well. (Note that unchecking this option does *not* mean that you will never get email from RealNetworks – see p.19.)

The next page (Figure 10) lets you choose how much software to download.

As you can see, RealNetworks recommends a "standard" package which includes, in addition to RealPlayer, RealJukebox, a download manager, and some AOL support. If you plan to listen to MP3s, RealJukebox is a good MP3 player, and so the "standard" package may in fact be your choice. For the purposes of listening to Internet radio, however, you need only the minimum package. As you can see, it is much smaller than the downloads with all the options.

The next page will give you a choice among many sites from which to download the software. The sites are all the same, the

Select your RealPlayer Basic download option			
Features Include:	**RealPlayer 8 Basic Complete**	**RealPlayer 8 Basic Standard**	**RealPlayer 8 Basic Minimum**
RealPlayer Basic - Play Streaming Audio & Video	✓	✓	✓
RealJukebox Basic - Digital Music, CD Recording, MP3s	✓	✓	
RealDownload Basic - Internet Download Manager	✓	✓	
AOL Icon	✓	✓	
Spinner - Listen to 140+ exclusive music channels	✓		
Make Your Selection ▌▌▌▌▌➡	○	○ Recommended	◉
Download FREE RealPlayer Basic Now			

RealPlayer Download Options (Figure 10)

installing and using RealPlayer

software is all the same, the only thing that may vary is the speed of the connection between you and the download site. Choose the closest site to you physically, and if you do not get a satisfactory connection, choose another. (You may also notice, as the download proceeds, various other screens popping up to advertise various other products, perhaps utterly unrelated to RealPlayer, but, obviously, not to RealNetworks' revenues.)

At the end of the download, installation of RealPlayer will begin, without any prompting from you. Most software vendors ask you whether to install now; RealNetworks just jumps right ahead. Your sign that installation is beginning is an authenticity alert such as the one illustrated below:

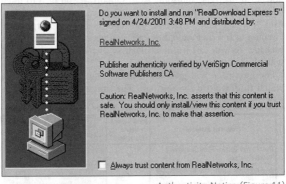

Do you want to install and run "RealDownload Express 5" signed on 4/24/2001 3:48 PM and distributed by:

RealNetworks, Inc.

Publisher authenticity verified by VeriSign Commercial Software Publishers CA

Caution: RealNetworks, Inc. asserts that this content is safe. You should only install/view this content if you trust RealNetworks, Inc. to make that assertion.

☐ Always trust content from RealNetworks, Inc.

Authenticity Notice (Figure 11)

As explained in the section "Installing and Using Windows Media Player," this alert, though it is labeled a "Security Warning," is actually more appropriately considered a "Security Reassurance." It tells you that the software you are installing is truly from RealNetworks and not some pretender, and it tells you that the software has not been altered in any way since RealNetworks digitally signed it. Say yes to this alert.

You will next be prompted to close all other applications,

RealPlayer Install Options (Figure 12)

which is a good idea. RealNetworks then displays a long license agreement to which you must agree if you want to install the software. Then you are asked where to install the software. Unless you have another place in which you normally keep applications, there is no reason to change the default that is displayed for you. Next up is a list of options, illustrated in Figure 12.

Uncheck all the boxes, each of which represents an attempt to make RealPlayer more visible on your computer. RealPlayer will be plenty visible enough without any of these options.

Next you are given the chance to change your browser's home page to one which advertises content in RealNetworks formats. You will probably want to decline this opportunity. Following is a screen giving software registration options.

Go ahead and register the software, or it will nag you mercilessly. Definitely uncheck the box inviting RealNetworks to send you junk email. (They will still send you junk email, but unchecking this box will reduce the amount somewhat.)

RealPlayer Registration Options (Figure 13)

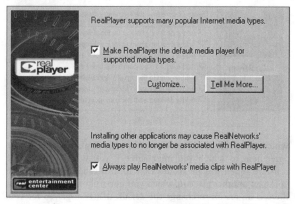

RealPlayer supports many popular Internet media types.

☑ Make RealPlayer the default media player for supported media types.

Customize...   Tell Me More...

Installing other applications may cause RealNetworks' media types to no longer be associated with RealPlayer.

☑ Always play RealNetworks' media clips with RealPlayer

Supported Media Types (Figure 14)

The following screen merely asks your Internet connection speed. The next is a portion of the format wars referred to above.

This screen asks you whether RealPlayer should be "associated" with various media types. That is, if Windows sees one of those media types, should it invoke RealPlayer to play it? As explained above, RealPlayer, Windows Media Player, and other media players will compete vigorously for this honor. To reduce contention, uncheck the top box, and check the bottom one. Roughly translated, this tells Windows "don't try to give *all* media types to RealPlayer, because I know that will start a fight, but if any other players try to take responsibility for Real media formats, don't let them."

The next screen gives you the opportunity to set up one-click access to various RealNetwork "channels." You will probably want to uncheck all the boxes, which is choosing not to have these channels in your face. The next screen gives you the chance to receive "flashes" from RealNetworks, about news, movies, etc. Unless this sounds like something you really want, uncheck all these options as well. Following is *another* opportunity to be mar-

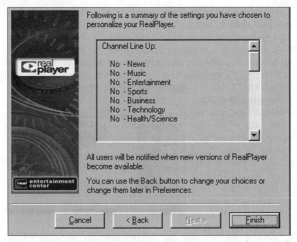

RealPlayer Options Summary (Figure 15)

keted to. Click these boxes if you'd like to find out what RealNetworks thinks is a special offer.

Finally there will be a review of the options you clicked.

Note that although you have declined every opportunity to get marketing mail from RealNetworks, this screen informs you that "*All* users will be notified" when new versions become available. Expect to get mail.

(You should also know that from this moment on, you will continually be sending RealNetworks information about your activities. Using the "Preferences" section of RealPlayer, you can exercise some choice about how much information to send to RealNetworks and to content providers, but don't count on turning it all off).

Most software vendors ask you at this point whether you would now like to launch their product. RealPlayer doesn't ask. It just takes control of your computer and starts giving you marketing

installing and using RealPlayer

pitches. It also pops up several windows trying to get you to buy the paid version, sign up for their guide, etc., etc. Then it opens up a browser and takes you to RealGuide.

As you did with Windows Media Player, this might be the time to explore RealPlayer's user interface and to decide for yourself whether you'd ever like to see it again. It is illustrated below in Figure 16.

As with Windows Media Player, you see that most of the screen is devoted to a media guide, Real Guide. Makers of software would love to have you use their software as the center of your world. Then they can sell you to

RealPlayer (Figure 16)

advertisers. You will probably find that this guide does not deliver the sort of thing you are very interested in, but now is the time to explore it and see.

Along the left you'll see the "Channels" of various partners of RealNetworks. Across the bottom are other functions. *Search* is a generic search across various media types. If you're interested in radio, the search function in the radio tuner will work better for you. To the right of the *Search* button is a *Messaging Service* Button. This is for managing messages you get from RealNetworks. This is best avoided entirely. On the far left is the button for *Radio Tuner*.

When you bring up the tuner, it will default to showing you "Featured" stations. There is no explanation for how stations get to be "Featured," but the selection process does not bring to the fore those most interesting to listeners. Click on the "Find a Station" tab, and you will see the screen illustrated in Figure 17 below.

This is worth spending some time with. Pull down the list of

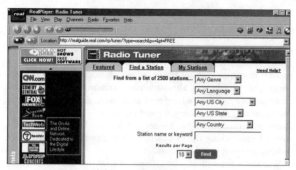

RealPlayer's "Find a Station" Function (Figure 17)

US cities, for example, to see what is available from your old hometown. Or pull down the language list to see what is streaming in Italian. This search facility is far too limited (only 2500 stations), and it's ordered by some other priorities than serving the listener, so it will probably not serve you as a primary search facility on a regular basis. But it is definitely worth playing with the first time you bring it up.

The rightmost tab is labeled *My Stations*. The first time you use RealPlayer, the list of "My Stations" will be empty. Whenever you are listening to a station you like, you can click the "+" button next to the station, and it will be added to the list. Then you can use the "My Stations" tab to return to it later. This can be handy, but because it only works for stations streaming in RealAudio format, it is not as handy as keeping track of favorites in your web browser.

If you have any questions about the RealPlayer user interface or configuration options, pulling down the "Help" menu will probably answer them. If not, a more complete manual is available online at **www.realnetworks.com/devzone/documentation**.

installing and using RealPlayer

Firewalls

The Internet grew up in a setting of research institutes and campuses, and Internet protocols were fairly open, depending on a cooperative user code of behavior, which made sense in the setting and which was almost universally maintained. When Internet use became widespread in a more general and diverse population of less collegial people, the wide-open quality of Internet protocols was no longer appropriate. System administrators started locking things down. One indispensable security tool widely adopted was the firewall.

Without a firewall, if your computer is on the Internet, anyone else on the whole Internet can access it, probe its ports, exploit its security weaknesses, possibly take control over it, and wreak damage. The concept of a firewall is to keep your computer *off* the Internet. Think of a firewall as a literal wall, prohibiting all access from your computer to the Net, and all access from the Net to your computer. Obviously, you wouldn't want to leave it completely locked up like that. But, for security purposes, it makes more sense to lock *all* the doors, and then only open the few you really need to use. This is just what firewalls do. They prohibit all access to the Internet, except for selected communications ports that are absolutely necessary. For example, you have to open up the HTTP port, so you can see the World Wide Web. You probably need to open up the SMTP and POP ports, so you can send email. Imagine a wall with a thousand windows, all but three of them locked. That's the firewall.

Given this situation, you can imagine that Internet radio would not get through. It needs to travel through one of those locked "doors." (In networking parlance, they are called *ports*.) If your media player (such as RealPlayer or Windows Media Player) encounters a firewall problem, it will present you with a message suggesting that a firewall is probably the problem. What you need to do then is to *see your network administrator*. In a corporate setting, this is probably the Information Technology (IT) department – whomever you would normally call to fix a problem with your computer or network. On a campus, it will be the computer services group, the people who hand out computer accounts.

Tell the network administrator you suspect that Internet radio ports are being blocked by the firewall. It is a simple and easy matter to open the ports. The network administrator can do so quickly, and you can verify that your problem is now solved.

If your administrator refuses to configure the firewall to allow radio traffic, you can configure your media players in a more limited way that will still work. For RealPlayer:

▸▸ Click the View menu and choose Preferences.
▸▸ Click the Transport tab.
▸▸ Click Automatically Select Best Transport.
▸▸ Click the Auto-Configure button.

Your network administrator may tell you that manual configuration is necessary. If so, there are instructions on the RealNetwork website explaining how to manually configure RealPlayer.

For Windows Media Player, pull down the Tools menu and choose Options. Click on the Network tab. Set the Protocols as directed by your network administrator.

The final situation to consider is one in which you are the network administrator. For example, you may have installed a firewall on your home network. (And if you haven't, you probably should.) The firewall was easy to install, and you left it in the default configuration, and the person who now needs to go in and open up the radio ports is you. The good news is that doing so is easy. The Internet radio ports are listed by name in the configuration menu of almost every commercial firewall sold today. Find the configuration screen for your firewall. (Perhaps this requires finding the documentation first!) Don't be intimidated. It's as simple as checking a checkbox. Find the ports for RealAudio and Windows Media and enable those ports. Your firewall vendor's web page or support personnel can help you if you encounter any difficulty, but it's usually just a matter of clearing a checkbox.

firewalls

Proxy Servers

A proxy server is similar to a firewall, except that no window is ever opened for Internet traffic to pass through. Instead, the proxy server talks to the Internet on your behalf (acting as your *proxy*). For example, your web browser never really accesses a web page out on the Net. Instead, the web browser accesses the proxy server. The proxy server goes out on the Net, gets the page, brings it back, and serves it up to your browser. As you can see, proxy servers have the potential to be even more secure than firewalls. As you can also imagine, they make everything more complicated. A proxy server can only imitate software if it knows how the software works.

Many firewall products incorporate proxy features, and the two words may be sometimes used interchangeably. Proxy servers are also employed for other purposes than security (most commonly to share a single Internet connection among multiple users). Essentially everything said above about firewalls holds true for proxy servers. You will need to get your administrator to config-ure the proxy server to allow radio traffic to pass. If *you* are the administrator of your proxy server, consult the documentation. There is also documentation on the Microsoft and RealNetworks websites that can be of assistance.

You may also need to configure your media player to work with the proxy. In RealPlayer, click the View menu and choose Preferences, and click on the Proxy tab. The Proxy tab appears as shown in Figure 18.

Illustrated is the default configuration, which is to not use a proxy server. If you are using a proxy server, you may need to check the boxes for "Use PNA proxy" and "Use RTSP proxy," filling in the name of the proxy server in the edit box. In some extremely rare cases, your network cannot use the default ports for RealMedia (1090 and 554). The small edit boxes to the right allow these ports to be changed. If you are proxying RealMedia, you will probably proxy HTTP (web traffic) as well. The boxes at

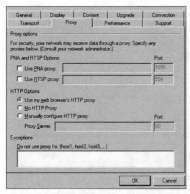

RealPlayer Proxy Tab (Figure 18)

the bottom allow you to manually set an HTTP proxy. Note that the default is to use whatever the web browser uses. So long as your web browser is working, this will ensure that your Internet radio works as well.

The situation is similar with Windows Media Player. From Full-Screen mode, pull down the Tools menu and choose Options. Click on the Network tab. The Network tab is illustrated in Figure 19.

This is the default setting. If your network administrator asks you to manually configure the protocols used by Windows Media Player, you may need to uncheck some of the protocols in the top section, or to change the ports used to receive data. In the Proxy Settings, in the lower portion of the tab, you will notice that the HTTP protocol is configured to use the same

Windows Media Player Network Options (Figure 19)

proxy servers

settings as your web browser. If your web browser works, this should work. The Windows Media protocols themselves are configured not to use a proxy. If you are using a proxy, you need to click the Configure button. Doing so will bring up the screen shown in Figure 20.

If you click "Autodetect proxy settings," the player will attempt to find the proxy server and configure itself appropriately. If you know the address of the proxy server, you can enter it manually in the edit field, which also allows you to set the port to a configuration other than the default 1755.

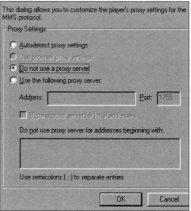

This dialog allows you to customize the player's proxy settings for the MMS protocol

Proxy Settings

○ Autodetect proxy settings
○ Use browser proxy settings
● Do not use a proxy server
○ Use the following proxy server:

Address: _____ Port: 1755

☐ Bypass proxy server for local addresses

Do not use proxy server for addresses beginning with:

_____

Use semicolons (;) to separate entries

OK   Cancel

Windows Media Player Configure Protocol Dialog (Figure 20)

Other Internet Radio Software

Media Players

In addition to the big two media players described above, there are others worth considering, particularly those designed to play streaming MP3 and Apple formats. Below are the most popular.

Itunes
www.apple.com/itunes

Itunes is Apple's impressive MP3 package (for Macintosh only). It can also serve up streaming MP3.

MusicMatch Jukebox
www.musicmatch.com

MusicMatch Jukebox is a versatile program for managing audio files. (For ripping and burning CDs, it's as good as or better than anything else you'll find on a PC). MusicMatch claims 18 million users. As a radio, it's a bit of a throwback to the early days of broadcast radio, when RCA both sold radios and ran radio stations. In addition to providing a player, MusicMatch is also a web site that wants to provide you radio. For a fee. It's called MusicMatch Radio MX. One of the services is "My Station," which allows you to create a "personalized radio station." That is to say, you can create a playlist and play it. The most interesting part of this is a taste-matching service, which works by noticing that other MusicMatch listeners who like these three things you like also like this *other* thing. (Hence the name.) Currently the fee is $4.95 per month. There's a free trial period. It's definitely worth trying out.

QuickTime
www.apple.com/quicktime

Apple claims that QuickTime is the world's leading cross-platform multimedia technology, noting that more than 150 million copies of QuickTime Player are in distribution. It is a great multimedia player, and the ongoing QuickTime development is some of the most impressive technology in this area. It's not all that important to an Internet radio experience, however, as very few of the world's radio staitons broadcast in QuickTime.

other internet radio software

Sonique

sonique.lycos.com

Sonique is an audio player for Windows capable of handling MP3, streaming MP3, and Windows Media audio formats. This means you could use it as a replacement for Windows Media Player. It is free.

WinAmp

www.winamp.com

WinAmp is a very popular, much-loved, free MP3 player. It is also the center of the effort to use streaming MP3 for Internet radio. WinAmp was developed by Nullsoft, now a division of AOL Time-Warner. WinAmp is also the default player of Shoutcast **www.shoutcast.com**, home of 37,000 home-brew radio streams. (You can also hear these streams via RealPlayer.) WinAmp has many advantages as an MP3 player. One is an open architecture that allows third parties to develop plug-ins. There is a great variety of free plug-ins available from the WinAmp site.

Tuners

There is a widespread notion that it would be good to have a "tuner" to help manage your favorite Internet radio stations. The metaphor behind tuners is a dashboard radio with several pre-set buttons, to make it easy for you to click back and forth between your five or ten favorite stations as you drive down the highway. One reason these are not more successful is that the current tuners work only on some subset of the radio world – for example, only on RealAudio files, not Windows Media files, not streaming MP3. So most users find it easier to use the web browser to get around. It's fast, it's easy, it's available on any computer you use. And it doesn't require you to bring up yet another software application, of which there are probably too many open on the desktop already. Finally, you'll want the browser up any way, to look at the radio station's web site, which has program information, playlists, DJ profiles, and news of special events. Most users find themselves excited about a tuner for a while, and

other internet radio software

then, without really thinking about it or planning to, they just find they have stopped using it. Sometimes the cessation coincides with the end of the free trial period, when the tuner provider wants to be paid.

There is also a tendency of tuner providers to serve up what they are paid to promote. Back in the broadcast radio days, this was called payola, and people went to jail for it. Out on the Internet, it's standard business practice.

iMtuner   www.iMnetworks.com

iMtuner (formerly Sonicbox) is a solid, full-featured, free tuner. It plays stations in the RealAudio format. The name makes sense

if you consider "IM" to be a radio band like AM and FM.

iMtuner comes with 1,000 stations, and it's a good list of stations. iM Networks also offers this tuner on a piece of hardware, a remote control device that lets you switch stations without having to go over to your PC. This is described in the section on hardware p.37.

iMtuner (Figure 21)

Vtuner   www.vtuner.com

Vtuner is the classic Internet radio tuner. It is a front-end to RealPlayer. (That is, it will not work for all Internet radio stations, only for those in RealAudio format.) Vtuner was the first tuner and remains the most fully developed. If you want to try out a tuner, it is the one to look at first. There is a free version and a $19.95 version. The free version assaults you with banner ads and lacks the most useful features, particularly the ability to search for programs that are on now.

other internet radio software

Skins and plug-ins

Some people like visual displays while they're listening to music. One variety of visual is the "skin." The skin is a way to individualize the appearance of your music player on screen. For example, if you are a serious fan of a particular musical group, you can get their skin for your player, so that you are visually reminded of them while you listen to music. One impetus for skins is to replace the lost visual experience of album covers and CD jewel cases, now that music comes to you invisibly via the Internet. Skins have the advantage over jewel cases in that they can be animated, so many skins crawl, swirl, zoom, or flash. You can get skins at the website for your media player.

One step beyond the skin is the plug-in. Plug-ins are bits of third-party software added to your players to give them additional functionality. Some tend toward the practical – massaging the sound, cross-fading, fixing gaps in the output. Most are less practical games and special effects, especially "visualizers," which show an animated visual representation of what you're listening to. The most popular among these are the dancers: animated dancers on your screen, gyrating in time to the beat of the music. See Holiday Dancer or Magic Iris at **www.winamp.com**.

Internet Radio on the Macintosh

The Macintosh is a great Internet listening device. (It is a great machine for all musical purposes.) All the players are available for the Macintosh. The process of installing and using Windows Media Player and RealPlayer is essentially no different than that described above. The Mac version of QuickTime is of course unsurpassed, and Itunes provides excellent support for streaming

MP3. The built-in Macintosh speakers are good. With the optional subwoofer, the sound is better than many home stereo systems.

A fairly recent Macintosh is required. The requirements for RealPlayer are typical:

➾ OS 8.1 or later

➾ 32 MB RAM

➾ 604 PowerPC (200 MHz or better)

Internet Radio on Linux

A Linux system will serve as a very good Internet radio platform, excepting that it won't allow you to listen to streams in the Windows Media format. There are a few installation differences worth noting, which are described below. Once you are past the installation stage, information in the remaining sections of this book should all apply without change to your system as well.

Installing RealPlayer on Linux

The process of installing RealPlayer on Linux begins with the same process as described in the section "Installing and Using RealPlayer," above. When you choose "Unix" from the pull-down box "Select OS," however, your path diverges, and you are presented with the information illustrated in Figure 22 below.

This page lets you know your status with RealNetworks. RealPlayer on Linux is a "community supported" version, and RealNetworks takes no responsibility for its functionality or suitability. Notice that this page, like the one you came from, has a "Select OS" pull-down list. This list, however, consists of various flavors of UNIX, including, at present, six different versions of Linux. Choose the version of Linux you are using and proceed to download the software. Figure 23 shows the dialog asking you where in your Linux file system to save the downloaded file.

If you do not have a conventional practice for where you keep your binary

Community Supported RealPlayer Download Page

NOTICE: RealNetworks has provided this software at the request of customers in the UNIX community. In addition, RealNetworks does not guarantee functionality, maintenance, upgrades, fixes, or suitability for any purpose.

This software is not formally supported by RealNetworks. However, a special public forum has been provided by RealNetworks to give users of these products a place to share their thoughts and experiences. We encourage you to use this forum for this purpose.

Community Supported Player Forum

First Name: [   ]
Last Name: [   ]
E-mail: [   ]
Country: [Select country ▼]
1. [Select OS ▼]
2. [Select CPU ▼]
3. [Select connection ▼]
4. ☑ Notify me of important news about RealNetworks consumer products and special offers. (Note: GoldPass Subscribers will receive e-mail notices about GoldPass services even if this box is not checked.)

Community Supported RealPlayer
(Figure 22)

files, the default provided will suffice. On most versions of Linux, the next required step is to set Execute permissions on the file, so you can run it. If you are using the Gnome user interface, you can start File Manager, browse to the location where you saved the file, right click on it, select "Properties," and choose the "Permissions" tab. You will see the set of permissions similar to those illustrated in Figure 24.

Click on the "Exec" box in the User row, as illustrated, to allow you to execute the file. Other user interfaces will allow you to do something similar. From the command line, you

Save As Dialog (Figure 23)

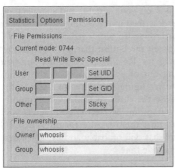

File Permissions Dialog in Gnome's File Manager (Figure 24)

can type "chmod 744 <filename>", where <filename> is the name of the file you downloaded.

When you have made the file executable, execute it. From Gnome's File Manager, you can double click on it. From the command line, you can type its name. This will begin the process of installing RealPlayer. You will be required to accept a license agreement, then asked where you wish to install the software. If you do not have a systematic practice, the default provided by the system will work. The dialog illustrated in Figure 25 suggests installing a Netscape plug-in and installing MIME types. Accept the defaults and say okay.

A confirmation dialog will then appear to let you know that the MIME types have been registered. This dialog will tell you where the installer wrote a log file detailing the results of this process. It is worth recording this information to look at in case you have problems. A final screen will ask you to register. Be sure to unselect the option to receive notifications from RealNetworks.

Register MIME Types (Figure 25)

internet radio on Linux

RealPlayer is now installed on your system, and its operation should be identical to that described in the section on RealPlayer above. To test it, use your browser to visit a radio station. KUT (**www.kut.org**) will do. Click on the button that says "Listen now in RealAudio." You should see RealPlayer come up, and you should hear music coming out of your speakers. If this is not what happens, and you can't figure out why, go back to the RealPlayer page and follow the links to Online Community Support. Describe your symptoms as clearly, completely, and concisely as you can and post them to the forum. There's a knowledgeable community that will probably answer your question, although it may take a little time.

Other Internet Radio Software for Linux

QuickTime is available for Linux. Get it at **www.apple.com/quicktime**. There's also a Linux version of MusicMatch Jukebox. It can serve admirably as a streaming MP3 player. Go to **www.musicmatch.com** and follow the directions for installation.

Many Linux systems ship with XMMS (the X Multimedia System). Although XMMS serves primarily to play media files from your hard drive, it can be used to access streams. The user interface of XMMS is illustrated in Figure 26.

XMMS (Figure 26)

Menus are accessed by clicking on the blaze in the upper left-hand corner. From the File Menu, choose "Open Location." You will see a dialog box in which you can type the full URL for a radio stream and click OK.

Internet Radio Hardware

Specialized hardware for listening to Internet radio is making its way on to the market, though not so rapidly as envisioned in the heady Internet boom of 2000. One device to look for is Intel's Dot.Station web appliance, expected soon and intended to be an easier, less-expensive way to access the Web than a PC. While not designed exclusively as a radio, Linux-based Dot.Station features good sound and has RealPlayer built in.

The consumer electronics giant Philips has announced and demonstrated a 220-watt standalone stereo system called the FW-i1000, which plays CDs, MP3s, and Internet radio. (Just plug it into your network.) The FW-i1000, which uses the iM Networks tuner, is supposed to ship by the beginning of 2002.

Bose, the sound equipment vendor, has introduced the Wave/PC, which combines a remote control tuner and an external sound unit. As illustrated in Figure 27, the external sound unit is essentially the same hardware as the well-known Bose tabletop radio unit.

The Bose Wave/PC (Figure 27)

(Besides functioning as an Internet radio, it continues to function as a broadcast receiver.) Installation involves connecting this unit to your PC with not one but two cables – one, carrying sound, to the output of your sound card; one, carrying control signals, to a serial port. Immediately this has the effect of producing much better sound from your PC. You install tuner software on your PC, and then, using the small and very well-designed remote-control unit, you

internet radio hardware

can surf Internet radio stations without touching your PC. (Provided, that is, you restrict your surfing to RealAudio stations, which are all the tuner knows about.) This is a commendable attempt to provide Internet radio hardware, and it will be an improvement to almost any PC, but it is expensive, lacks stereo separation in the speakers, and still ties your Internet radio experience to the PC by very short cables.

Many non-PC devices are in the works, and the media player vendors have been scrambling to set up bundling deals, in an attempt to establish their formats as a standard. RealNetworks has licensed RealPlayer to Symbian, the consortium of manufacturers representing cell phones and personal digital assistants. The terms of the license offer RealPlayer to Symbian users for free. So if the Symbian operating system becomes the default for handheld wireless devices, RealAudio will become the standard for handheld wireless devices. RealPlayer has also been licensed to Sony for inclusion in PlayStation2. Windows Media Player, of course, will be part of Microsoft's game machine Xbox.

Improving Your Sound

If you are interested in improving the sound you hear when you listen to Internet radio, there are some things that might help. One thing that probably won't help is upgrading your computer itself. You can improve many computer-related experiences by spending extra money on your computer. This is not necessarily so for Internet radio. Limitations tend to be more matters of bandwidth (yours or your favorite stations') than of computer hardware. Any system capable of running the latest web browser is adequate to run Internet radio, and a faster processor or more memory is unlikely to improve your radio reception.

Sound Cards

It is entirely possible that you can improve the sound you hear by investing in a more expensive sound card. The best way to test whether this is the case is to connect your sound card to the amplifier of your sound system. (See below.) Then compare the sound generated from the PC to the sound generated from other sources. For the most accurate comparison, if you have the ability to copy CDs, take two copies of the same CD, and place one in your PC's CD player and one in your sound system's CD player. Switch back and forth between the two sources while listening. A muddy, compressed, limited sound, which mushes the bass and drops out high sounds like cymbals, is probably caused by the limitations of your sound card.

Manufacturers of good sound cards include:

▸▸ Voyetra Turtle Beach (Santa Cruz) **www.voyetra-turtle-beach.com**
▸▸ Creative Labs (SoundBlaster) **www.soundblaster.com**
▸▸ Digital Experience **www.digitalexperience.com**

A good tutorial on sound cards, from the physics of sound to the technologies used by sound cards in sound reproduction, is available at **www.pctechguide.com/11sound.htm**. There is a guide to shopping for sound cards at **www.zdnet.com**. Choose "Help & How-To," "Hardware," then "Sound Cards." Included is a step-by-step guide for upgrading your sound card, aimed at those who have never opened the case on their computer. CNET has reviews and prices: **www.cnet.com**. Choose "Hardware Reviews," "Graphics and Sound," "Sound Cards."

Speakers

One of the first places to turn in trying to improve your Internet radio sound is your speakers. Computer systems are coming equipped with better and better speaker systems, as manufacturers realize that people are purchasing their products

improving your sound

for use as multimedia devices. Still, better speakers will sound better. If you are ordering a new computer, better speakers are usually an option from the manufacturer. Later on, you can usually order speakers from the manufacturer as an add-on. Many speaker companies now make a line of products designed specifically for computer use. If you have a favorite speaker manufacturer, their web page is a good place to begin looking. Altec Lansing has some solid multimedia speakers, as do Harmon Kardon. and VideoLogic

One particularly cost-effective solution is provided by Cambridge Soundworks **www.cambridgesoundworks.com**. Even before the advent of the Web, Cambridge Soundworks had a direct-to-customer sales model, sending speakers out mail order for customers to try at home. Sound designer Henry Kloss, familiar to many audiophiles for two or three companies before Cambridge Soundworks, creates speakers that sound as good as – often better than – extremely high-end competitors, yet they're dirt cheap. Listening to his PCWorks system, for example, one would never believe it costs under $50.

Headphones

Finally, don't forget the option of *headphones*. Not only do headphones deliver a much higher quality sound than all but the very best speaker systems, but they also have two other very important advantages. First, they allow you to listen without imposing your sound on others. Second, they mask the distracting noise of others. This is why it is common in high-tech industries to walk down a line of cubicles and see the majority of the workers wearing headphones. Cutting out distraction can be a major improvement in productivity. Headphones designed for

Headphone Adapter (Figure 28)

use with stereo systems are what you want, not the junky things that ship with computers.

One of the jacks on the back of your sound card will be for headphones. It will probably have a picture of headphones above it. Unfortunately, the jack is a "1/8 inch stereo mini jack." High fidelity headphones use a larger connector called a "1/4 inch stereo plug." Because bridging these two connector systems is a common need, an adaptor to do so is available at any electronic store. One is illustrated above in Figure 28.

Connecting your Computer to your Sound System

You probably already have a sound system in your house, and it may make the most sense to direct your Internet radio sound through it. It is optimized for the purpose. That's where your CD and tape deck and broadcast radio connect to the major speaker systems you own. Why not pump Internet radio through it? One fear sometimes expressed is that the inferior quality of the Internet radio sound might be painfully exposed when amplified through a real stereo system. You should not find this so. Under most circumstances, Internet radio will sound *better* than FM radio.

Stereo gear and computer gear use two different sets of connectors. You'll need an adapter between them. The computer gear uses "1/8 inch stereo mini" jacks and plugs. Stereo gear uses "phono" jacks and plugs. Your neighborhood electronics store should be well stocked with 1/8 inch stereo mini to phono stereo adapters. One is illustrated in Figure 29.

You can run normal phono patch cords from this adapter to the amplifier of your sound system, where any open input jacks ("Tuner," "Auxiliary," etc.) will work. There is a limit to how far you can run unamplified signals in patch cords before causing sound degradation; unfortunately, no one agrees on what the limit is. Your corner audio or electronics store will sell you patch cords 30 feet long, which should cause no audible grief.

improving your sound

Most current sound cards have more than one speaker jack. If your sound card has only a single speaker jack and you want to continue using your PC's speakers as well as your stereo system, you probably need yet another adapter, a "Y" with one 1/8 inch stereo mini jack on one end and two 1/8 inch stereo mini plugs on the other. Plug this Y into your sound card. Plug the PC's speakers into one half of the Y. Plug the above adapter into the other.

Another option for connecting to your sound system is the IRhythm Remote Tuner from iM Networks (formerly Sonicbox). This device transmits Internet radio to your stereo system via – get this – *radio*. 900 MHz radio, to be precise. So there's a device you hook to your PC, and a device you plug into your stereo, and then a remote control, so you can change stations when you're away from your PC. The tuner is a hardware version of the iMtuner described above in the "Tuners" section. It is an inventive design that is not only easy to use but fun to pass around to friends. The only problem with this

Adapter for Connecting a PC Sound Card to a Stereo System (Figure 29)

otherwise excellent concept is that the sound quality degrades considerably in the 900 MHz transmission – enough for critical listeners to write the whole package off as unusable. The cost is $89.95. For details, see **www.imnetworks.com**.

Turtle Beach's AudioTron works similarly, except that it uses household electrical wiring for the connection between the PC and the sound system. It costs $299.95. More information is available at **www.voyetra-turtle-beach.com**.

part two

the directory

A Guide to the Directory

This directory adopts, for the most part, the philosophy of the *Whole Earth Catalog*, which is to include only positive reviews. It is a busy, crowded world full of more things than any one lifetime could take in. Why waste space on anything not worth your attention? So, though you may find a few minor gripes and complaints herein, essentially, if a station's content is unexceptional, or its stream is just too hard to receive, the station is not included here. This is a guide to what's good.

This directory does not pretend to be either comprehensive or objective: it is highly selective, and the selection criteria are personal. One obvious and explicit bias favors the non-commercial over the commercial.

Most of the radio stations in the world play the same things, over and over again – they are little more than catalogs of corporate product. Whether it's adult contemporary, young country, or easy listening, it's all packaged, and it's the same in Cleveland as it is in Tucson. This isn't the same thing as teenagers dressing alike because they copy each other. These stations are largely interchangeable because they're owned and run by the same people. A couple of giant corporations own most of the radio stations in America (this is true in other countries as well), and in many cases, the signal that is broadcast in your town isn't even programmed in your town. A single staff in a building somewhere in Kentucky turns out the programming for hundreds of teen-oriented stations all over the country. It's cheaper that way. Instead of paying two dozen DJs in two dozen cities, the giant corporation pays one in the building in Kentucky. Well, this may be an effective way to increase shareholder value, but it is not a way to create memorable radio. This is why most commercial radio stations today are boring and having difficulty holding their audiences. In any event, you certainly don't need a guide to commercial radio. You turn to Internet radio for what you can't get on commercial radio. So although there are a few commercial stations sprinkled here and there in this guide, marked as commercial so you aren't surprised when they start pitching beer, cars, and beauty products, mostly they've been left out. Even when the commercial station has excellent original programming, such as, say, KING, which receives high praise for its classical music programming, there is still the likelihood that if you went to listen to it, instead of classical music you would hear an advertisement for a diamond store. Since there are dozens of classical music stations in the world that *don't* interrupt the music to tout diamonds, there seems to be no compelling reason to add one that *does*, unless it is a truly exceptional station. (This bias against the commercial has been greatly relaxed in the case of foreign-language stations, since if you're listening to practice your Portuguese, you might well find the commercials even more valuable than the news.)

While there is a high percentage of American radio stations in this book – after all, the U.S. has far more radio stations than the rest of the world combined – and this is particularly true of Internet radio – one of the most exciting promises of Internet radio is that it brings the rest of the world to us. So the guide includes as many stations from elsewhere in the world as possible, intentionally giving them favored treatment. If more aren't here, the main reason is that radio stations in places like Vietnam, Cape Verde, and Latvia are less likely to be on the Net, and, if on the Net, are more likely to have bandwidth limitations or other problems that make them harder to listen to.

Finally, while you will see Internet-only audio streams listed in this guide, there is a discernible bias toward radio stations that are *radio stations*. That is, rather than being just some web page with an audio stream, they also have a transmitter somewhere. The reason is that, at this point in history, real radio stations just tend to be better. Their extensive history, their community connections, and their audience have created programming that is more alive and more interesting. As Internet-only stations thrive, grow, get fanatically devoted and supportive audiences, and develop more interesting programming, expect to see more of them here.

If you love a radio station or program that is on the Internet but not in this guide, please write and explain what is great about it. Send email to radio@heberlein.net.

Subject to Change

Note that although pains have been taken to make this guide up-to-the-minute, stations do change their schedules from time to time. A current schedule is in almost every case available on the station's website.

A Note About Time

If the Internet hasn't entirely eliminated geography, it sure has mangled time. Radio is a live medium. Most of what's available on the Internet is not tape recordings of old shows, but something happening right *now*. This guide attempts to tell you a certain insanely brilliant DJ can be heard on a certain obscure station at 10pm on Mondays. But when is 10pm, to you?

Americans grow up hearing "9pm, 8 Central," so if it were merely a matter of our continental time zones, that would not take much adjustment. But many of the radio stations in this book broadcast from time zones we've never heard of, where the time right now is sometime tomorrow.

The obvious choice would be to list all times in this guide in Greenwich Mean Time, also sometimes referred to as Universal (UTC) or Zulu time. This is the global standard, and it has become the Internet standard. It's a relatively simple matter to learn that where you might be right now is, say Greenwich +8. So if the guide said that a certain show came on at 1400 GMT, you could work out that that means 10pm your time.

One problem with listing all times in Greenwich is that many places on earth, and in particular most of the United States, have an inconsistent relationship with Greenwich time. Twice a year, for the ostensible purpose of "saving daylight," we change all our clocks. So that if the guide were to say that our DJ was on at 1400 Greenwich, this would be true from November to April, but untrue from May through October. A more mundane objection is that it would require the majority of the readers to convert the majority of the listings. So instead this guide uses local times for stations on the American continent, and Greenwich elsewhere. This compromise lacks technical elegance, but should hopefully provide the most convenience to the most readers.

A Note About Listening to Foreign Stations

The stations in this guide have been selected partly on the basis of reliability. That is, preference was given to streams that are relatively easy to get, and that drop out less often. Nevertheless, more frustration is likely when attaching to a stream on the other side of an ocean. If you can't get a station, try again at a different time of day. Because part of the problem is Net congestion, you will have your best luck during times that are not peak business hours in the United States. The websites for some stations are in languages other than English, but the button to push to listen is usually fairly obvious. When you browse a web page in, say, Chinese, your browser may ask whether you would like to install a language pack to correctly display Chinese characters. Choosing not to do so will not affect your ability to browse the site (assuming that you don't read Chinese anyway), but allowing the installation has the advantage that the browser will stop asking the question in the future.

Some Stations to Start With

Before wandering out to explore the wide variety of Internet radio in the world, here is a very short list of some particularly excellent and interesting stations to serve as appetizers and benchmarks.

All Songs Considered   NPR **www.npr.org/programs/asc**
Many listeners of NPR's afternoon news program *All Things Considered* have long enjoyed the snippets of music used as breaks between news stories; in fact, one of the largest categories of mail received by NPR has been of the form "what was that song you played after the story about…?" *All Songs Considered* is a Web-only program playing the full versions of the music played on *All Things Considered*. It is archived and searchable.

KCSN   **www.kcsn.org**
California State University Northridge. KCSN is a superb classical station by day, fringe-seeking alternative station by night, home to over a dozen expertly programmed shows on various kinds of music from *Citybilly's* country/rock to *L'Chaim's* Jewish fusion. You might try just leaving KCSN on for a couple of weeks and seeing what you discover.

KEXP   **www.kexp.org**
University of Washington/Experience Music Project. KEXP provides some excellent examples of how to *use* the technology. To take the simplest example, live playlists on the website. This is something everyone should do. If you are listening and hear something that you would like to know what it is, your choices with most stations are a) wait 20 minutes until the DJ (maybe) identifies it; or b) call them on the telephone and (possibly) get through to ask the DJ. The Web is *perfect* for this. It's visual. It doesn't take one away from the sound. It's instant. Every radio station should do it. Specialty shows are

a guide to the directory

Amanda Wilde

scheduled evenings and weekends. Tune in any weekday for impeccably mixed music, mostly extremely current. Particularly sharp is Amanda Wilde, daily 2–6pm Pacific.

KPFA   www.kpfa.org

The first listener-sponsored station. When KPFA went on the air April 14, 1949, nothing like it existed. The Pacifica Foundation, created by World War II conscientious objector Lewis Hill, broadcasting via the new, experimental technology of frequency modulation, had no sponsors, and expected its listeners to become members. It teetered on the edge of financial ruin until... well, it is still teetering on the edge of financial ruin. But its existence served as a model for every public radio station that followed. Its eclectic format, featuring folk songs, classical music, science fiction, and Zen, featured the talents and helped launch the careers of Anthony Boucher, Alan Watts, Pauline Kael, and Jerry Garcia. Television arrived before FM receivers became widespread. The red scares of the 1950s caused continual government harassment. A pro-marijuana broadcast in 1954 brought down the wrath not only of police, but also of listener/sponsors and the Pacifica Board. Throughout its growth, KPFA received more passionate engagement with its listeners than any radio station before – and possibly since. When the Pacifica Board brought in armed guards to take control of the station in 1999, amidst reports they intended to sell the frequency, thousands of protestors occupied the streets outside the studio, and the City Council of Berkeley forbade the police department to take action against them. The Board backed down, somewhat (and the chair subsequently resigned), but the KPFA community is still shaken, polarized, and fearful.

KSUT
www.ksut.org

The program *Music Blend*, from 9am to 4pm Mountain, with an hour off at noon for *The World Cafe* and similar programming, is a relaxed eclectic mix heavily biased toward Americana: folk, roots, and bluegrass, with a modicum of rock, blues, world, and jazz mixed in.

KVMR
www.kvmr.org

KVMR is a community-supported, volunteer-based, non-profit, non-commercial radio station in Nevada City, California. It is a model of what a community radio station can be, offering up a profuse variety of music and public affairs programs – all of which are locally produced by people working without pay. Stations claiming they need to act more like commercial stations because of the requirement to raise more funds should take a few steps back and ask themselves if their communities really possess fewer resources than Nevada City, California. It is heartening as well to hit KVMR's website and see the proposed schedule changes (which are all minor) being advertised for public comment. There is a tendency in our culture to think of *process* and *results* as essentially opposed, to lament the messiness of democracy and envy the supposed relative efficiency of the ruthless dictator. What makes KVMR serve as such an excellent model is how great the resulting programming is. The day is filled with a progress of one gregarious program after another. Tune in at any random time of the day or night and see.

A Net Station
www.anetstation.com

A Net Station would be of interest if only for its location: it streams from the Ross Island Ice Shelf on the continent of Antarctica. But its repeat listeners aren't there for the novelty of listening to radio from the South Pole. They're there for the excellent music. It's a non-commercial mix of original music, most of it independently released by its creators, so listening to A Net Station is a bit like going to the farmers' market rather than a grocery store. As George Maat, A Net Station's creator explains it, "Most radio broadcasts generate income for the station owners through paid advertising. They demographically 'cover the odds' to get a broad base of listeners for those ads. The result is a music venue showcasing music generated by record companies with a similar profit motivation. We play music by artists who perform internationally at clubs, cafés, and concerts. Most prefer not to compete for the record industry's favor. This music is owned, published and distributed by the musicians themselves. That is why we provide links to their websites." The website also has Antarctica news and photos. The only drawback is that A Net Station provides only a short stream, usually only about 72 songs long.

a guide to the directory

Classical Music

Classical Music Stations

Allegro FM   **www.allegrofm.com**
This Colombian station streams easy-listening classical hits of the ages, extending through jazz all the way to Windham Hill.

Classical Favorites	
CBC Saturday Afternoon at the Opera	see p.66
ClasicaOnline	see p.53
Hear and Now	see p.72
KCSN	see p.60
Lyric FM	see p.54
Opera on 3	see p.67
Radio B.A.C.H.	see p.54
Radio Canada Chaîne Culturelle	see p.54
RDP Antena 2	see p.55
Sunday Opera	see p.68

CBC Saturday Afternoon at the Opera — see p.66
ClasicaOnline — see p.53
Hear and Now — see p.72
KCSN — see p.60
Lyric FM — see p.54
Opera on 3 — see p.67
Radio B.A.C.H. — see p.54
Radio Canada Chaîne Culturelle — see p.54
RDP Antena 2 — see p.55
Sunday Opera — see p.68

classical music

Australian Broadcasting Corporation
www.abc.net.au/classic

The highest-quality classical programming, 24 hours a day, with playlists on the website in advance.

BBC Radio 3
www.bbc.co.uk/radio3

Classical music throughout the day.

Cesky Rozhlas 3–Vltava
www.rozhlas.cz/vltava

This station from the Czech Republic has some folk, jazz, and other specialty shows, but its programming is mostly classical. In case you can't find the stream, it's at **www.rozhlas.cz/vltava/zive/288s.ram**.

ClasicaOnline
www.clasicaonline.com.ar

Superb station from Argentina, with many programs archived on the website. It features an impressive array of adventurous contemporary material. (Click on "escúchenos.")

Classic FM
www.classicfm.co.za

From Johannesburg, South Africa.

Eesti Raadio Klassikaraadio
www.er.ee/eng/klassik

The Estonian national broadcast system's Klassikaraadio streams classical music 24 hours a day. "Classical" here is a broad category that ranges from baroque and Renaissance music to jazz and folk. Specialty programs include premieres of new musical compositions. (The URL above is for the English version of the website.)

ERA 3
http://ert.ntua.gr

This Greek site offers several streams of a variety of audio. ERA 3 is classical, and it's a satisfying classical stream to listen to for an extended time.

KBPS
www.kbps.org

If what you want is a station that plays good classical music *all* the time, so you don't have to get up from what you're doing and turn off some talk show that comes on, KBPS is your station.

KBYU
www.kbyu.org/fm

Serious program of classical music almost all the time.

classical music

Klassik Radio
www.klassikradio.de

Although this German station's content is excellent, you may have some difficulty receiving its stream, particularly if you are on the opposite side of the Atlantic. Selecting the lowest-quality stream ("mit Analog-Modem") will help.

Klasyka FM
www.bor.com.pl/radio93

Classical music with a distinctly Polish flavor.

Korean Broadcasting System FM 1
www.kbs.co.kr

Very solid classical music programming around the clock.

KUSC
www.kusc.org

Solid all-classical station. Full playlists on the website in advance.

Lyric FM
www.lyricfm.ie

This Irish station streams a lineup of solid classical music programs. Particularly good is Evelyn Cockburn's afternoon program, *The Full Score*, which plays major full-length pieces.

Radio B.A.C.H.
www.platforma.pl/bach

Not only all-Bach all the time, but *eight channels* of Bach – a channel for cantatas, a channel for harpsichord works, etc. Although the station is from Poland, the website is available in English. (Click on the Union Jack.)

Radio Beethoven de Chile
www.beethovenfm.cl

Playlists on the website in advance.

Radio Canada Chaîne Culturelle
radio-canada.ca

Francophone Radio Canada has two streams. The cultural one offers exceptionally good classical music, with a few breaks, from 6am to 10pm Eastern weekdays.

Radio Classique
www.radioclassique.fr

Solid classical station from France.

Rádio de la Universidade
orion.ufrgs.br/radio

From the Federal University of the Rio Grande Do Sul in Brazil.

Radio K
www.radiok.net

This Mexican station's *Música Clásica* stream features the warhorses, but often versions you haven't heard.

classical music

Radio Television Hong Kong (RTHK) Radio 4
www.rthk.org.hk

Radio 4 presents a variety of cultural programming, including substantial amounts of classical music. Edward Morton Jack's *Masterpiece Studio,* daily 0600–0800 Greenwich, plays longer selections. All playlists are on the website in advance (in English).

RAI Radio 3
www.rai.it

(Click "Radio," then on the international forward arrow for play beside "Radio 3." In case you have trouble, the stream is **www.radio.rai.it/live/radio3.ram.**) It should probably not be surprising that the classical station of Italy is seriously committed to presenting the highest quality music.

RDP Antena 2
www.rdp.pt/antena2

Excellent classical station from Radiofusão Portuguesa. Complete schedule including playlists is on the website in advance.

Ríkisútvarpid (RUV) Channel 1
www.ruv.is

The National Broadcasting Service of Iceland's Channel 1 mixes classical music and informational programming.

Sveriges Radio P2
www.sr.se

Excellent classical programming from the national radio service of Sweden. (Click on "Lyssna direkt P2 Musick.")

Symphony 92
symphony.mediacorpradio.com

A very decent commercial station in Singapore.

Universidad Técnica Federico Santa María
www.utfsm.cl

From Valparaiso, Chile.

WCPE
www.wcpe.org

Classical music 24 hours a day, in every format you could want: RealAudio, Windows Media, QuickTime, and MP3.

WFMT
www.networkchicago.com/wfmt

Solid programming includes a featured artist or composer each month. WFMT broadcasts The Chicago Symphony Orchestra in concert Sundays 1-2pm Central. The 8-10pm slot weeknights (except Friday) features special shows,

classical music

such as *Music in Chicago*, *International Konzert*, *Rising Stars at Ravinia*, and *Salzburg Festival*. WFMT is the home of the Beethoven Satellite Network, which, among other programs, creates and distributes Peter Van De Graaff's *LaSalle by Night*. One annoyance is that you have to listen to WMFT through Yahoo, which means suffering through Yahoo's annoying Media Helper before you can get to the music.

WOSU   **www.wosu.org**
Another all-classical-all-the-time station. (Be sure you get WOSU-FM; WOSU-AM is all jazz.)

WPLN   **www.wpln.org**
Classical music from Nashville? Yes, good coverage through much of the day. Weekday schedule: 9am–3pm, Eastern 7:30–10pm, Eastern 10pm–5am Eastern (*Music Through the Night*).

WQED   **www.wqed.org**
Classical music almost all the time, from this very good station in Pittsburgh.

WRTI   **www.wrti.org**
Classical music weekdays 6am–6pm Eastern, with classical specialty shows on the weekend.

WWFM   **www.wwfm.org**
Very good locally produced shows, with fewer interruptions (news, traffic reports, etc.) than you will find elsewhere. A symphony every weekday evening 8-10pm Eastern.

XLNC1   **www.xlnc1.org**
The transmitter is in Tijuana, but this is a San Diego station, and the website and announcing are in English, featuring the best known pieces of the best-known composers.

NPR Classical Stations

Across the United States, particularly in small university towns, can be found radio stations that broadcast NPR's *Morning Edition* in the morning, *All Things Considered* in the afternoon, a mix of shows such as *Pipedreams*, *Thistle and Shamrock*, *Prairie Home*

classical music

Companion, and *Car Talk* on the weekends, and the rest of the time – that is, most of the day weekdays, much of the evening, and all night – they broadcast classical music. If you have ever lived in a small Midwestern town, such a station may have served as your lifeline, your companion, evidence that Western Civilization exists. Throughout much of the Midwest, the stations are rebroadcast on multiple repeaters, so that you do not have to be in Lawrence, Kansas, to hear the University of Kansas station – its reach extends to remote farms in distant corners of the huge state. Even though you do not live in the regions dependent on these radio stations, you might still find them a good source of classical music. The quality of programming varies from tame to more adventurous, but it's never bad and often quite interesting. Even if you have a favorite classical station, it's good to get out of your rut once in a while (perhaps during a pledge drive?) and see what they're listening to today in Iowa.

Alabama Public Radio
www.wual.ua.edu

Classical music weekdays 9am–4pm Eastern.

KAMU
kamu-fm.tamu.edu

This station from the Brazos Valley in Texas has classical music from 9am–2pm Central, and then a symphony most nights at 8pm Central, before streaming classical music through the night.

KANU
kanu.ukans.edu

Classical music 9am–3pm Central.

KCCU
www.cameron.edu/admin/kccu

Broadcasts the Beethoven Satellite Network via three transmitters across Oklahoma, weekdays 9am–4pm and 7pm–6am Central.

KOSU
www.kosu.org

Classical music weekdays 9am–3pm Central, with playlists on the website in advance.

Radio Kansas
www.radioks.org

Classical music all day and all night weekdays.

classical music

WBAA

www.wbaa.purdue.edu/wbaa

WBAA, from Purdue University in Indiana, is an exception to the "Classical Music between NPR News" format in that it has split itself in two. All the talk, the *All Things Considered*, etc., is moved to the AM dial, and thus to a separate stream on the Web. On the FM side, and therefore on its own Internet stream, is essentially uninterrupted classical music. (The availability of AM frequencies has led other public radio stations to experiment with this approach, which may become widely adopted.)

WCBU

www.bradley.edu/irt/wcbu/

WCVE

www.wcve.org/fm_ric/fm.html

Classical music weekdays 9am–4pm, midnight–5am Eastern.

WEKU

www.weku.com/

WFCR

www.wfcr.org

From the University of Massachusetts in Amherst, classical music weekdays 9am–4pm Eastern.

WFIU

www.indiana.edu/~wfiu/

WGCS

www.goshen.edu/wgcs

WGTE

www.wgte.org

Classical music weekdays 9am–4pm and 6:30pm–6am Eastern. The 8–10pm slot is for concert shows, with Tuesdays produced locally.

WKAR

www.wkar.org

WSHU

www.wshu.org

Classical music 9am–3pm Eastern.

WUOT

www.sunsite.utk.edu/wuot/

Classical music weekdays 9am–noon, 1–4pm, and 8pm–6am Eastern.

WYSU

www.wysu.org

Classical music weekdays 9am–5pm and 8pm–5am Eastern, with playlists on the website in advance.

classical music

Classical Music Programs

Adventures in Good Music
Host: Karl Haas. It would be interesting to know how many adults there are today who would say they received a substantial portion of their education in classical music from Karl Haas. His program has a heavier mix of the didactic than most, meant to be more like a good college lecture than easy-listening music for the office. Syndicated on PRI stations, such as WWFM (**www.wwfm.org**) weekdays 7–8pm Eastern.

Canadian Music Centre Presents   CJSW **www.cjsw.com**
Tuesday 9–10am Mountain. Host: John Reid. Reid is director of the Canadian Music Centre, a library and promotional archive of new music by Canadian (primarily classical) composers. The show airs music from the CMC's library and covers styles ranging from jazz, through world music, electroacoustic and avant-garde, to contemporary classical music – focusing always on the newest releases.

Coming Out   5UV **www.adelaide.edu.au/5UV**
Thursday 2340–Friday 0130 Greenwich. Host: Ewart Shaw. A preview of the latest CDs.

Deutsche Welle Concert Hour
Host: Martin Goldsmith. This program is a collaboration of Germany's public broadcasters, with symphonic, chamber and solo pieces from the early baroque to the 20th century, live concerts and exclusive studio productions, playlist favorites and seldom-heard gems. Only a few of these recordings are available on CD. Each program revolves around a central theme, from "The Century Past" to "Games and Pranks." It is syndicated (free) to numerous public radio stations; one place to hear it is WOSU (**www.wosu.org**) Saturday 8–9pm Eastern. For more information, see the Deutsche Welle website: **http://www.dwelle.de/english**.

Rick Martin (left) and Martin Goldsmith

classical music

From the Top
www.fromthetop.org

Host: Christopher O'Riley. This PRI syndicated program gives young classical musicians a chance to stand in the spotlight. Each one-hour program features five musicians of pre-college age. All programs are archived on the website for listening any time.

KCSN
www.kcsn.org

Hosts: Mara Zhelutka (daily 2–6pm Pacific); Tony Hanover (daily 6–10:30am Pacific). Mara Zhelutka is a master of radio. You should learn her name and follow her career, wherever she goes and whatever she plays. Many listeners first encountered her on KCRW in Santa Monica, where of everyone who handled the flagship program *Morning Becomes Eclectic*, she was far and away the best. Currently she is at the California State University Northridge station KCSN hosting an afternoon classical program. It is an extremely savvy, well-arranged presentation of classical music. Where else do you hear Marcello Zarvos? The "Chamber Hour" at 2pm is particularly enjoyable. Tony Hanover also does an excellent show in the morning, with a "Morning Symphony" at 10am.

Northern Lights
CBC Radio One **www.cbc.ca**

Weeknights 11pm–1am Eastern. Host: Andrea Ratuski. This very well produced classical program is archived on the CBC website so you can listen to years of it any time.

Time Bandits
KUCR **www.kucr.org**

Saturday 11pm–1am Sunday Pacific. Host: Michael Smith. An interesting show featuring rare historic classical music.

Early Music

Early Music
Australian Broadcasting Corporation Classic FM
www.abc.net.au/classic

Saturday 1200–1400 Greenwich.
Host: Simon Healy.

Harmonia
WFIU **www.indiana.edu/~wfiu**

Thursday 9–10pm Eastern. Host: Angela Mariani. Mariani, a performer and scholar of early music, has been producing this excellent (and now widely syndicated) program for WFIU for a decade. Many programs feature conversations with, and studio performances by, early music ensembles. All programs are archived on the website for listening any time.

Chamber Music

Chamber Music New York
WNYC **www.wnyc.org**
Friday 8–9pm Eastern. Host: John Schaefer. Performances from the music room at the Frick Collection, as well as from elsewhere around the city.

Spoleto Chamber Music Series
WRJA **www.scern.org**
April–June, Thursday 8–9pm Eastern. Host: Charles Wadsworth. This 13-week series is recorded live at the Dock Street Theatre in Charleston, South Carolina, produced by the South Carolina Educational Radio Network, and syndicated on PRI.

John Schaefer

St. Paul Sunday
Minnesota Public Radio **sunday.mpr.org**
Host: Bill McLaughlin. Chamber music, broadly conceived, and superbly executed live in the St. Paul studios, with host McLaughlin's effective questioning eliciting interesting comments from the performers. Widely syndicated. Archives of past shows available any time on the website.

Choral

With Heart and Voice
WXXI **www.wxxi.org**
Sunday 8–10am Eastern. Host: Richard Gladwell. Sacred choral and organ music.

Guitar

Classical Guitar Alive
You can hear this syndicated program on KAMU (**kamu-fm.tamu.edu**) Sunday 1–2pm Central. More information at **www.guitaralive.com**.

classical music

part two

La Guitarra in el Mundo
Radio UNAM FM
Monday 8:30–9:30pm Central.
www.unam.mx/radiounam
Host: Esteban Escárcega. This program is devoted to the place of the guitar in the world's panorama of music. From the Universidad Nacional Autónoma de México. Note that Radio UNAM has two streams. This program is on the FM stream.

Organ

Pipedreams
Minnesota Public Radio pipedreams.mpr.org
Host: Michael Barone. Weekly 90-minute show devoted to the organ. Widely syndicated; archives of past shows available any time on the website.

Piano

Au piano avec Glenn Gould
Radio Canada Chaîne Culturelle
Sunday noon–1:30pm Eastern.
radio-canada.ca

Live Performances

Adelaide Concert Hour
5UV www.adelaide.edu.au/5UV
Monday 0330–0430 Greenwich. Live performances from Adelaide, Australia.

BBC Proms
BBC Radio 3 www.bbc.co.uk/radio3
Eight weeks of live concerts, usually late July through mid-September. Concerts daily. Times vary, but usually 1930–2300 Greenwich. A number of proms also receive repeat broadcasts at 1400 weekdays.

Central Florida in Concert
WMFE www.pbs.org/wmfe
Saturday 1–2pm Eastern.

Concerts du Soir
Radio Canada Chaîne Culturelle radio-canada.ca
Weeknights 8–10pm Eastern. Live performances from Europe.

Concierto OFUNAM
Radio UNAM www.unam.mx/radiounam
Sunday noon–2:30pm Central. Selected live performances from the Universidad Nacional Autónoma de México.

classical music

Friday Concert
Lyric FM **www.lyricfm.ie**

Friday 2000–2230 Greenwich. Host: Aedin Gormley. Various symphonic concerts recorded live.

Houston in Concert
KUHF **www.kuhf.uh.edu**

Sunday 1–2pm Central. Host: Elaine Kennedy.

Hunter Rostrum
2NUR **www.newcastle.edu.au/cwis/ra**

Sunday 0900–1000 Greenwich. Host: Ray Hugo. Performances recorded at the Concert Hall of the Conservatorum of Music at the University of Newcastle in Australia.

In Performance
CBC Radio Two **www.cbc.ca**

Weekdays 8–9pm Eastern. Host: Eric Friesen. A variety of performances from around Canada.

Live Broadcast from Estonia Concert Hall
Eesti Raadio Klassikaraadio
www.er.ee/eng/klassik

Friday 1700–1900 Greenwich.

OnStage
CBC Radio One **www.cbc.ca**

Sunday 9–10pm Eastern. Winter and spring broadcasts of *OnStage* are recorded before live audiences in CBC's 340-seat Toronto concert hall, the Glenn Gould Studio. Summer and fall broadcasts come from Europe's orchestral concert series and festivals. The program is archived on the website.

Our Music
CBC Calgary **www.calgary.cbc.ca**

Sunday noon–1pm Mountain. Host: Catherine McClelland. Choral, chamber, and orchestral music recorded live in concerts around Alberta.

Performance in Pittsburgh
WQED **www.wqed.org**

Sunday 5–7pm Eastern (repeated Thursday at 10pm). Host: Paul Johnston. This program features local and visiting artists recorded in performance in Pittsburgh.

Performance Today

Host: Fred Child; Sundays Korva Colman. On NPR's *Performance Today* listeners can experience concert hall performances in this two-hour program, which offers intriguing interviews and commentary intended to educate the listener about the music. A representative recent show included the following live performances:

classical music

part two

▶▶Clarinetist James Campbell and pianist Leonard Hokanson playing Claude
Debussy's *First Rhapsody* in clarinet, recorded at a concert February 2001
at the Ithaca College School of Music
▶▶Cellist Heinrich Schiff's performance of Camille Saint-Saens' *Cello Concerto
No. 1 in A minor* in the summer of 2000 at the Ascona Music Festival in
Switzerland
▶▶A performance the Trio Fontenay gave in 1999 of *Piano Trio No. 1 in B
major*, by Johannes Brahms

Performance Today is available on various NPR stations at various times, often
at night. For example, Yellowstone Public Radio **www.yellowstone
publicradio.org** carries it weekdays from 9–11am Mountain.

Played in Oregon
KBPS **www.kbps.org**
Tuesday 8–10pm Pacific.

Sunday Afternoon Live From Elvehjem
Wisconsin Public Radio **www.wpr.org**
Sunday 12:30–2pm Central, October through May. Chamber concerts
broadcast live from the Elvehjem Museum of Art in Madison, Wisconsin.

Sunday Live
Australian Broadcasting Corporation Classic FM Classic
Sunday 0500–0600 Greenwich. **www.abc.net.au/classic**
Australian musicians in live performance, from different cities in Australia, in
collaboration with local venues and communities.

Sunday Live
BBC Radio 3
www.bbc.co.uk/radio3
Sunday 0900–1200 Greenwich.

Symphony Cast
www.npr.org
Host: Korva Coleman. Weekly concert program
featuring performances by a wide variety of
orchestras. Picked up by many NPR stations,
including WHYY **www.whyy.org** Sunday
8–10pm Eastern.

Symphony Hall
CBC Radio Two
www.cbc.ca
Sunday 10:05. Host: Katherine Duncan. *Symphony
Hall* is CBC Radio Two's showcase for Canada's
orchestras and their musicians. Each program

Korva Coleman

classical music

64

presents one concert by one orchestra, not only from Toronto, Montreal and Vancouver, but also from smaller cities such as Victoria and Saskatoon.

Take Five
CBC Radio Two **www.cbc.ca**

Weekdays 10am–3pm Eastern. Host: Shelley Solmes. There is one full concert in each day's program. (Solmes plays requests for the remainder of the five-hour show.) Upcoming performances are listed on the website. There is a wide variety of performers and material.

Thornton Center Stage
KUSC **www.kusc.org**

Sunday 8–9pm Pacific. Host: Alan Chapman. A magazine-style program of live performances at the University of Southern California's Thornton School of Music.

Specific Orchestras

Australian Symphony Orchestra
Australian Broadcasting Corporation
Classic FM **www.abc.net.au/classic**

Saturday 1000–1200 Greenwich. Host: Simon Healy.

Chicago Symphony Orchestra
KBPS **www.kbps.org**

Saturday 1–3pm Pacific. (among many other stations).

Detroit Symphony Orchestra
KTXK **tc.cc.tx.us/ktxk**

Friday 8–10pm Central.

Indiana Symphony Orchestra
WFIU **www.indiana.edu/~wfiu**

Thursday 10–11pm Central.

Milwaukee Symphony
Wisconsin Public Radio **www.wpr.org**

Sunday noon–2pm Central July–September.

Minnesota Orchestra
Hour-long program broadcast weekly from December through July. Syndicated by Minnesota Public Radio. See **www.mpr.org** for a full list of stations and times. You can catch it on KBPS **www.kbps.org** Tuesday at 8pm Pacific.

Philadelphia Symphony
WHYY **www.whyy.org**

Sunday 8–10pm Eastern, October–June.

classical music

(Outside the Philadelphia Symphony season, WHYY picks up NPR's *Symphony Cast* at this time.)

Pittsburgh Symphony Radio
WQED **www.wqed.org**

Sunday 2–4pm Eastern (repeated Tuesday 7–9pm). Host: Jim Cunningham. This 26-week series, syndicated on PRI, features recent concerts and archival tapes.

Royal Concertgebouw Orchestra of Amsterdam
KCSN **www.kcsn.org**

May–July Thursday 7–9pm Pacific.

San Francisco Symphony
KDFC **www.kdfc.com**

Tuesday 8–10pm Pacific.

The St. Louis Symphony Orchestra
KTXK **tc.cc.tx.us/ktxk**

Thursday 8–10pm Central.

The Evening Concert
WILL **www.will.uiuc.edu**

Weeknights 7:04–9pm Central. Monday: Milwaukee Symphony Orchestra. Tuesday: San Francisco Symphony Orchestra. Wednesday: Chicago Symphony Orchestra. Thursday: St. Paul Chamber Orchestra.

Opera

Full-Length Opera Broadcasts

CBC Saturday Afternoon at the Opera
CBC Radio Two **www.radio.cbc.ca**

Saturday 1:30–5:30pm Eastern. Superb productions from sites such as Teatro Alla Scala, Milan; Concertgebouw, Amsterdam; Lyric Opera of Chicago; Opera Garnier, Paris; and the National Opera House, Helsinki. During the Metropolitan Opera season, CBC streams the live performance from the Met. Every opera lover should know this show.

Lyric FM
www.lyricfm.ie

Saturday 2000–2230 Greenwich. Host: Ray Lynott. This Irish station streams some extremely high-quality productions from Europe that you won't hear elsewhere.

classical music

Lyric Opera of Chicago

Many stations fill the Metropolitan Opera time slot with the Lyric Opera of Chicago during May and June. One is WFIU (**www.indiana.edu/~wfiu**) Saturday 12:30–4pm Central.

Metropolitan Opera

Saturdays December–April, usually 1:30–4pm Eastern. This long-running program has such an established audience on radio stations around the world that it has become the opera hour on many of them, even outside the Met season. One station streaming the Metropolitan Opera is WOI (**www.woi.org**).

NPR World of Opera   www.npr.org

Saturday 1–4pm Eastern, July–November. During off-season for the Metropolitan Opera, NPR offers full-length operas from around the world. For example, in 2001, the 200th anniversary of the death of Giuseppe Verdi, the program featured *Il Trovatore* from La Scala, *Macbeth* from a Carnegie Hall performance of the Collegiate Chorale, *Jerusalem* from Genoa, and *Falstaff* from the Munich National Theatre. The program is picked up by some 135 NPR stations (the NPR website will help you find one), for example WOI (**www.woi.org**).

L'Opera du Samedi   Radio Canada Chaîne Culturelle

Saturday 1:30–5pm Eastern.   **radio-canada.ca**
Host: Jean Deschamps.

Opera on 3   BBC Radio 3 **www.bbc.co.uk/radio3**

Saturday 1930 Greenwich. Offers a complete opera weekly, from such venues as the Royal Opera House, English National Opera, Aldeburgh Festival, Glyndebourne Festival Opera, Sadler's Wells Theatre, and Cheltenham Festival.

Radio France   **www.radio-france.fr/chaines/**
france-musiques/opera/

From October through June, full operas on Saturday evenings (usually beginning at 1730 Greenwich). Operas from Paris Bastille, the Châtelet, Théâtre des Champs-Elysées, Palais Garnier, Anvers, Bologne, Lausanne, as well as elsewhere in the world.

RDP Antena 2   **www.rdp.pt/antena2**

Great schedule of full-length operas from around the world from Radiofusão Portuguesa. Most Saturday evenings at 1600, 1730, or 1800 Greenwich.

classical music

Seattle Opera

KING **www.king.org**

The second Saturday performance of each opera in the Seattle Opera season is simulcast on KING, beginning at 7:30pm Pacific. For details, see the website of KING or the Seattle Opera (**www.seattleopera.org**). The schedule for 2002 includes *Madama Butterfly* on January 19, *Salome* on March 30, and *Un Ballo in Maschera* May 11.

Sunday Opera

Radio Television Hong Kong (RTHK) Radio 4

www.rthk.org.hk

Host: Michael Rippon (Rupert Chan first Sunday of the month). Unlike most of the listings in this section, RTHK's Sunday opera does not present original live opera productions. What you will hear is a recording, albeit of a complete opera, with an introduction by the host; Rippon's programs are in English, Chan's in Cantonese. What makes Sunday Opera particularly valuable is that the program is archived for a year afterwards on the website.

Opera Programs

At the Opera

NPR **www.npr.org**

Saturday 12:30–1pm Eastern (July–November). *At the Opera* is a half-hour educational program airing before *NPR World of Opera*, an introduction to the opera that listeners are about to hear. The current week's show is archived on the NPR website for listening on demand.

Classic Soaps

Classic FM **www.classicfm.co.za**

Sunday 1900–2100 Greenwich. Host: Mary Rorich. Each episode of this program from South Africa is organized around a single topic. For example, one recent show was devoted to the career of Renate Tebaldi.

Eesti Raadio Klassikaraadio

www.er.ee/eng/klassik

Monday 1700–2000 Greenwich. The Estonian national broadcast system's Klassikaraadio streams monthly opera evenings, with live music from concert halls both in Estonia and abroad.

KCSN Opera House

KCSN **www.kcsn.org**

Wednesday 8–11pm Pacific. Host: Bill Toutant and Don Cummings, of California State University Northridge. Features full-length performances of operas performed around the world, introductions, education, quizzes, and contests.

classical music

Musiques en Liberté
Friday 1600–1700 Greenwich.

A Night at the Opera
WQED **www.wqed.org**
Sunday 7–10pm Eastern. Host: Ken Meltzer.

Opera in Action
BBC Radio 3 **www.bbc.co.uk/radio3**
Saturday 1830–1930 Greenwich. Host: Michael White. A light and entertaining program featuring more talk than music, on themes in opera and the practical details of the opera world. One recent program, for example, pondered the seven deadly sins as they appear in opera, whereas another set out to discern the extent to which opera's major funders get to influence artistic decisions. The program can be fun as well, particularly when White stages his "Fantasy Opera," picking from opera stars past and present to assemble dream operatic casts. (Radio 3 also frequently airs short, one-time features, interviews with singers and directors. Look at the current schedule, particularly for Sunday.)

Operadio
www.operadio.com
Operadio offers *ten channels* of opera, on demand. It is easy to get excited when you first see the options. The Bel Canto Channel! The Romantic Channel! The Interviews Channel! The playlists are pretty short, and the novelty wears off, but Operadio is certainly a sketch of what *could be*. While Operadio is free, it does require registration, during which they mention the possibility of voluntary contributions. It uses its own little front-end tuner which requires ActiveX and also involves downloading a plug-in for RealAudio.

Opera Show with Duff Murphy
KUSC **www.kusc.org**
Saturday 9am–noon Pacific (shorter during Met season).

Opera with Robert Swedberg
WMFE **www.pbs.org/wmfe**
Sunday 1–2pm Eastern. Host: Robert Swedberg, General Director of the Orlando Opera.

Saturday Allegro at the Opera
KUMR **www.kumr.org**
Saturday 12:30–4pm Central. Host: John Francis. Complete, recorded operas.

Sunday Evening at the Opera
Australian Broadcasting Corporation Classic FM Classic **www.abc.net.au/classic**
Sunday 0900–1100 Greenwich. Host: Colin Fox. Each two-hour program is organized around a topic, for example, "The Verdi Century."

classical music

Sunday Morning Opera with Sandy
WPRB www.wprb.com

Sunday 7–10am Eastern. Host: Sandy Steiglitz.

Sunday Night at the Opera
WHRB www.whrb.org

Sunday 8pm–midnight Eastern. From recordings, this program plays one opera in its entirety each week, plus selections from other recordings for comparison.

Their Greatest Bits
BBC Radio 2 www.bbc.co.uk/radio2

Tuesday 1900–2000 Greenwich. Host: Alan Freeman. Opera highlights and selections from the light classical repertoire.

Opera Lectures

Opera World
http://www.operaworld.com/prompter/distance.shtml

San Diego Opera Opera Talks
http://www.sdopera.com/

Host: Nick Reveles. Several half-hour educational programs, mostly introductions to specific operas, are available any time from the website.

New Music

Categories are only a convenience, to make it easy to look things up. There is a discernible genre of contemporary music, often performed on symphonic instruments and composed by people with classical training, but not generally (or at least not yet) considered "classical" music. This music is often challenging, attracting only a small audience. One could waste time arguing as to the exact definition of this genre and who should be included in it. But the work you have in your hand is not an essay in the philosophy of music history. It is merely a radio guide. If you like music by Harry Partch, Havergal Brian, Richard Barrett, Robert Minden, and Meredith Monk, below are some radio programs featuring that kind of music. Look also in the "Experimental" category.

classical music

The Amoeba Weeps
CFRC www.queensu.ca/cfrc

Monday noon–2pm Eastern. Substantive program from a student station in Ontario.

CKUT
www.ckut.ca

CKUT, the student station at McGill University and community station for Montreal, has an exceptional lineup of new music programs. The schedule changes fairly frequently; below is listed what was streaming in Autumn, 2001. (All times Eastern):

▸▸ The Hearing Trumpet Sunday 1–2pm

▸▸ More Like Space Sunday 9–11pm

▸▸ Contemporary Madness Tuesday 7:30–8pm

▸▸ Where's the Beat? Wednesday 9–11:15am

▸▸ The Music of Sound Wednesday 2–4pm

▸▸ Chaud pour le Mont-Stone, alternating with Francis et les Exercices
    Thursday 9–11pm

▸▸ Entertainment Through Pain Thursday 11pm–1am

The program description for Where's the Beat? might serve much of the New Music community well: "Classical music without the answers."

Cranial Nerve
WHPK whpk.uchicago.edu

Thursday 1:30–3pm Central. Host: Greg Whitman. Music from the 20th-century Western classical tradition, particularly for piano, small ensemble, or voice.

De Concertzender
www.omroep.nl/concertzender

This Dutch station is dedicated to all facets of New Music from 20th-century composition to a monthly session from the experimental music magazine The Wire.

Fast Forward
KUSP www.kusp.org

Monday 9am–noon Pacific. Hosts: Susan Alexander and Phil Collins. 20th-century classical music.

Hacia Una Nueva Música
Radio UNAM FM
www.unam.mx/radiounam

Wednesday 6–7pm Central. Host: Ana Lara. A program dedicated to helping promote contemporary concert music, from the Universidad Nacional Autónoma de México. Note that Radio UNAM has two streams. This program is on the FM stream.

classical music

Hear and Now
BBC Radio 3 **www.bbc.co.uk/radio3**

Hosts: Sarah Walker and Verity Sharp. This excellent contemporary music program features live concerts, studio sessions, interviews with composers, and premieres of BBC-commissioned works.

Les Avante-Gardes du XXe Siècle
Radio Canada Chaîne Culturelle
radio-canada.ca

Sunday 7–8pm Eastern.

New Music Australia
Australian Broadcasting Corporation Classic FM Classic **www.abc.net.au/classic**

Wednesday 1000–1130 Greenwich. Host: Julian Day. This program, which has been running on ABC Classic FM for more than a decade, commissions new works and the recording of new works. It usually contains interviews with composers and musicians.

New Music New Haven
WPKN **www.wpkn.org**

Second Tuesday 10–11pm. Host: Martin Bresnick. Performances of 20th-century music recorded at Yale University. Bresnick is a composer at Yale.

Social Service
WREK **www.wrek.org**

Sunday 6–7pm Eastern (but available any time on the WREK website). An hour of 20th-century composed music, "the stuff that they'll be calling classical in 200 years."

21st Century Classical
WMUC **wmuc.umd.edu**

Monday 9–11am Eastern. Host: Greg Mol.

Wired for Sound
CHRW **www.usc.uwo.ca/chrw**

Tuesday 10pm–midnight Eastern. Host: Chris Meloche. "Contemporary classical music and strange progressive sounds from around the world."

Martin Bresnick

classical music

Rock

In the categories that follow, popular music is divided into genres such as jazz, blues, hip-hop, dance, gospel, bluegrass, and conjunto. Since at least the 1950s, however, the most popular music in the world is rock or rock-based. This remains true even despite the growing popularity of hip-hop music and all its derivatives. Radio programming devoted to specific rock categories such as metal, punk, and oldies is also listed below. Before those categories is a list of some of the most interesting stations in the world that play the currently popular varieties of primarily rock-based music. This blend is usually described as "alternative." (Its immediate predecessor was "indie," denoting that its artists distributed their music on independent labels.)

Missing from the listings below is what is indisputably the most *popular* music in the world: mainstream corporate pop rock star power music. A tour of the world's radio stations turns up the amazing diversity described in this guide, but it also measures the extent of the entertainment monoculture around the globe. At any given moment, a huge portion of the world's radio stations are playing the same very few songs. In Namibia, in Jamaica, in Venezuela, in Thailand, they are listening to Britney Spears, N'Sync, and Madonna. This mainstream pop music has been intentionally omitted from this guide for the simple reason that no one needs a guide to find it. It is hard to escape it when one tries.

The stations and programs below, while sometimes overlapping with the mainstream, have been selected for some flavor or another that differentiates them from the monoculture. In addition to the stations and programs listed below, anyone with an

rock

interest in alternative music should immediately consult the section of this book on college stations, which are the primary vectors of this music today.

Rock Favorites

Euro Hit 40	see p.78
Killer Oldies	see p.86
The Live Room	see p.81
OzRock	see p.75
Radio Tuzla	see p.78
WNUR	see p.75
WONC	see p.76

Rock Stations

Coast FM
local.abc.net.au/goldcoast/radio
The Australian Broadcasting Corporation's stream from the Gold Coast in Queensland features an "adult contemporary" blend of roots music, highlighting Australian artists.

KAOS
www.kaosradio.org
The community radio station of Olympia, Washington, fed by The Evergreen State College, is an extremely eclectic place, with numerous specialty shows covering the musical spectrum. Somewhere near the station's vibrantly beating heart, however, is alternative/indie rock music. Of particular note are the following programs (all times Pacific):

▶▶ *What's New, Pussycat?* Monday 9–11pm Host: Michelle Noel
▶▶ *Six-Foot Spine* Monday 11pm–1am Host: Mike Duggan
▶▶ *Strange Attractors* Tuesday 11pm–1am Host: Chris Scofield
▶▶ *Free Things Are Cool* Wednesday 9–11pm Host: Diana Arens – a program which has been on KAOS for ten years, often featuring live performances with groups from the area (which hosts one of the world's most thriving indie scenes) or visiting the area

rock

KAOS at the circus

KFJC
www.kfjc.org

From Foothills-DeAnza Community College in Los Altos, California. Music programming is largely oriented to recent material: programs must play at least 35 percent (by song count) tracks from material released in the last eight weeks.

OzRock
www.ozworld.com.au

On-demand stream of Australian rock.

PBS
www.pbsfm.org.au

This public station from Melbourne, Australia plays all kinds of music; the label applied more than any other to its programs is "Contemporary Alternative." Of particular interest is Phoena Donohoe's show *Auscultation* (Wednesday 0300–0500 Greenwich), which spins new Australian releases.

WLUW
www.wluw.org

WLUW puts Chicago's independent music scene on the Net whenever it's not airing community affairs programs and specialty shows. Roughly that works out to all afternoon, all evening (with a break from 6-6:30pm Central), and overnight, usually from 9 or 10pm Central to 9am the next day. On Thursdays, from 6:30 to 10pm Central, is the program *Radio Free Chicago*, hosted by Jed James, with interviews, music and guests focusing on the local independent music scene.

WMSE
www.wmse.org

WMSE streams a wide diversity of musical programs, but about half of their shows feature alternative rock music. Best of all, the shows are archived so that you can listen to them any time.

WNUR
www.wnur.org

Chicago's WNUR, which is an interesting eclectic station in its own right, has

rock

one stream devoted just to rock. On the main page, look in the upper left corner for "Streams" and choose "Rock."

WONC   **www.wonc.org**

This is an exceptional station. It is similar to those jazz stations where one show features the swing years, one show bop, and a late night guy plays the Art Ensemble of Chicago – various kinds of jazz, on various shows, but all jazz. The difference is that on WONC, all those shows are about *rock*. Examples of the programming:

- ›› *Vintage Rock*: *The best from the psychedelic era, 1964–1974* Daily 10pm–midnight Central
- ›› *Rock News* Weekdays 3:30–4pm
- ›› *The Pure Rock Happy Hour* Weekdays 5pm–8pm
- ›› *The Bassment* Weekends 4–8am

Everyone who loves rock music should have this station in their list of favorites.

WVBR   **www.wvbr.com**

Specialty shows on the weekend; the weekdays are rock.

XFM   **www.xfm.co.uk**

Commercial station from the UK with a solid stream of alternative music.

Rock Programs

All Ages   WUSB **www.wusb.org**

Wednesday 10pm–midnight Eastern. From Weezer to Trembling Blue Stars, with occasional live guests.

Canadian Bacon   CKDU **is2.dal.ca/~ckdufm**

Sunday 9–10:30pm Atlantic (one hour ahead of Eastern). Hosts: Derek Huffman and Kathy Crosby. Canadian Indie rock.

The John Peel Show   BBC Radio 1 **www.bbc.co.uk/radio1**

Tuesday–Thursday 2100–2300 Greenwich. His tireless championing of new and challenging music (everything from punk to African music) for over 30 years has made John Peel one of the world's most famous and influential radio DJs.

The New Afternoon Show

WNYU www.wnyu.org

Weekdays 4–7:30pm Eastern. For more than 20 years, this program has been New York's main showcase for underground and independent rock.

The Oz Music Show

Australian Broadcasting Corporation Triple J

Wednesday 1200–1500 Greenwich.

www.abc.net.au/triplej

Host: Richard Kingsmill. For over a decade this weekly show has been chronicling the latest in Australian rock, including interviews and always a live performance in the Triple J studios.

The Record Hospital

WHRB www.whrb.org

Monday–Friday 10pm–5am Eastern, Sunday night (Monday morning) midnight–5am. For 20 years, this late-night program from the student station at Harvard University has aired underground rock, including punk, pop, hardcore, emo, grindcore, new wave, no wave, indie, and crust.

Radio Therapy

CKLN ckln.sac.ryerson.ca

Monday (that is, Sunday night) 2–7am Eastern. A show dedicated to the promotion and support of new independent Canadian music. There are interviews with bands from Toronto and around the country.

World Cafe

Host: David Dye. This is a contemporary popular music show, with just a sprinkling of relatively accessible popular music from elsewhere in the world. If you're just beginning to experiment outside pop radio, this might provide a gentle introduction. The show is syndicated on so many stations that the list of stations at the World Cafe website (www.worldcafe.org) will usually present you with at least one that is streaming right now.

Rock Around the World

Anteroom

SWH www.radioswh.lv

Saturday 1100–1200 Greenwich. New Latvian bands.

Eesti Raadio Raadio 2

er.ee/eng/r2

This stream from the national radio of Estonia is oriented towards youth, with a strong component of dance music. (The link above is to an English version of the website.)

rock

Euro Hit 40   Radio Nederland www.rnw.nl/en/html/euro_hit_40.html
Radio Nederland surveys the charts of 18 European countries every week to compile this hour-long Top 40 list. You can listen to it from the website any time. Available in several languages, one of which is English.

FM Champla   www.fm-champla.co.jp
Straight-ahead rock station from Okinawa. The website is in Japanese; click where it says "RealPlayer." If you have any difficulty, the stream is www.fm-champla.co.jp/champla.ram.

Katsushika FM   www.kfm789.co.jp
This Japanese station has a diverse roster of interesting specialty shows, including some extremely engaging and innovative pop music and rock sliding right down the edge of the future. The website is in Japanese. The stream is www.kfm789.co.jp/live789.ram.

Radio J 93.5   www.radioj935.com
From Acadia. Nice beat, easy to dance to… wait, the lyrics are in *French*!

Radio 94.7   www.94-7.com
This Costa Rican station mixes oldies with contemporary music in Spanish.

Radio Tuzla   www.slon.tuzla.net
For an entirely different view of Bosnia than the one that has appeared in newspapers the last few years, one can drop in on this radio station, where the power of rock 'n' roll seems determined not only to endure but to prevail. Power chords but with lyrics in Bosnian.

Rock Radio 101   www.101.ru
Rock both Russian and Western, website available in English.

Rock in Spanish

Latin Rebel-ution   WHFR whfr.hfcc.net
Thursday 2–4pm Central.
Host: Alfonso Gutiérrez. Latin alternative scene music, from groups such as Café Tacuba, Maná, Control Machete, Molotov, Jaguares, Illya Kuryaki, Julieta Venegas, Aterciopelados, and Zurdok.

rock

Música Alternative
Radio UNAM AM
www.unam.mx/radiounam

Saturday 4–4:30pm Central.
This program from the radio station of the Universidad Nacional Autónoma de México focuses on noncommercial and "marginal" rock music. (Note that Radio UNAM has two streams. This program is on the AM stream.)

Radioacktiv
www.radioactiva.com.co

This commercial station from Colombia plays mostly the same music you'd hear on a commercial "alternative" station in the United States: Blink182, Weezer, Papa Roach, etc. But about ten percent of their music is Spanish rock. (Solid stream with good sound.)

Rock en Español
www.radiok.net

This is a stream, available any time, on Mexican station Radio K.

Rock Latino
KCSB **www.kcsb.org**

Thursday 10am–noon Pacific. Host: Angel Lopez.

Salario Minimo
CITR **www.ams.ubc.ca/citr**

Monday 6–8pm Pacific. Spanish rock, ska, techno and alternative music, "porque no todo en esta vida es salsa."

Sin Fronteras
KNON **www.knon.org**

Sunday 10pm–midnight Central. Host: Jesús Chaírez. Rock en Español and Alternative Latino – very popular youth show in Dallas. In Spanish.

Spanish Rock
WLUW **www.wluw.org**

Wednesday 10pm–2am Central.

Live Music Shows

Audioasis
KEXP **www.kexp.org**

Saturday 6–8pm Pacific. Host: John Richards. Local music show from the Pacific Northwest, with in-studio guests and live performances.

The Basement
www.basement.com.au

The Basement is an Internet-only music stream from Sydney, Australia, primarily the creation of long-time broadcaster Doug Mulray. The Basement is

rock

conveniently situated contiguous to a nightclub by the same name, from which they can stream live musical performances by musicians as diverse as Janis Ian and Elvis Costello. These performances are then repeated more than once later on the stream, and clips from many of them are archived in "The Replay Room" for listening on demand later. The website has a list of upcoming guests. In addition, there are studio visits galore, with everyone from Morgan Freeman to Monsieur Camembert.

John Richards

Basement Tapes   WQNA
www.wqna.org
Monday 9pm–midnight Central. Host: Joe Ryan.

Brave New World   KCRW www.kcrw.org
Saturday (that is, Friday night) midnight–2am Pacific; archived on the website for listening any time. Host: Tricia Halloran. Live sessions with a wide variety of guests, from Robyn Hitchcock to the Pastels. The Los Angeles location brings in major talent, but there are unsigned bands as well.

The Basement Studio

rock

Fries to Go

URB **www.bath.ac.uk**

Friday 2300–Saturday 0200 Greenwich. Live from the Venue in Bath, England, courtesy of the student station of the University of Bath.

From the Vault

KFJC **www.kfjc.org**

Tuesday 6–7pm. Host: Pete Dixon. This program has an unusual premise. Dixon phones a band and the band plays a live set over the phone connection. The music is recorded on the band's side (because the phone line would destroy the sound quality), mailed in, and spliced together with the phone interviews. So the program is not "live" in the sense of real-time, but no overdubs or re-takes are allowed. Since they don't have to physically appear in the Los Altos, California studios of KFJC, bands from as far away as Sweden have appeared. Guest list includes Pelt, ST 37, Juneau, Nick Saloman, The Alchemysts, Mick Wills, The Linus Pauling Quartet, Bari Watts, Salamander, Rake, Charalambides, The Double Leopards, The Falcon Project, Tonalamotl, and Klak.

Pete Dixon

The Joint

WBRS **www.wbrs.org**

Wednesday and Thursday 9:30pm–midnight Eastern. Music of all genres live from the Student Center at Brandeis University. Also *The Coffeehouse* Friday at 3pm Eastern.

KALX Live

KALX **kalx.berkeley.edu**

Saturday 9pm–midnight Pacific. Ninety minutes from the studios of KALX, then 90 minutes from a local (Berkeley, California) club

Live Music Special

WPKN **www.wpkn.org**

Fourth Saturday of the month 6–10pm Eastern. Musicians from any genre, live from the Bridgeport, Connecticut studios of WPKN.

The Live Room

KEXP **www.kexp.org**

Saturday 8-9pm Pacific. Host: Abe Beeson. Northwest bands play a one-hour set live from the studios of Jack Straw Productions. Archived shows at **www.jackstraw.org**.

rock

Live Set
KUT **www.kut.org**

Sunday 8–9pm Central. There are few better places on earth to hear live music than Austin, Texas. The variety and quality of talent on this show is exceptional.

Local Noise
5UV **www.adelaide.edu.au/5UV**

Tuesday 1130–1230 Greenwich. "Local" in this case meaning Adelaide, Australia.

Loud Live Acts
WFMU **www.wfmu.org**

Thursday 11pm–2am Eastern. Host: Pat Duncan. Live bands, primarily punk, in the studio every week. All programs are archived on the WFMU website so you can listen to them later.

Sonarchy Radio
KEXP **www.kexp.org**

Saturday 11pm–midnight Pacific. Host: Doug Haire. Live from the studios of Jack Straw Productions in Seattle, showcasing Northwest artists. Archives at **www.jackstraw.org/studio/sonarchy**.

Third Rail Radio
WMUC **wmuc.umd.edu**

Sunday 6–9pm Eastern. Host: Jim Thompson. Live bands appearing at the University of Maryland. A few of the programs are archived.

Universal Buzz
WBER **http://wber.monroe.edu/**

Sunday 11–midnight Eastern. A weekly radio show of live concerts recorded exclusively for this program. Recent guests include Steve Earle, Caustic Resin, and Cursive.

Wisconsin Jukebox Radio Show
WMUR **www.marquette. edu/stumedia/wmur**

Saturday 5–7pm Central. Several Wisconsin bands appear in the studios of this student station at Marquette in Milwaukee each semester.

Gothic

Bats in the Belfry
WMBR **wmbr.mit.edu**

Saturday 6–8pm Eastern.

From the Grave
95B **www.95bfm.com**

Wednesday 1200–1300 Greenwich. Gothic, industrial, and dark ambient. From

rock

the University of Auckland in New Zealand.

Out of the Coffin

WRVU **http://wrvu.org**

Thursday 10pm–midnight Central.

Metal

Aggressive Rock
CKLN **ckln.sac.ryerson.ca**

Sunday 9:30–11:30pm Eastern. Hardcore and black/death/doom metal.

Bad Hair Day Radio
www.bhdrocks.com

If you fondly remember the days when metal bands had more hair spray than talent, this 24-hour stream of Poison, Warrant, Autograph, Britny Fox, etc. is for you.

Cries in the Night
KVCU **www.colorado.edu/ StudentGroups/KVCU**

Thursday 8–10pm Mountain.

Disciples of Dr. Demento
CFUV **cfuv.uvic.ca**

Sunday 3:30–5pm Pacific. "Way out distortion-drenched satanically powered metal."

Hellhole
WNYU **www.wnyu.org**

Tuesday 7:30–9pm Eastern. A decade old, *Hellhole* presents thrash, gore, death, and black metal.

Metal Forge
WQNA **www.wqna.org**

Friday noon–3pm Central. Host: Chris Hupp.

MetalGina
KDVS **www.kdvs.org**

Sunday 3–6am Pacific. "The most brutal metal show in the history of mankind. Death metal, black metal, grind and gore."

Nasty Habits
WERS **www.wers.org**

Sunday 11pm–2am Eastern.

Nocturnal Dimension
95B **www.95bfm.com**

Monday 1300–1400 Greenwich. Death, black metal and doom, from the University of Auckland in New Zealand.

rock

Power Chord
CITR **www.ams.ubc.ca/citr**

Saturday 1–3pm Pacific. From Vancouver, British Columbia.

Steel Mill
WNUR **www.wnur.org**

Saturday 8–10pm Central.

Stonehenge
WMUL **www.marshall.edu/wmul**

Weeknights midnight–3am Eastern.

Van Halen Radio Network
www.vhradio.com

All Diamond Dave all the time.

WSOU
www.wsou.net

Seton Hall University's radio station is almost exclusively devoted to metal of all shades and stripes. With the exception of Sundays and the occasional sports broadcast, WSOU is 24 hours of metal mayhem.

Punk

Attention Deficit Radio
KUCR **www.kucr.org**

Tuesday midnight–3am Pacific. (That's Monday night.)

Crucial Chaos
WNYU **www.wnyu.org**

Thursday 9–10:30pm Eastern. The successor to Tim Somer's legendary *Noise*, *Crucial Chaos* plays both vintage and contemporary hardcore and punk.

Fresh Fruit for Rotting Vegetables
CJSF **www.cjsf.bc.ca**

Monday 8–10pm Pacific. Punk and nerd. Also give an ear to *No Values*, Monday 9–11am.

Green Dyed Fingernails
CHSR **www.unb.ca/chsr**

Sunday 9–11pm Atlantic (an hour ahead of Eastern). Every kind of punk: old school, Calpunk, hardcore, emo, ska-punk, ska, pop-punk, garage, etc.

I'd Rather Eat Glass
CFUV **cfuv.uvic.ca**

Thursday 4–5pm Pacific. Grrl Punk.

KDVS
www.kdvs.org

KDVS is a student station (from the University of California at Davis), so the

rock

schedule changes frequently. The website has a convenient color-coded grid to let you know when punk is played. Currently it's:

▸▸ Sunday (that is, Saturday night) midnight–3am Pacific
▸▸ Tuesday 4–8:30am
▸▸ Wednesday 2–4 am, 9:30am–noon
▸▸ Thursday noon–2:30pm
▸▸ Saturday midnight–3am

Please Kill Me   CKLN **ckln.sac.ryerson.ca**
Thursday (that is, Wednesday night) 2–7am Eastern.

Punk Off   Radio Campus Paris **www.radiocampusparis.org**
Archived on the website for listening any time.

Revolution Rock   KUGS **www.kugs.org**
Tuesday (that is, Monday night) midnight–2am.

Schizophrenia   WUSB **www.wusb.org**
Friday 2:30–5:30pm Eastern.

Turmoil   WUSB **www.wusb.org**
Wednesday 8–10pm Eastern. Hosts: Steve Kreitzer and Ron Pitt. *Turmoil* claims to be the longest running punk/hardcore program on radio.

Vengeance is Mine   CITR **www.ams.ubc.ca/citr**
Tuesday (that is, Monday night) midnight–4am Pacific.

Viva La Hardcore   95B **www.95bfm.com**
Wednesday 1100–1200 Greenwich. Punk and hardcore from New Zealand and around the world.

WQNA   **www.wqna.org**
WQNA offers a strong run of various punk music on Friday afternoon and evening (Central Time):

▸▸ *Pandora's Box* 3–6pm: Punk and ska featuring some local (Illinois) music
▸▸ *Suburban Warfare* 6pm–9pm: Suburban punk
▸▸ *Sound System* 9pm–midnight: Reggae, punk, and dub

rock

Oldies/Roots Rock

Oldies Stations

Killer Oldies   www.killeroldies.com

This Internet-only, all-oldies station features the work of Art Laboe. Laboe has been a radio disk jockey since 1956 (when he had the top-rated show in Los Angeles), and his program *Art Laboe Sunday Night Special* is still heard on several stations, as well as on Killer Oldies. Laboe is recognized as the first person to package up an album of oldies by assorted artists and market it, under the title "Oldies But Goodies," a phrase he is credited with inventing.

Radio 94.7   www.94-7.com

This Costa Rican station mixes oldies with contemporary music in Spanish.

Slagerradio   www.slagerradio.hu

Interesting oldies station from Budapest, Hungary. (It's a commercial station, but the commercials are in Hungarian.)

VinylFM   vinylfm.com

Internet-only stream from Canada devoted to the 1960s and '70s, "an authentic representation of the soundtrack of the time when music on the FM radio came from vinyl."

WS-FM   www.wsfm.com.au

Commercial station in Sydney, Australia.

Oldies Programs

American Routes

Host: Nick Spitzer. An adventure in American music, a cross-country excursion spanning eras and genres, roots rock, soul, blues, country, gospel. Usually features interviews with musicians. Syndicated on PRI. You can catch it on KCSN www.kcsn.org Saturday and Sunday 7–8pm Pacific.

Nick Spitzer

rock

Backwoods
WMBR **wmbr.mit.edu**

Saturday 8–10am Eastern. Host: John Funke. Vintage rock, blues, country, and R&B.

CKUA Documentaries
www.ckua.org

Athabasca University professor David Gregory and CKUA producer Brian Dunsmore produce a superb series of documentaries on the history of popular music. Installments have included *Ragtime to Rolling Stones*, *The Long Weekend* (popular music between the two World Wars), *From Bop to Rock* (from World War II to 1960) and *The Rocky Road* (1960–1980). Check the CKUA website to see what this duo has come up with recently.

Classic Rock
KSHU **www.shsu.edu/~rtf_kshu**

Saturday 9am–6pm and Sunday noon–6pm Central.

Crap from the Past
KFAI **www.kfai.org**

Monday (that is, Sunday night) midnight–2am Central, archived for listening any time. Host: Ron Gerber. Gerber's show is original, iconoclastic, often funny. Here is what he says about it: *"Crap From The Past* is a weekly radio show that plays the very best and very worst of the pop music of the last 30 years. Although this simple, one-line description of CFTP seems to lump it into the 'retro' category, the actual show is light years away from the bland/cheeseball/ syndicated 'retro' shows that currently pollute the airwaves. Some examples: You won't hear Soft Cell's 'Tainted Love,' but you will hear Gloria Jones's 1964 original version of 'Tainted Love.' You won't hear Mariah Carey or Puff Daddy, but you will hear the songs they're ripping off, in the 'New Stuff Rippin' Off Old Stuff' feature. You won't hear The Beatles, but you will hear the Stars On 45 and dozens of other atrocities in the 'God-Awful Medley of the Week' feature. Any old 'retro' show can play Milli Vanilli and snicker, but where else will you hear tracks from the second Milli Vanilli album (never released in the U.S.), or from the independently released Rob and Fab album? Who else would dare to play an entire show of common pop songs sung in the wrong language? Or an entire show where the music is sped up by 12%? Or cuts from *The Ethel Merman Disco Album*? If there exists a more obsessed pop music historian than me, I have yet to meet him."

Dusties
WHPK **whpk.uchicago.edu**

Thursday 9pm–midnight Central.

Finkleman's 45s
CBC Radio One **www.cbc.ca**

Saturday 8:05–10pm Eastern. Host: Danny Finkleman.

rock

Gardening at Night
WQNA **www.wqna.org**

Monday 7–9pm Central. Host: Dave Antoine. 1970s and '80s hits and should-have-been-hits.

Land of 1,000 Dances
KUSP **www.kusp.org**

Saturday 5–8pm Pacific.

Oldies with J.R.
KCSB **www.kcsb.org**

Saturday 6–8am Pacific. Host: Josie Ramos. Music from between 1950 and 1970.

Querido Señor Fantasia
Radio UNAM AM

Tuesday 5:30–6:30pm Central. **www.unam.mx/radiounam**

Host: Leonora Alonso Pinzón. Rock music from the 1960s and '70s. (Note that Radio UNAM has two streams. This program is on the AM stream.)

Radio Rumpus Room
KFAI **www.kfai.org**

Friday 9–10:30pm Central, archived for listening any time. Surf, hot rod, rockabilly, hillbilly, 1960s garage, psychedelia, primal pop, and country.

Reach Out in the Darkness
KPFT **www.kpft.org**

Tuesday midnight–4am Central.

Rock House
WEVL **www.wevl.org**

Friday 7–9pm Central. Host: Brian Stuhr. Classic rockabilly from the town that brought you Elvis.

Rockin' Remnants
WVBR **www.wvbr.com**

Saturday 6–9pm Eastern.

Rockin' Roots
WOJB **www.wojb.org**

Friday noon–1pm Central. Hosts: Tom Boyd and Ann Sternberg. Blues, jazz, country, world, rock, and folk music from the 1920s through the present.

Shake, Rattle and Roll
BBC Radio 2 **www.bbc.co.uk/radio2**

Monday 2130–2230 Greenwich. Host: Mark Lamarr. Dedicated to excavating rock 'n' roll gems.

Southbound Train
WEVL **www.wevl.org**

Tuesday 10am–noon Central. Host: Brian Stuhr. Rockabilly, Western swing, psychobilly and current roots rock.

rock

This Little Girl's Gone Rockin' KFAI www.kfai.org
Tuesday (that is, Monday night) 2–5am Central. Host: Mick Novak. Featuring female vocalists and girl groups, including lots of obscure singles and rare tracks.

Uncle Bri's Early Morning Funhouse CFUV cfuv.uvic.ca
Thursday 6–8am Pacific. A wacky program of music from the 1950s and '60s.

The Vault TNL Radio www.lanka.net/tnl/
Tuesday 1700–1800 Greenwich. Rock from the 1970s through '90s. (The station is from Sri Lanka, but the rock is not.)

Before Oldies

The Music Shelf WVXU www.wvxu.org
Saturday 3–5pm. Host: Jim King. The '50s, but not *those* '50s. Doris Day, Rosemary Clooney, Andy Williams, the Ames Brothers, and Tony Bennett. Sample some of the archived programs on the website.

Play it Again CKUA www.ckua.org
Sunday 9–10am Mountain (rebroadcast Monday at 8pm). Host: Tony Dillon-Davis. Popular music from 1920–1950.

Seems Like Old Times CFRU www.uoguelph.ca/~cfru-fm
Thursday 10–11am Eastern. Host: Doug Blackwood. Music and radio memories from the 1930s to the '50s.

When the Melody Is Right WHUS www.whus.org
Sunday noon–2pm Eastern. A salute to the golden age of songwriting, what Johnny Mercer called "The Melody Era," the age of Cole Porter and George Gershwin, a time when melodies and lyrics were king.

A Year to Remember BBC Radio 2 www.bbc.co.uk/radio2
Sunday 1300–1500 Greenwich. Host: Desmond Carrington. This is music from a time before oldies. Think Bing Crosby and Doris Day. Think Ethel Merman. Think "Yes Sir, That's My Baby." (Following this program is a sing-along show!)

rock

part two

'50s

Fast Eddie's Oldies Caravan
WQNA **www.wqna.org**
Friday 9pm–midnight Central. Host: Fast Eddie Ruebling.

Surf

Beach Party
RTL **www.rtl.fr**
Friday 2300–Saturday 0100 Greenwich. Host: Georges Lang. If you'll accept a wide mix of '60s pop along with your surf music (Diana Ross???), you might enjoy this French program.

Walk Don't Run
WREK **www.wrek.org**
Saturday 11:30pm–midnight Eastern (but available any time on WREK's web site). Host: Burt Ives. The Astronauts, The Ventures, Link Wray and The Mummies.

'60s

Garage
CFUV **cfuv.uvic.ca**
Sunday (that is, Saturday night) midnight–1am Pacific. "Farsifa-drenched, Vox-powered, Boss garage '60s punk."

Rock 'n' Blues Zone

KAOS **www.kaosradio.org**
Sunday 8–10pm Pacific.
Host: Tony Moreland. Rare rock and blues from the 1960s.

Sounds of the '60s
BBC Radio 2 **www.bbc.co.uk/ radio2**
Saturday 0805–1000 Greenwich. Host: Brian Matthew. Matthew often manages to dig out something totally obscure.

Brian Matthew

rock

Teenage Wasteland   WFMU **www.wfmu.org**
Sunday 3–5pm Eastern. Host: Bill Kelly. Punk, garage, and rock from the 1960s.

Psychedelic

Longhair's Jukebox   CFUV **cfuv.uvic.ca**
Sunday (that is, Saturday night) 1–3am Pacific.

Psychedelic Airwaves   CITR **www.ams.ubc.ca/citr**
Tuesday (that is, Monday night) 3–6am Pacific. From the student station at the University of British Columbia.

Psychedelic Revue   WHUS **www.whus.org**
Thursday 8–10pm Eastern. A reprise of the music from the "underground" FM stations of the 1960s.

'70s

KEOM   **www.keom.fm**
1970s Top 40 almost all the time on this community radio station from Texas.

Sounds of the '70s   BBC Radio 2
                                 www.bbc.co.uk/radio2

Thursday 2103–2130 Greenwich. Host: Steve Harley.

'80s

Better Eat Yer '80s   KUGS
                           www.kugs.org
Wednesday 10pm–midnight Pacific.
"Pop, old school, and big hair butt rock from the most radical of decades."

Flashback Radio   **www.flashback radio.com**
This is an Internet-only stream devoted exclusively to music of the 1980s.

Steve Harley

rock

91

Retro Radio

TNL Radio **www.lanka.net/tnl**

Saturday 1200–1500 Greenwich. Host: Boo Ray Daniels. In addition to the music, this program from Sri Lanka includes countdowns from different weeks of the 1980s, and lots of background information.

The '80s at Eight

SWH **www.radioswh.lv**

Weekday 1700–1800 Greenwich. Heartfelt Eighties show from Latvia.

The Ultimate '80s Show

WVBR **www.wvbr.com**

Saturday 3–6pm Eastern. Host: Nicky Wood.

Beatles

Beatles-a-Rama

www.Live365.com (Search for "Beatles")

Particularly good for covers of Beatles songs.

Beatles Archives

www.thebeats.com

It is a bit awkward to get the stream started, but an interesting stream once you do.

Beatles Radio

www.beatlesradio.com

Internet-only Beatles music. (Click on the apples.)

Club de Los Beatles

Universal Stereo
radiocentro.com.mx/universal92.1

Daily 8–9am and 1–2pm Central.

Saint Johnn's Wood

Radio UNAM AM
www.unam.mx/radiounam

Tuesday 6:30–7pm Central. Host: José Carlos García. Analysis and commentary (in Spanish), along with rare Beatles tracks. (Note that Radio UNAM has two streams. This program is on the AM stream.)

Dylan

Buckets of Bob

CHMA **www.mta.ca/chma**

Sunday 5:30–6pm Atlantic (an hour ahead of Eastern). Dylan and scripture.

rock

Street Legal
KVMR **www.kvmr.org**

Alternate Thursdays, 4–7am Pacific. Hosts: Danny and Julie Chauvin. Features lots of covers, some rarities.

Elvis

The Elvis Hour
Ritz Radio1035 **www.ritz1035.com**

Tuesday 2100–2200 Greenwich. Host: Randall Lee Rose. An hour devoted to the King on a country music station in England.

Grateful Dead

Dead Air
KLCC **www.klcc.org**

Saturday 7–9pm Pacific. When they find the last Deadhead 600 years from now, he or she will probably be living in Eugene, Oregon. This program has been on KLCC for a decade, and it's still full of fresh energy.

Dead Air
KVMR **www.kvmr.org**

Friday 9–11pm Pacific. Host: Jonathan Winfield or Richard Dunk.

Dead Air
WNCW **www.wncw.org**

Wednesday 10pm–1am Eastern (following *The Grateful Dead Hour*).

Dead to the World
KPFA **www.kpfa.org**

Wednesday 8–9:30pm Pacific. Host: David Gans. David Gans is the dean of Grateful Dead radio, host of the long-running syndicated show *The Grateful Dead Hour*, author of more than one book on the band, and a relative insider given wide and frequent access to the vault. The first hour of this program is Dead-related, the second hour free-form.

Field Trip
WFHB **www.wfhb.org**

Alternate Fridays 11pm–1am Eastern. Host: David Novak. Recordings of live performances, including those by the Grateful Dead. (On alternate weeks is *Extended Shelf Life*, an exploration of old vinyl from the station's record library.)

rock

The Grateful Dead Hour

Host: David Gans. This widely syndicated radio program is all but the official house organ of the Grateful Dead, and for years it has served as the town square for all Deadheads. The miniature collages Gans makes by slicing Dead snippets together are a high art form of their own, as well as fascinating evidence of just how finely tuned the musical recognition faculty of the human being is – Gans will slice in just the barest sliver of a song, so thin you wouldn't think it would be still recognizable, but yet never actually so thin that you can't identify it. You can hear *The Grateful Dead Hour* on KSUT **www.ksut.org** 9–10pm Mountain.

Lone Star Dead
KNON **www.knon.org**
Friday 8–10pm Central.

Morning Dew
WBAI **www.wbai.org**
Saturday 9pm–midnight Eastern. Host: Lance Neal.

The Music Never Stops
KPFK **www.kpfk.org**
Friday 8pm–midnight Pacific. Host: Barry Smolin. Good coverage of other jam-rock bands.

The Music Never Stops
WUSB **www.wusb.org**
Alternate Mondays 8:30–10pm Eastern. Host: Bill Frey. The website lists in advance what you can hear on the upcoming show.

Radio Daze
KUCR **www.kucr.org**
Tuesday 11pm–1am Wednesday Pacific. Heavy on Phish.

Sarcastic Deadhead
KCSN **www.kcsn.org**
Sundays 11:30pm–midnight. Host: Les Perry.

Wall of Sound
KYDS **www.sacramento.org/voice**
Sunday 6–8pm Pacific.

Zappa

Frank on Friday
WNCW **www.wncw.org**
Friday 12:30–1pm Eastern. Host: Marshall Ballew.

rock

Other Popular Music

Ambient/New Age

Alpha Rhythms
WYSO www.wyso.org
Sunday 8pm–midnight Eastern. Hosts: Jerry Kenney and Lori Taylor.

Ambient Overnight
KVCU www.colorado.edu/
StudentGroups/KVCU
Daily 1–7am Mountain.

Dreams of a New Age
WMBR wmbr.mit.edu
Monday 8–10pm Eastern.

Galactic Voyager
KCSN www.kcsn.org
Tuesday 9pm–midnight Pacific. Host: Meishel Menachekanian. Electronic music – Jean Michel Jarre, Vangelis, Mike Oldfield – offshoots, and related music.

Hearts of Space
www.hos.com
Host: Stephen Hill. Nowadays *Hearts of Space* includes ambient music, techno, and quite a bit of world fusion. Its mission, though, is to promulgate "space music," which in itself is a river that meanders over a wide plain. Although much space music is purely electronic, *HOS* program #592, for example, was devoted to space music performed on pedal steel guitar, while #589 made space music on the Irish whistle. You can listen to the current program any time on the website, and if you're willing to pay a membership fee, the archives as well.

ambient/new age

Hybrid
PBS **www.pbsfm.org.au**

Sunday 1000–1200 Greenwich. Host: Andrew Hollo.

Music for a New Age
WKAR **www.wkar.org**

Sunday–Wednesday 11pm–midnight Eastern. Host: Dan Bayer. Broader than just "New Age" music; a recent show, for example, featured Pat Metheny, The Loma Mar Quartet with the London Symphony Orchestra, Sara McLachlan, and Kronos String Quartet (performing Philip Glass).

New Frontiers
WXDU **www.wxdu.duke.edu**

Saturday 10am–noon Eastern. Two hours of space music.

Parallel Universe
95B **www.95bfm.com**

Thursday 1100–1300 Greenwich. Ambient, electronic, and experimental music, from the University of Auckland, in New Zealand.

Sunday New Age Morning
WAER **www.waer.org**

Sunday 9am–noon Eastern. *Sunday New Age Morning* often features a different artist or group by playing a number of selections from their latest release.

Blues

Blues Stations

KFAI
www.kfai.org

When one thinks of the blues, Minneapolis-St. Paul is not the first locale that springs to mind. But nowhere is there better blues programming than on KFAI. A different program every day 3–6pm Central, plus the great vintage show *Blueslady's Time Machine* Tuesday 9–11am, along with several other programs that blend blues, R&B, and jazz.

KNON
www.knon.org

Very extensive, and very good, blues lineup. Weekdays 9am–noon Central. (Thursday emphasizes Texas blues.) Weekdays 6–8pm Central.

KPFT
www.kpft.org
Blues all day Sunday 6am–6pm Central.

WMSE
www.wmse.org
Three hours of blues every weekday afternoon 3–6pm Central. *Saturday Morning Blues Jam* Saturday 9am–noon Central. But the best news is that you can listen to the extensive archives any time.

WWOZ
www.wwoz.org
Jazzy New Orleans station plays blues each weekday 2–4pm Central.

Blues Programs

All Blues
KPLU **www.kplu.org**
Saturday and Sunday 6pm–midnight Pacific.

Antique Blues
WPKN **www.wpkn.org**
Sunday 6–10pm Eastern. Host: Bill Nolan. Documents the source and history of this music with research from around the U.S. Nolan has hosted the show on WPKN since 1969.

Back Porch Blues
WUNC **www.wunc.org**
Saturday (that is, Friday night) midnight–2am Eastern. Saturday night 11pm–1am Eastern.

Blue in the Face
Trent Radio **www.trentu.ca/trentradio**
Tuesday 8–11pm Eastern. Host: Al Kirkcaldy.

Blue Monday
WFHB **www.wfhb.org**
Monday 9–11pm Eastern.

Blues
WBFO **www.wbfo.org**
Saturday and Sunday 11am–4pm Eastern, and Saturday 10pm–midnight. Hosts: Jim Santella, Kim Buckner (3–4pm Saturday), Debbie Sims (Saturday night).

Blues
KMDH **www.kmdh.org**
Friday 4pm–2am.

Blues
WHPK **whpk.uchicago.edu**
Saturday 7pm–midnight Central, Monday 9pm–midnight.

blues

Blues Avalanche
PBS **www.pbsfm.org.au**

Monday 1200–1400 Greenwich. Host: Kaye Frost.

Blues Beat
Hot FM **www.hotfm.org.au**

Thursday 1200–1400 Greenwich. Host: Geoff Pegler.

Blues Hangover
WHRB **www.whrb.org**

Sunday 7–11am Eastern. A wide range of acoustic and electric blues, including well-known standards and less-frequently played recordings of country blues, Chicago blues, and contemporary musicians.

Blues Never Die
CHRW **www.usc.uwo.ca/chrw**

Wednesday 6:30–8:30pm Eastern. Hosts: Chris Murphy and John Hoevenaars.

Blues with Phil
KVMR **www.kvmr.org**

Monday 2–4pm Pacific. Host: Phil Givant.

Cha Cha Cha in Blue
CKUT **www.ckut.ca**

Sunday 9–11pm Eastern. Montreal's longest-running blues program.

Blues Legacy
KGNU **www.kgnu.org**

Friday 6–9 pm Mountain.

Blues Power
KLCC **www.klcc.org**

Saturday 1–5pm Pacific. Host: Carl Stolz. The full spectrum of blues, from the traditional to the contemporary, including Delta and Chicago blues as well as Zydeco, soul and funk.

Blues Roots
KVNF **www.kvnf.org**

Sunday 1–4pm Mountain.

The Blues Session
KSHU **www.shsu.edu/~rtf_kshu**

Saturday 7pm–midnight Central. Nice five-hour run from the station at Sam Houston State University in Texas.

The Blues Show
WUSB **www.wusb.org**

Tuesday 7–9pm Eastern. This program features electric blues, often with live performances from guests.

blues

Bluesology
WERS www.wers.org

Saturday 11pm–2am Eastern.

Crossroads
WVBR www.wvbr.com

Saturday 9am–1pm Eastern. A mix of blues from Chicago to the Delta, even hopping across the pond from time to time.

El Blues Inmortal
Radio UNAM FM www.unam.mx/radiounam

Saturday 4–5pm Central. This program from the radio station of the Universidad Nacional Autónoma de México brings together blues music from many countries. (Note that Radio UNAM has two streams. This program is on the FM stream.)

Friday Night Blues Party
CKUA www.ckua.org

Friday 9pm–midnight Mountain. Host: Cam Hayden.

Friday Night Fish Fry
WREK www.wrek.org

5–7pm Eastern (but available any time on WREK's website). The *Friday Night Fish Fry* brings you all kinds of blues from Robert Johnson to Albert King to some of today's players. Also occasional live performances from local Atlanta artists.

Hall of Fame Blues
WYSO www.wyso.org

Monday 7–9pm Eastern. Host: Dave Hussong. One solid blues program, followed by another, *Red-Eye Express*, which lasts until 11pm.

House of Blues
HBC www.hbc.com.np

Friday 1300–1400 Greenwich. Host: Sachin Rai. Blues programming from Katmandu, Nepal (in English).

In the Evening
WPKN www.wpkn.org

Thursday 6:35–10pm Eastern. Host: Bob Shapiro. This program covers blues from the 1920s to the present day, with emphasis on the 1950s and '60s.

Jumpin' the Blues
KCSB www.kcsb.org

Saturday 4–6pm Pacific. Host: Matt Cohen. Blues, R&B, and Zydeco, from the 1940s to the present.

King Biscuit Time
KFFA www.kffaradio.com

Weekdays 12:15–1pm Central. On air since 1941, the program which made Sonny Boy Williamson a blues superstar is most likely the longest-running blues program in the world.

blues

Ninth Alley Blues

KNBA www.knba.org

Sunday 7–10pm Alaskan.

Nothin' But the Blues

KLON www.klon.org

Saturday and Sunday 2–7pm Pacific. Host: Doug MacLeod.

One More Shot

KCSB www.kcsb.org

Monday 6–8am Pacific. Host: Mike Wilkinson.

Out of the Blues

WMBR wmbr.mit.edu

Saturday noon–2pm Eastern. Host: David Herwaldt. Country blues, classic blues, jump blues, Chicago blues – with admixtures of jazz, gospel, and rock 'n' roll.

Pickin' the Blues

Rádio Universitária www.proex.ufu.br/links/radio.html

Friday 2300–2400 Greenwich.

Portraits in Blue

WBGO www.wbgo.org

Friday 7–8pm Eastern; repeated Saturday 7pm Eastern. Host: Bob Porter. Each week, Porter considers a slice of the career of a major (postwar) blues artist. For example, there have been five programs on Lightnin' Hopkins and two so far on Junior Parker and Big Maybelle.

David Herwaldt

Preachin' the Blues

KEXP www.kexp.org

Sunday 9am–noon Pacific. Host: Marlee Walker. Excellent program with unusually strong coverage of women in blues. Archived for listening any time.

Pure Blues

KCSB www.kcsb.org

Friday 8–10pm Pacific. Host: Mike Petrini.

Saturday Night Blues

CBC Radio One www.cbc.ca

Saturday 11:05pm–midnight Eastern. Host: Holger Petersen. Centers on

blues

classic blues, but also features concerts, interviews, artist features, new releases.

Saturday Night House Party
WNCW **www.wncw.org**

Saturday 8pm–midnight Eastern.

Sunday Night Blues
WAER **www.waer.org**

Sunday 6–10pm Eastern. Host: Tom Townsley. For over ten years, Syracuse blues harmonica player Townsley has been hosting this show which combines local (central New York State) talent such as Dirty Pool and Roosevelt Dean and national talent such as Luther "Guitar Jr." Johnson, and Little Charlie and the Nightcats.

Sunday Night Blues
WBGO **www.wbgo.org**

Sunday 7–10pm Eastern. Host: Walter Wade.

Trouble in Mind
KUSP **www.kusp.org**

Saturday 3–5pm Pacific.

True Blues
WBRS **www.wbrs.org**

Monday–Thursday 10am–noon Eastern.

Two Steps from the Blues
KUSP **www.kusp.org**

Monday 7–9pm Pacific. Host: Charlie Lange.

Live

Beale Street Caravan

Hosts: Pat Mitchell and Daren Dortin of the Blues Foundation, sometimes celebrity hosts such as Sam Phillips, Tracy Nelson, and Alvin Youngblood Hart. Live blues performances from places such as B.B. King's Blues Club, The King Biscuit Blues Festival and Manny's Car Wash. Heard on some 260 stations, listed at **www.bealestreetcaravan.com**.

Bluesland
KCSB **www.kcsb.org**

Thursday 2–5pm Pacific. Host: Leo Schumaker. Music, live interviews, and live music productions.

House Party Live
WNCW **www.wncw.org**

Saturday 11pm–midnight Eastern. The last hour of WNCW's blues program

blues

Saturday Night House Party features music recorded live in venues in North Carolina.

Bluegrass

American Anecdotes
KAOS www.kaosradio.org

Thursday 6–8pm Pacific.

Banjo Signal
KUAC www.kuac.org

Second Saturdays 7–8pm Alaska (one hour earlier than Pacific). Host: Trudy Heffernan.

Bluegrass
WBFO http://www.wbfo.buffalo.edu/

Sunday 9pm–midnight Eastern. Hosts: Rob Campbell and Randy Keller. Features a healthy dose of progressive bluegrass.

Bluegrass Breakdown
WPLN www.wpln.org

Saturday 8–9pm Eastern. Host: Dave Higgs. Great show, all over the bluegrass map. Particularly good coverage of new releases. Being based in Nashville, Higgs has particularly good opportunities for conversations with artists. Recent studio visitors have included The McLains, Lynn Morris and Marshall Wilborn, Crucial Smith, Tim O'Brien, Dirk Powell, the Larry Stephenson Band, and the Mark Newton Band.

Bluegrass Breakdown
WYSO www.wyso.org

Saturday 6–10pm Eastern. Host: Aaron Harris.

Bluegrass Café
WHUS www.whus.org

Sunday 2–4pm Eastern. This program from the college station at the University of Connecticut is particularly open to music that pushes the edges of the definition of bluegrass, including jazz and classical, but it does not neglect the core.

Bluegrass Country
www.bluegrasscountry.org

Host: Ray Davis. *Bluegrass Country* is an amazing 24-hour-a-day bluegrass program. It has grown out of station WAMU (**www.wamu.org**) which has offered large quantities of excellent bluegrass programming for over 30 years. Among his many other activities in promotion of bluegrass music, host Davis brings forth recordings on his Wango label. *Bluegrass Country* is supported by The National Endowment for the Arts.

bluegrass

Bluegrass Etc. KCSN www.kcsn.org
Sunday 7:30–10am Pacific. Host: Frank Hoppe, a bluegrass musician, dancer, and bluegrass festival organizer.

Bluegrass Express KCSN www.kcsn.org
Saturday 7:30–10am Pacific. Host: Marvin O'Dell (replacing long-time veteran Frank Javorsek). Long-running, extremely popular show.

Bluegrass for a Saturday Night KUMR www.kumr.org
Saturday 7–10pm Central. Host: Wayne Bledsoe. Also *Firstar Bluegrass Hour*, Sunday 8–9pm Central, devoted to new releases. Archives of both programs are on the website for listening on demand.

Bluegrass Overnight WAMU www.wamu.org
Sunday midnight–6am Eastern. Hosts: Les McIntyre and Gary Henderson. For over 30 years, WAMU's support of bluegrass music has been exceptional, measured not only by the sheer number of hours devoted to the genre, but also by the stellar musical quality. This six-hour show is just one example.

Bluegrass Saturday Morning KBEM http://www.jazz88fm.com/
Saturday 8am–noon Central. Host: Phil Nussbaum.

Bluegrass State of Mind CKUA www.ckua.org
Sunday 11am–noon Mountain. Host: David Ward.

Bluegrass Time WUSB www.wusb.org
Wednesday 6:30–8pm Eastern. Host: Buddy Merriam. Frequent studio guests.

Chris Teskey WPKN www.wpkn.org
Wednesday 7:30–10pm Eastern.

County Line Bluegrass Show KVMR www.kvmr.org
Saturday 10am–noon Pacific. Host: Eric Rice.

Down on the Pataphysical Farm KUSP www.kusp.org
Sunday noon–2pm Pacific. Hosts: Leigh Hill and Chris Jong. This show's been going since 1972. (Stick around after for *Lost Highway*, a "bluebilly" program.)

Going Across the Mountain WNCW www.wncw.org
Sunday noon–6pm Eastern. Hosts: Jerry McNeely and Dennis Jones. Six hours of traditional and contemporary bluegrass.

bluegrass

Music for the Mountain

WNEC **www.wnec.org**

Saturday 7–11pm Eastern. Host: Jonathan Colcord.

Old Grass GNU Grass

KGNU **www.kgnu.org**

Saturday 6–9am Mountain.

Out Behind the Barn

KFJC **www.kfjc.org**

Tuesday 10am–2pm Pacific. Bluegrass, some gospel, an emphasis on the fiddle.

Peach State Festival

WRFG **www.wrfg.org**

Weekdays 7–9pm Eastern. Radio Free Georgia's Peach State Festival is dedicated to acoustic Americana, with programs like *Old Strings New Strings* (Monday), *Bluegrass Festival* (Wednesday), and *Amazing Grass* (Friday) dedicated exclusively to bluegrass and Old Time music.

Pickin' and Swingin'

KPFT **www.kpft.org**

Saturday 3–6pm Central.

Pickin' Bluegrass

KVNF **www.kvnf.org**

Saturday 1–4pm Mountain.

The Ray Davis Show

WAMU **www.wamu.org**

Sunday 10am–1pm Eastern. In addition to his extensive collection of bluegrass music, host Davis also has a deep collection of tapes he has made himself over the years. (See also *Bluegrass Country*, Davis's 24-hour-a-day bluegrass stream.)

WAMC Bluegrass Time

WAMC **www.wamc.org**

Sunday 1–3pm Eastern. Host: Nick Barr.

Bluegrass Gospel

Most bluegrass contains a large strain of gospel; these programs focus on it exclusively.

Rise When the Rooster Crows

WYSO **www.wyso.org**

Sunday 6–8am Sunday. Host: Joe Colvin.

Stained Glass Bluegrass
WAMU **www.wamu.org**

Sunday 6–10am Eastern. Host: Red Shipley. This program, which has aired on WAMU for over 25 years, is a particularly rich source of Southern hill country spiritual music.

Old Time

Many of the programs listed under Bluegrass above play Old Time music. These programs concentrate on it.

The Salt Creek Show
WVBR **www.wvbr.com**

Sunday 6–10am Eastern. Old Time string band and a little bit of country mixed with bluegrass.

This Old Porch
WNCW **www.wncw.org**

Sunday 3–5pm Eastern. Host: Joe Cline or John Fowler.

Cajun/Zydeco/New Orleans

Bayou Country
KVMR **www.kvmr.org**

Saturday 4–6pm Pacific. Host: Dick "LeBlanc" Johnson. Cajun, Creole, Zydeco, and swamp pop.

Cajun & Zydeco Radio Guide
www.cajunradio.org

A listing of Cajun radio on the Net.

Cajun Hour
KNON **www.knon.org**

Monday 8–10pm Central.

China Mike's Swamp Jazz Culture Hour
CFUV **cfuv.uvic.ca**

Tuesday 1–2pm Pacific.

Crawfish Fiesta
WFHB **www.wfhb.org**

Friday 7:30–9pm Eastern.

Down Home
KCSN **www.kcsn.org**

Saturday 3–5pm Pacific. Host: Chuck Taggart. Chuck is from New Orleans, but he plays "whatever tastes good in the gumbo."

Louisiana Gumbo
CJSW **www.cjsw.com**

Sunday 7–8pm Mountain. Host: Wayne Brideaux. In addition to Cajun and zydeco, "Chef Wayne" will play Louisiana blues, folk, country, rock, R&B, and rap. He emphasizes the Francophone Cajun and Creole traditions and occasionally throws some traditional or contemporary Acadian artists into the mix.

Louisiana Rhythms
KFAI **www.kfai.org**

Friday 9–11am Central.

New Orleans Music Hour
WLUW **www.wluw.org**

Saturday noon–1pm Central. Host: Tom Jackson.

Pe-Te's Cajun Bandstand
KPFT **www.kpft.org**

Saturday 6–8am Central. Preceded by *Zydeco Dawn* 4–6am Central.

WWOZ
www.wwoz.org

WWOZ, from New Orleans, broadcasts "blues, jazz, cajun, zydeco, gospel, Brazilian, Caribbean and a whole lot more." The *New Orleans Music Show* streams weekdays 11am–2pm Central.

Conjunto/Tex-Mex/ Norteño/Tejano

Canción Mexicana
KUVO **www.kuvo.org**

Sunday 9am–1pm Mountain. Hosts: Mercedes Hernandez and Flo. *Canción Mexicana* is hosted in English, for English-speaking Latinos and Latinas who want to hear "roots" music, predominantly conjunto.

Howlin' at the Moon
WUNH **www.wunh.org**

Sunday 4–5pm Eastern. Host: Dave Pasiuk.

KNON
www.knon.org

KNON is a great community radio station in North Texas that devotes four hours each day to Tejano music (Monday–Saturday, noon–4pm Central). You would think it would be only natural for radio stations to emphasize local musical flavors, but it is actually uncommon. Perhaps Internet audiences, uninterested in syndicated sameness, can help support locally flavored stations. In the meantime, don't miss KNON. If you like Tejano music, they've got it fresh and juicy.

KSCA
www.netmio.com/radio/ksca

Commercial norteño station in Los Angeles. Top 40 countdown on Sunday morning.

Radio Aztlan
KUCR www.kucr.org

Friday 6:30pm–Saturday 7am Pacific. A variety of musical styles having in common a geography and a language:

» 6:30 *Que Pasa Raza* DJ Tripp "Brownsounds"

» 8:30 *Tejano Sounds* El Guapo Lapo Tex-Mex

» 10:00 *Rolas de Aztlan* Mr. Blue Movimiento Music

» 12:30 *Cruisin' thru Midnight* Mr Beto Man Oldies and Dedications

» 2am *Dreaming Casually* Angel Baby "Souldies" and Dedications

» 5am *La Madrugadoras* Mana y Paloma Rancheras

Texas Music
KUT www.kut.org

Sunday 9pm–midnight Central.

Country/Alternative Country/ Americana/Rockabilly

For the same reason that the rock section of this guide does not list all the thousands of the world's radio stations that play the Top 40, this section does not include many mainstream Nashville stations. Instead, it primarily lists less-produced country music, often more acoustic, usually on smaller labels, and nearly always from other parts of the world than the big recording studios of Nashville. This music goes by various names, most commonly "alt-country."

Although more and more people are finding they like it, nobody can agree on what alt-country is. One could dispute all day about whether this group or that group should be put in this category or that. There are people out there who would tell you that the titles given here for this category refer to *completely* different things and that lumping them together insults them all. Nonetheless, there is an indigenous American music, in whose ancestry we find the blues, Irish fiddle tunes, the banjo, and the English ballad. It is associated with rural people of the South and Southwest.

The radio stations below play contemporary music that seems closer to the spirit of Hank Williams, Hank Thompson, Bob Wills, and the Carter Family than does the music you hear on Country Music Television. (It is likewise more probably closer to the heart of rock 'n' roll than anything you will see on MTV.) Its practitioners cover a lot of territory, from the murder ballad harmonies of Gillian Welch and David Rawlins, to the sharp dance tunes of The Derailers. On the stations listed below, you'll hear Steve Earle, BR549, Two Tons of Steel, Ray Wylie Hubbard, The Great Divide, Charlie Robison, Allison Moorer, Chris Knight, Robert Earl Keen. The best of the stations and programs tend to be more inclusive than exclusive, more interested in enjoying music than in establishing categories. Names and slogans range from "the best rockabilly, boogie, and rhythm and blues" to "absolute twang."

country/alternative country/americana/rockabilly

Country Favorites

Country Stations

KHYI
www.khyi.com
Commercial station in Plano, Texas.

KNBT
www.radionewbraunfels.com
The number one Alternative Country station in the world has to be Radio New Braunfels from Texas. Last year it was picked as "Americana Station of the Year" by Gavin's, an organization that is doing much to promote the label "Americana."

KNON
www.knon.org
Great community station in Dallas that plays lots of Texas-flavored music. The program *Texas Renegade*, weekdays 4–6pm Central, is the most explicitly alt-country. Also check out *Rockabilly Revue* Tuesday 8–10pm Central. But you'll probably like the whole of KNON's lineup: lots of Tejano, Texas blues, and with Western rock.

WDVR
www.wdvrfm.org
This New Jersey station streams many kinds of music; a large percentage of the programs drift towards the "traditional country" corner. See particularly:
- ‣ *Honky Tonks and Heart Aches* Monday noon–3pm Eastern.
- ‣ *Country Roundup* Tuesday 9am–noon
- ‣ *Happy Valley Echos* Wednesday 6–9am
- ‣ *Tiny's Country Cafe* Thursday midnight–4am
- ‣ *Honky Tonk Roadhouse* Thursday 6–9am
- ‣ *The Country Store* Friday 7–10pm
- ‣ *Country Classics* Friday 10pm–1am
- ‣ *Bick at Night* Saturday 1–6am

WFDU
www.wfdu.fm
This student station from Farleigh Dickinson University is not all Americana all the time. Weekday afternoons are given over to soul and the blues, and weekends are mostly alternative rock. But most of the weekdays are devoted to a "Music America" format. In the fall of 2001, its playlist was topped by Rhonda Vincent, Del McCoury, String Cheese Incident, BR549, Lucinda Williams, and Rosie Flores.

WNCW
www.wncw.org
The mainstay of WNCW's programming is *Crossroads*, which runs other times

country/alternative country/americana/rockabilly

as well but you can always count on it from 8am to 7pm Eastern. Although *Crossroads* includes world music, blues, jazz, and quite a bit of Celtic, it is at its heart Americana , and this North Carolina station plays it all day.

Country Programs

Acid Country
PBS **www.pbsfm.org.au**

Thursday 0500–0700 Greenwich. Host: David Heard. Innovative program from a community radio station in Melbourne, Australia.

Americana
Radio Active **www.radioactive.co.nz**

Sunday 0200–0400 Greenwich. Americana as seen from New Zealand.

Arctic Cactus Hour
KNBA **www.knba.org**

Saturday 6–8pm Alaska. Hosts: Eric Smith and Jim Stratton. The word "Arctic" in the name of the program refers to the fact that KNBA is the station of the Koahnic Broadcast Corporation in Anchorage, Alaska. The "Cactus" refers to the music, which ranges from Vassar Clements to The Bastard Sons of Johnny Cash, by way of the New Riders of the Purple Sage.

Back Alley Porch Roost
WREK **www.wrek.org**

Saturday 9–10pm Eastern. (But available any time on WREK's website.) "The music that Nashville has forgotten or doesn't want you to hear – The Good Stuff!! Classic country, bluegrass, folk, rockabilly, punkabilly, country-influenced rock, rock-influenced country, etc., etc."

Blood on the Saddle
KWVA **gladstone.uoregon.edu/~kwva**

Saturday 4–7am Pacific. Wide-ranging and extremely vigorous show from the student station at the University of Oregon in Eugene.

Boot Heel Drag
CJSW **www.cjsw.com**

Tuesday 7:30–9pm Mountain. Host: Allen Baekland. Traditional country and western music: honky-tonk, Western swing, bluegrass, rockabilly, Bakersfield, Canadian fiddle, yodeling, pedal steel, chicken pickin', and truckers' favorites, from Calgary, Alberta, where Baekland has been on radio for 23 years. The program also usually contains interviews.

Chicken Shack
WMSE **www.wmse.org**

Friday 9am–noon Central., but archived on the website so you can listen to it any time.

Citybilly
KCSN www.kcsn.org

Sunday 5–7pm Pacific. Host: René Engel. This is a great show. As Engel describes it, "truckers, twang, and torch… cowboy and gospel, country and city. Any dividing lines just disappear." Sometimes has on-air guests.

Country Fried Radio
KVRX www.kvrx.org

Friday 5–7am Central. Host: Mason Dixon. This entertaining show from the student station at the University of Texas serves up a mess of bluegrass, classic country, Western swing, and rockabilly, prominently featuring Texas artists without neglecting other honky-tonk favorites.

Down Home Country
WUSB www.wusb.org

Sunday 11am–12:30pm Eastern. Hosts: Debbie de Waltoff or Walt Simpson.

Front Porch
KLCC www.klcc.org

Saturday 6–7pm Pacific. Host: Dan Plaster. Americana music – rockabilly, alt-country, bluegrass, rock – focusing on new releases.

Hardcore Country
CHRW www.usc.uwo.ca/chrw

Wednesday 10pm–Eastern. Hosts: Fred Smith and Ryan Spence.

Hillbilly at Harvard
WHRB www.whrb.org

Saturday 9pm–midnight Eastern. Hosts: Lynn Joiner and Brian Sinclair. This widely respected program has been bringing a variety of American music to New England for over 50 years. The program draws from its pick of touring musicians as well as recordings.

Home Grown
CFRU www.uoguelph.ca/~cfru-fm

Wednesday 7–8pm Eastern. Agricultural information and country music from Ontario.

Honky-Tonk Heroes
KGNU www.kgnu.org

Saturday 6–9am Mountain.

KEXP
www.kexp.org

If you've been through Seattle, you might remember this station as KCMU, the student station at the University of Washington. Now it has been taken under the wing of the Experience Music Project, but all the same DJs are still there doing all the same shows, particularly the outstanding honky-tonk show Swinging Doors Wednesday 6–8pm Pacific. Host: Greg Vandy. A mix of American music, including Louisiana, Kentucky, and contemporary Nashville.

country/alternative country/americana/rockabilly

Lone Star Jukebox
KPFT
www.kpft.org

Saturday 9am–noon Central. Three hours of good acoustic Texas music, followed by three more entitled *Spare Change*.

Lost Highway
KUSP
www.kusp.org

Sunday 2–4pm Pacific. Hosts: Genial Johnny Simmons and Charlie Park. "Bluebilly" music: "a working hybrid of traditional country, blues, folk, gospel, and Western swing, plus the best of the new material that stands on the shoulders of the giants who came before."

Greg Vandy

Radio Thrift Shop
WFMU www.wfmu.org

Saturday noon–3pm Eastern. Host: Laura Cantrell. Fans of Cantrell's music will certainly appreciate the chance to listen to the music she loves, which she's good enough to volunteer to play three hours of each week on WFMU in New Jersey. The music she plays ranges beyond alt-country into ragtime, swing, and points beyond. Past shows are archived on the website, so that while you're in catch-up mode, it can be all Laura, all the time.

Ragged But Right
KVMR www.kvmr.org

Alternate Saturdays noon–2pm Pacific. Host: Thomas Greener. Country and Western focusing on the music of Austin, Texas, folk, Cajun, and more. The Gospel Corner is a regular feature at 12:45pm. On alternate Saturdays is *Hard Country*, with Rick Snelson. And following these shows, at 2pm, is Wesley Robertson's *Rockin' and Stompin'*, two hours of rearing and bucking country, country rock, bluegrass, Cajun, zydeco, blues and folk.

Ritz Radio 1035
www.ritz1035.com

Monday 2100–2400 Greenwich. Host: Mark Hagan. Alt-country and rockabilly program on a commercial country music station from England. See also Nick Stewart's Americana show *Captains America* at the same time on Fridays.

The Roadhouse
KEXP www.kexp.org

Thursday 6–8pm Pacific. Host: Don Slack. This is the music on the jukebox of the heart. One Thursday Slack played The Louvin Brothers, Farmer Boys, Gene O'Quin, Wayne Hancock, Roger Wallace, Whiskeytown, Joe Henry, Charlie Robison, Leslie Satcher, Justin Trevino, Gene Watson, Faron Young, and Conway Twitty.

Route 66
KJHK kjhk.ukans.edu

Sunday noon–3pm Central. This program from the student station at the University of Kansas in Lawrence frequently features studio visitors, from Saltgrass to Ben Harper. Programs are archived on the *Route 66* site so you can listen to them any time: www.route66radio.net.

Route 78 West
KVCU www.colorado.edu/StudentGroups/KVCU

Saturday 6–7pm Mountain. Old 78's, LPs, trucker's songs, honky-tonk, hot rod music, Western swing, alt-country, and surf.

Sangamon Valley Roots Revival
WQNA www.wqna.org

Wednesday 7pm–9pm Central. Host: Sean Burns. Hillbilly, rockabilly and Western swing.

Shake the Shack
KEXP www.kexp.org

Fridays 6–8pm Pacific. Host: Leon Berman. Berman tirelessly repeats junior high school jokes, with incessant references to body parts and excretion, but his playlist is unsurpassed: Sid King and the Five Strings, Ray Smith, Calvin Bose, Hank Thompson, Hank Snow, Sonny Burgess, The Rockin' Saints, Cave Cat Sammy, Crazy Love, The Barnshakers, Cat Scratch Fever, Wylie and the Wild West… as Berman says, "rockabilly, boogie, rhythm and blues."

The Songwriter Sessions
WPLN www.wpln.org

Saturday 7–8pm Eastern. Each week three guests swap songs and tell stories in this Nashville studio. Recent guests include Mathew Ryan, Danny Tate, Eric Taylor, Terri Corker, Michael J. McEvoy, Vince Bell, Joe Nolan, Pam Gadd, and Larry Bastian.

Sound from the Mother Road
KUGS www.kugs.org

Saturday 8–9am Pacific. "A musical journey across the vast landscape of American roots music."

Southbound Train
WNUR **www.wnur.org**

Sunday 8–10pm Central.

South by Southwest
WMPG **www.wmpg.org**

Monday 9–11am Eastern. Host: Lincoln Pierce. Honky-tonk, Western swing, and straight ahead country music from the likes of Webb Pierce and Bill Boyd, often compiled into a theme show. Recent themes: Steel Guitar Rag Extravaganza, Carl Butler & Pearl Appreciation, Kitty Wells' "Answer Songs", and Train Songs.

Southern Rail
WBRS **www.wbrs.org**

Friday and Saturday 1–3pm Eastern. Contemporary bluegrass, folk and country, mixed with a variety of Old Time, acoustic and traditional music.

Trash, Twang and Thunder
WFMU **www.wfmu.org**

Wednesday 10pm–midnight Eastern. Host: Meredith Ochs. Twang rock, gutbucket blues, front porch bluegrass, American soul of all sorts. Lots of live music too. Archives of past shows on the WFMU website for listening any time.

Tupelo Blue Whiskey
CJAM **venus.uwindsor.ca/cjam**

Monday 9–10:30am Eastern.

Classic Country

Most of the programs listed above feature ample portions of classic country music; the ones listed below concentrate primarily or exclusively on it.

Classic Country
2NUR **www.newcastle.edu.au/cwis/ra**

Saturday 0430–0630 Greenwich. Host: Warren Fuller.

Country Classics
WNCW **www.wncw.org**

Sunday 5–6pm Eastern. Host: Joe Bussard. Music from 1910 to 1950.

Country Classics
WQNA **www.wqna.org**

Monday 6pm–10pm Central. Host: Ed Reubling. Mainstream country from 1940 to 1990.

The Cowboy Cultural Society
**www.cowboycultural
society.com**

Host: Laura Ellen. Internet-only channel with a good selection of sentimental favorite cowboy songs, from Gene Autry to Ian Tyson. (If you enjoy this channel, you might also want to check out KPIG **www.kpig.com**, where Ellen is the program director.)

Debbie Does Dallas
WMBR **wmbr.mit.edu**

Deb Rich

Wednesday 6–8am Eastern. Host: Deb Rich. Don't miss this show. Also don't miss Rich's page on the WMBR website, which among other treats contains a "Name Game" section where you can count the country songs with your name in the title.

The Eddie Stubbs Show
WAMU **www.wamu.org**

Saturday 3–6pm Eastern. Stubbs, the fiddle player for the Johnson Mountain Boys, plays country music from the 1940s through the 1960s.

Good 'n' Country
KFAI **www.kfai.org**

Saturday 1–3pm Central. Host: Ken Hippler. Archived on the KFAI website for listening any time.

Hillbilly Heaven
CFUV **cfuv.uvic.ca**

Saturday 4–5pm Pacific. Host: David P. Smith. Old Timey country music.

Honky-Tonk
WOJB **www.wojb.org**

Friday 7:30pm–midnight Central.

Loud Fast and Out of Control
CFUV **cfuv.uvic.ca**

Monday 3–4pm Pacific. Rockabilly program featuring B-sides and unreleased songs from the 1950s and early '60s.

Midnight Ramble
WYSO **www.wyso.org**

Saturday 10pm–midnight. Host: Ray Garrison. Country music from the 1920s through the 1960s.

country/alternative country/americana/rockabilly

The Old Record Shop

WRVU http://wrvu.org

Thursday noon–2pm Central.

Radio Boogie

CKLN ckln.sac.ryerson.ca

Wednesday 10pm–midnight Eastern. Host: Steve Pritchard. This program spotlights traditional bluegrass, gospel, Western swing, cajun, cowboy and string band music going back to the 1920s.

Rhythm Ranch

WFHB www.wfhb.org

Monday 6:30–9pm Eastern. Host: Greg Adams. Rockabilly, country, and R&B from the 1940s through the 1960s.

The Truck Stop

KNBA www.knba.org

Sunday noon–3pm Alaska. Classic country music, from a truck stop at the north end of a very long road.

Country All Over The World

Bob Harris Country

BBC Radio 2
www.bbc.co.uk/radio2

Thursday 1900–2000 Greenwich. Frequently includes interviews with artists.

CJMS

www.cjms.ca

Pure country feeling, in French, from this commercial station in Montreal.

CJSE www.capacadie.com/capradio

On CJSE one can find a variety of country-flavored music in French, including (what must be somewhat of a rarity) quite a bit of French bluegrass.

Bob Harris

Country Radio

www.countryradio.cz/

From Prague in the Czech Republic, a sprightly mix of banjo, Old Time fiddle, and folk melodies. It can sound like the hills of Tennessee, if you ignore the fact that they're singing in a foreign language.

country/alternative country/americana/rockabilly

Daybreak Country
2NUR **www.newcastle.edu.au/cwis/ra**

Saturday 1900–2300 Greenwich. Host: John Slaven. This program from the station at The University of Newcastle, in New South Wales, Australia, emphasizes local country music.

Good 'n' Country
Trent Radio **www.trentu.ca/trentradio**

Saturday 7am–noon Eastern. Hosts: Barb Bell and Barb Holtman. Includes quite a bit of local country music from Ontario, Canada.

Hot FM
www.hotfm.org.au

This community radio station in Mildura, Victoria, Australia has a variety of specialty shows, from jazz and blues to ethnic broadcasting in foreign languages. But if you tune in at any random time, the chance is better than 50 percent you'll hear Australian country music. To improve your chances, it's all country from 1400 to 2100 Greenwich daily.

Lider Contry Company
Lider FM **www.liderfm.com.br**

Saturday 2200–2300 Greenwich. Country music from Brazil and around the world.

Nick Barraclough
BBC Radio 2 **www.bbc.co.uk/radio2**

Wednesday 1900–2000 Greenwich. Provides a good summary overview of the new releases from Nashville. Awfully mainstream, but there are occasional gems.

Ritz Radio1035
www.ritz1035.com

Tuesday 2100–2200. Country music from England.

Saturday Night Country
ABC Coast FM **local.abc.net.au/ goldcoast/radio**

Saturday 1000–1400 Greenwich. Host: John Nutting. Australian country music from Queensland. Each edition of the program features a guest artist. Recently appearing were the Topp Twins, New Zealand's amazing lesbian yodelers.

Today's Country
Radio Television Hong Kong (RTHK) Radio 3 **www.rthk.org.hk**

Saturday 0515–0700 Greenwich. Host: Anders Nelsson. The best feature of this program is that it is archived for a year after broadcast, so there are 52 episodes on the RTHK website at any time.

country/alternative country/americana/rockabilly

Wide Cut Country
CKUA www.ckua.org

Saturday 10:30am–noon Mountain. Host: Allison Brock. Alberta itself is wide, and covering it with a radio signal requires the CKUA Network to put up over a dozen transmitters. This program manages to communicate that open expanse.

WRTL Country
RTL www.rtl.fr

Thursday 2300–Friday 0100 Greenwich. Host: Georges Lang. An interesting mix of country music, including a lot of straight Nashville.

Dance/Electronica/Techno/ House/Trance/Acid Jazz

Electronic media have played a major role in the diffusion and development of musical culture for almost eighty years. African musicians cite Jimmie Rodgers as a primary influence, and the British rock revival started in Liverpool because port cities got earlier and easier access to foreign records. But the Internet's immediacy and multidirectionality are so different from anything that came before that music evolves differently now. Rave music is arguably the first truly global music, in the sense that it is the first music that co-evolved all over the globe at once, rather than igniting in a single location and then spreading. It is as indigenous to London as to Detroit, and the Balearic Islands have a claim as its homeland. Its ancestry is diverse. You can detect in it features of disco, funk, soul, reggae, technopop, and industrial. If it has a most immediate source, it is probably the club music supported and developed by the gay scene. Early raves, like the early psychedelic scene, were not only musical events, but a setting in which optimistic youth could gather and reinforce each other's feelings of positive energy. The music promises to be with us for a long run, and on Internet radio now you can hear it morphing into thousands of pulsating new forms.

Dance favorites	
Dream Escape	see p.119
Groove FM	see p.119
PulseRadio	see p.121

Dance Stations

C-Dance
www.c-dance.be

High energy dance stream from Belgium.

Dream Escape
www.dream-escape.org

Excellent live techno channel.

Dubplate.net
www.dubplate.net

This collection of the latest dubplates, white labels and new releases from the UK garage scene is not necessarily a radio station, but if you don't live in London this is a good way to stay current.

Fresh FM
www.freshfm.com.au

This community radio station from Adelaide, Australia lives up to its name.

Groove FM
www.groovefm.net

Groove FM is a community radio station from Brisbane, Australia, with three different streams of R&B, soul, funk, acid jazz and other dance grooves.

Groovetech
www.groovetech.com

The site may be tied to an online record retailer, but with three bases of operation (San Francisco, Seattle and London) the range of material featured is impressive, covering the entire breadth of the electronic/club music spectrum.

Hyperdub
www.hyperdub.com

Not a radio station per se (there are also numerous articles on dance culture from R&B to UK garage), but the site hosts an excellent archive of DJ mixes organized by bpm, from downtempo and dub to drum 'n' bass and UK garage.

dance/electronica/techno/house/trance/acid jazz

Interface Pirate Radio

interface.pirate-radio.co.uk

Founded with the intention of beaming London's vibrant pirate radio scene across the globe, Interface hosts mixes from the likes of Andrew Weatherall, Metalheadz, The Orb's Dr. Alex Paterson, Botchit & Scarper and Red Snapper.

KCSB

www.kcsb.org

This station from the University of California at Santa Barbara has several very good dance programs. (All times Pacific.)

- ▸ *Bass Beat Swap Meet* Monday midnight–2am Drum 'n' bass, hip-hop, downtempo, and electro
- ▸ *Surface Tension* Monday 11am–1pm Ambient soundscapes and atmospheres
- ▸ *Domestic Blend* Tuesday 4–6am Hard-hitting drum 'n' bass
- ▸ *Journey Through Sound* Thursday 8–10pm Eclectic mix of electronic music
- ▸ *Astroantiquity* Friday 9–11am Lively dance mix including techno, house, and drum 'n' bass
- ▸ *Hypnotic State* Saturday midnight–2am Trance and psychedelic trance

1Groove

1groove.com

Excellent collection of mixes from an Internet-only site in Toronto, which brings to a single stream the work of DJs around the world. Everything on the site is archived for a week.

1Groove

dance/electronica/techno/house/trance/acid jazz

PulseRadio
www.pulseradio.net

This global dance stream has an impressive lineup of shows from all around the world, each featuring a different variety of dance music.

Radio Active
www.radioactive.co.nz

This station from New Zealand plays a variety of music. If you tune in at random, you might hit a specialty show playing jazz or country music. But most of the time they play interesting dance music.

Radio Italia Network
www.italianetwork.it

A decent mix of the same dance grooves you hear everywhere else and slightly more challenging fare.

RadiOK
www.radiok.net

The Dance and Electronica streams (available any time) of this Mexican station offer a unique flavor.

Radio Vitosha
www.radiovitosha.com

Bulgarian station.

Studio FM
www.gmw.be/sfm

This Internet-only station with studios in the Netherlands and servers in California plays dance hits all the time.

SWH+
www.radioswh.lv/swhplus.htm

High energy dance music from Latvia.

Tempo
live.tempo.fm

In addition to the live stream, this site from Belgium offers several dance streams on demand, including *Partyzone*, *Eternal Trance*, and *The Hottest Vinyl*.

Jimmy Degreef of Tempo FM's Party Zone

dance/electronica/techno/house/trance/acid jazz

u4ia   **www.trinidad-online.org/Underwire**
"Trancetastic" stream from Trinidad.

Dance Programs

Beats Per Minute   95B **www.95bfm.com**
Thursday 0900–1100 Greenwich. From the University of Auckland, in New Zealand.

Beta Lounge   **www.betalounge.com**
Thursday 8pm–midnight Pacific. Weekly showcase of excellent DJ talent, everyone from Goldie to I-Sound, Richie Hawtin to Z-Trip. Every show has been archived for listening any time.

Deeper Shade of House   CHRW **www.usc.uwo.ca/chrw**
Monday midnight–2am Eastern. House and techno. If you enjoy this show, you will probably also have a good time with *Deep Six*, a more techno-oriented program, at the same time on the previous night.

Didjilution   WNYU **www.wnyu.org**
Wednesday 9–10:30pm Eastern. Experimental electronica.

Dreem Teem   BBC Radio 1 **www.bbc.co.uk/radio1**
Monday 0000–0300 Greenwich. If you don't live within earshot of London's pirate radio community, this program is one of the best ways to hear the latest from the UK garage scene.

Electronic Air   KGNU **www.kgnu.org**
Saturday 9–11pm Mountain. "Techno tribal dance music."

Electronika   Radio Campus Lille **www-radio-campus.univ-lille1.fr**
Saturday 2200–2330 Greenwich.

Escape Velocity   CFUV **cfuv.uvic.ca**
Thursday 10:30pm–midnight. Pacific. Intelligent techno.

Esoterica   WQNA **www.wqna.org**
Tuesday 10pm–2am Central. Hosts: DJ MsLisa and Ted Keyton. Emphasizes experimental/electronic innovations in sound, from the likes of Gershon Kingsley's pop corn to the big beats of Fatboy Slim.

dance/electronica/techno/house/trance/acid jazz

The Essential Mix
BBC Radio 1 **www.bbc.co.uk/radio1**
Sunday 0100–0300 Greenwich. Two hour mixes from the leading house, techno, drum 'n' bass, garage and eclectic DJs.

The Essential Selection
BBC Radio 1 **www.bbc.co.uk/radio1**
Friday 1700–2000 Greenwich. Host: Pete Tong. This long-running program is perhaps the most influential radio show for the global clubbing community.

Fabio & Grooverider
BBC Radio 1 **www.bbc.co.uk/radio1**
Saturday 0100–0300 Greenwich. This DJ duo are credited with helping to kick-start drum 'n' bass and they're still bringing it to the masses.

Horizons
WREK **www.wrek.org**
Saturday 10–midnight Eastern (but available any time on WREK's website). Here is the program description: Hear the sound electronic unique sonic expanding understanding undemanding designed flowing into your mind beats underneath the street complete organic indeterminate heat marks the drum one place one space bass undeniable inconceivable yet believable house better non-stop dance in any weather global culture rhythm station needing no translation.

House of Jacq
JOY **joy.org.au**
Friday 1400–1600 Greenwich. Energetic dance and electronic program from a volunteer-operated community gay and lesbian radio station in Melbourne, Australia.

Kiwi Dance Music
Radio New Zealand **www.radionz.co.nz**
Kiwi Dance Music is a stream available any time from the Radio New Zealand website. To find it, choose "Radio NZ Audio," then "Audio Xtra."

LUSH
URY **ury.york.ac.uk**
Friday 1900–2100 Greenwich. This program from the student station at the University of York serves up house music for a Friday night. An hour of representative music is available for listening any time at the Lush Web archive **www.lushshow.com**.

Modular Trips
KUCR **www.kucr.org**
Monday 3–5pm Pacific., Saturday 7–9pm Pacific. RPM, dance, trance.

Oxy Dance
Lider FM **www.liderfm.com.br**
Saturday 2300–Sunday 0300 Greenwich. Dance music from Brazil and around the world.

dance/electronica/techno/house/trance/acid jazz

Re:mixit

CFUV **cfuv.uvic.ca**

Wednesday 11pm–1:30am Pacific. Remixes and cover tracks, with a focus on electronica.

Revolutions

WERS **www.wers.org**

Weekdays 11pm–2am Eastern. Three hours of electronica nightly.

Senseless Acts of Randomness

KVMR **www.kvmr.org**

Wednesday 10pm–midnight Pacific. Host: Chris Fluke. Liquid dub, trance, and mellow electronica.

Solid Steel

BBC London Live **www.bbc.co.uk/londonlive**

Monday 2300–0100 Greenwich. Host: Coldcut. Now over a decade old, this program hosted by the production duo Coldcut is the granddaddy of all beat-based eclectica mixes. Every show they've ever done is archived at **www.ninjatune.net/solidsteel**.

Soular Grooves

KPFT **www.kpft.org**

Friday 9–midnight Central. Great acid jazz show.

Tribalife

CFUV **cfuv.uvic.ca**

Wednesday 12:30–3am Pacific. Hosts: Tora Styles and DJ Rennie Dubnut Foster. House and funky techno.

Folk

Folk favorites

FolkScene	see p.125
WUMB	see p.125

Folk Stations

CFUV

cfuv.uvic.ca

Weekdays 8–10am Pacific. This Victoria, British Columbia station offers two hours of varied and excellent folk music programming each weekday morning.

Don't miss Jo Vipond's *Ode to Ani* on Tuesdays, a program which remembers the political roots of folk music, dedicated to the proposition that "the revolution is just a folk show away."

FolkScene
www.kpig.com

Hosts: Howard and Roz Larman. *FolkScene* is a channel at KPIG, meaning you

can hear it any time. (Actually, it's two channels: one for the current show, one an archive.) *FolkScene* is one of the longest-running folk programs around, heard on Los Angeles Pacifica station KPFK until recent purges cast the Larmans out. The Larmans' folk knowledge is encyclopedic, and their friendship with generations of folk musicians guarantees an unsurpassed guest list. The show is

Roz and Howard Larman

always a treat for the ears. In addition to the KPIG channel, the Larmans also host a *FolkScene* for Boston folk station WUMB **www.wumb.org** Saturday 9–11pm Eastern.

WUMB
www.wumb.org

This Boston station (with three affiliate stations) may be the world's only radio station devoted to folk music. There are specialty shows evenings and weekends, but they also tend to favor folk music and you will find a good solid block of traditional and contemporary folk and acoustic music weekdays 6am–6pm Eastern.

Folk Programs

The Acoustic Minstrel Show
KAOS **www.kaosradio.org**

Sunday 1–3pm Pacific. Host: Tom Wilson.

AM Americana
KCSB **www.kcsb.org**

Tuesday 6–8am Pacific.

folk

Back to the Blue Ridge
WVTF **www.wvtf.org**

Sunday 2–3pm Eastern. Hosts: Seth Williamson and Kinney Rorrer. This program is devoted to the traditional acoustic music of the Blue Ridge Mountains and the Piedmont region. There is bluegrass, sure, but also lots of Old Time, as well as blues and gospel.

Back Porch Music
WUNC **www.wunc.org**

Friday 9pm–midnight Eastern, Saturday 8–11pm Eastern, Sunday 7pm–midnight Eastern. Hosts: Freddy Jenkins and Keith Weston.

The Circle
HBC **www.hbc.com.np**

Tuesday 1330–1430 Greenwich. Host: Danny Birch. This program (from Nepal!) traces the evolution and development of 20th-century music from rural folk into jazz and rock, then follows it back to the roots.

Coast Ridge Ramble
KUSP **www.kusp.org**

Saturday 1–3pm Pacific. Host: Rachel Goodman or Michael Tanner.

Coffee House
WERS **www.wers.org**

Weekdays 6–10am Eastern.

Currents and Traditions
WDVR **www.wdvrfm.org**

Friday 10pm–4am Eastern. Host: Eileen Fisher. Much of the music on this New Jersey station is traditional. Check out Jen Elsworth's *The Music of Love* Wednesday 9am–noon.

Dakota Dave Hull Show
KFAI **www.kfai.org**

Thursday 9–11am Central. This well-known program in the Twin Cities often has guests, including some semi-regulars.

Dancing on the Air

www.dancingontheair.com
Hosts: Jay Ungar and Molly Mason. The *Dancing on the Air* website archives episodes of this monthly WAMC program for listening any time.

Jay Ungar and Molly Mason

folk

126

The Dick Spottswood Show
WAMU **www.wamu.org**

Sunday 1–3pm Eastern. Spottswood is an important collector, researcher, and author. The show is wide-ranging and various, but its center is in the "Songcatcher" period (around 1920-50) when musicologists were first dragging recording gear through the South, capturing the music as it was sung in homes and communities.

Festival Americana
KCSB **www.kcsb.org**

Wednesday 3–5pm Pacific.

Fine Tuning
KCSB **www.kcsb.org**

Saturday 8–10am Pacific.

The Folk and Acoustic Show
KSHU **www.shsu.edu/~rtf_kshu**

Sunday 6–11am Central. A nice relaxed, five-hour folk show from the student station at Sam Houston University in Texas.

Folk Beat
WRBC **www.bates.edu/wrbc**

Saturday 10am–noon Eastern. Host: Skip Mowry.

Folk Roots
CKUA **www.ckua.org**

Sunday 4–6pm Mountain. Host: Tom Coxworth. Includes good coverage of folk musicians and events in Alberta.

Folk Roots
Radio Television Hong Kong (RTHK) Radio 3
www.rthk.org.hk

Saturday 1015–1100 Greenwich. This program is archived for a year after broadcast, so there are 52 episodes on the RTHK website at any time.

Folk Salad
KWGS **www.kwgs.org**

Sunday 10–11pm Central. Hosts: Richard Higgs and Scott Aycock. From the University of Tulsa, Oklahoma, including some good local music.

The Folk Sampler

Host: Mike Flynn. A weekly one-hour program of folk, traditional, bluegrass, and blues, originating in the foothills of the Ozark Mountains. The website, **www.folksampler.com**, has a list of stations that stream it, including KUMR **www.kumr.org** Saturday 10–11pm Central.

The Folk Show
New Hampshire Public Radio **www.nhpr.org**

Sunday 7–10pm Eastern. Host: Kate McNally.

folk

The Folk Show
WUNH **www.wunh.org**

Sunday 10am–noon Eastern. Host: Jack Beard.

Folk Song Festival
WNYC **www.wnyc.org**

Saturday 7:30–8pm Eastern. Host: Oscar Brand. WNYC has aired *Folk Song Festival* since the 1950s, when the House Un-American Activities Committee attacked Brand. In those years, the program has introduced to New Yorkers such singers as Woody Guthrie, Leadbelly, Pete Seeger, Joan Baez, and Bob Dylan.

The Folk Tradition
WKAR **www.wkar.org**

Sunday 6–7pm Eastern. Host: Bob Blackman.

Folkways
WOJB **www.wojb.org**

Wednesday 8pm–midnight Central. This extensive program on Ojibwe station WOJB has a rotating pool of hosts and ranges widely.

Fretz
KVSC **www.kvsc.org**

Saturday 6am–noon Central. Host: Wayne Bergeson.

Friends and Neighbors
KLCC **www.klcc.org**

Monday 7:30–9:30pm Pacific. Host: Kobi Lucas.

InFOLKus
5UV **www.adelaide.edu.au/5UV**

Thursday 1030–1230 Greenwich. This Australian program is produced by the South Adelaide Folk Federation. It usually has live performances.

The K and K Corral
CFUV **cfuv.uvic.ca**

Sunday 6–7pm Pacific.

Loafer's Glory

Probably any four people convened to define folk music would come up with five different opinions. But certainly all would agree that it includes the music of U. Utah Phillips. It is simple and unadorned and it has a relentlessly

U. Utah Phillips

folk

populist message. Every episode of *Loafer's Glory* is a collectible classic, featuring Phillips telling railroad stories, Wobbly stories, organizing stories, and jokes about his family and neighbors, in addition to playing the obscure music he has collected. The program is syndicated on hundreds of PRI stations. One is KZYX **www.kzyx.org** Sunday 2–3pm Pacific.

The Long and Dusty Road   KVMR **www.kvmr.org**

Monday 10am–noon Pacific. Host: Don Jacobson. On the air for fifteen years, this program is often organized around a theme. Playlists available on the website.

The Midnight Special   WFMT **www.networkchicago.com/wfmt**

Saturday 9pm–midnight Central. Host: Rich Warren. The program is preceded at 8pm by *Folkstage*, but you can listen to archived shows of *The Midnight Special* any time: **www.broadcast.com/radio/archives/wfmt/midnight special/**

Mostly Folkly, Mostly Locally   WGDR **http:// www.goddard.edu/wgdr/**

Thursday 4–6pm Eastern. Host: Tom Arner. This is just a really comfortable show to listen to. Maybe it's a Vermont thing.

Mountain Jubilee   WUOT **http://www.sunsite.utk.edu/wuot/**

Saturday 9–10pm Eastern. Host: Paul Campbell. There are few areas of the United States as musically rich as the hill country of the Southeast. As WUOT says about *Mountain Jubilee*: "The Upland South is home to deep and powerful music traditions, both secular and sacred. In *Mountain Jubilee* we try to convey something of the richness of our music."

Music from the Mountains   **www.wvpubcast.org**

West Virginia Public Radio Friday 9–10pm Eastern. Host: Joe Dobbs. The mountains are the Appalachians, and Dobbs celebrates their music in all its forms, from Old Time fiddle to ragtime to gospel to contemporary.

Nonesuch   WVBR **www.wvbr.com**

Sunday 10am–2:30pm Eastern.

Profiles in Folk   WSHU **www.wshu.org**

Friday 10pm–midnight Eastern. Host: Steve Winters. On WSHU for 28 years. Each week features a different thematic exploration.

folk

Shrunken Planet
WFMU **www.wfmu.org**

Saturday 6–9am Eastern. Host: Jeffrey Davison. Traditional and folk music of England, Scotland, Ireland, and North America. Blues, country, bluegrass, Old Time, Cajun, Celtic, singer/songwriters, etc. Archived on the WFMU website so you can listen any time.

Simply Folk
Wisconsin Public Radio **www.wpr.org**

Sunday 5–8pm Central. Host: Judy Rose. The second Sunday of each month is listener request night.

Somebody Else's Troubles
WLUW **www.wluw.org**

Saturday 10am–2pm Central. The program sometimes has live visitors.

Sunday Night Folk Festival
WHUS **www.whus.org**

Sunday 7–10pm. In its 23rd year, this program usually includes visits from guests.

Sunday Street
WUSB **www.wusb.org**

Sunday 9–11:30am Eastern. Host: Charlie Backfish. On the air in Long Island for over 20 years, this program always features a Dylan segment and frequently also has conversations with and performances by studio guests.

Trail Mix
KANU **kanu.ukans.edu**

Sunday 1–7pm Central. Host: Bob McWilliams. This program is ordered less like trail mix, with all the elements mixed together, than like a layer cake. The first 90 minutes are Celtic, followed by 150 minutes of contemporary folk (2:30–5pm), then 60 minutes of more traditional folk (5–6pm), ending up with bluegrass (6–7pm).

20th Century Folk
WQNA **www.wqna.org**

Monday 11pm–2am and Thursday noon–3pm Central.

Urban Folk
KFAI **www.kfai.org**

Sunday 11am–1pm Central.

Valley Folk
WFCR **www.wfcr.org**

Saturday 9pm–midnight Eastern. Host: Susan Forbes Hansen.

folk

British

Many of the programs listed above play substantial amounts of the folk music of the British Isles; the ones below are devoted to it.

Black Jack Davy
WBRS **www.wbrs.org**

Monday 8–10:30pm Eastern. Host: Andy Nagy. A wide variety of contemporary and traditional roots-related music from England, Ireland, Scotland, Wales, France, Brittany, and beyond.

Lunch in the Pub
WYSO **www.wyso.org**

Saturday 2–4pm Saturday. Hosts: Mike Reisz and Bill Flint. This long-running program also includes quite a bit of Celtic music, as well as some electrified stuff.

The Mike Harding Show
BBC Radio 2
www.bbc.co.uk/radio2

Wednesday 2000–2100 Greenwich. A program of folk roots and acoustic music, broadcast from a cowshed in Harding's back garden in the Yorkshire Dales.

Tree and Root
WDVR **www.wdvrfm.org**

Monday 10pm–1am Eastern. Host: Bruce Pierson.

Canadian

Acoustic Routes
CKLN **ckln.sac.ryerson.ca**

Sunday 7–8pm Eastern. Host: Joel Wortzman. This program features (mostly Canadian) singer/songwriters.

Canadian Geography
CJSF **www.cjsf.bc.ca**

Wednesday 8–9pm Pacific.

Canadian Lunch
CITR **www.ams.ubc.ca/citr**

Thursday 11:30am–1pm Pacific.

Downeast Ceilidh
WMBR **wmbr.mit.edu**

Thursday 8–10pm Eastern. Host: Marcia Young Palmater. The folk music of Atlantic Canada. (You can hear a "Best of Downeast Ceilidh" program on Live365 – **www.live365.com**, look for "ceilidh.")

folk

Escapades
Radio Canada Première Chaîne **radio-canada.ca**
Saturday 11pm–midnight Eastern. From Winnipeg, in French.

Mostly Canadian Hour
CHMA **www.mta.ca/chma**
Sunday 6–7pm Atlantic (an hour ahead of Eastern). Hosts: Alex Keeling and
Andrew MacKinnon.

Québec–Acadie en musique
CKUT **www.ckut.ca**
Saturday 8–10am Eastern. Traditional music of Québec and Acadia.

Radio Newfoundland
www.radionewfoundland.net
Radio Newfoundland is a radio station devoted to the music of Newfoundland.
This fact would be unremarkable, almost obvious, were it not so rare. Almost
all radio stations serve up, instead of local fare, frozen music in jewel boxes
from distant climes. Surely there is a place in the world for more stations like
Radio Newfoundland. Located where performers live, where folk traditions still
thrive, the world's radio stations certainly could take a more active and
prominent role in collecting, supporting, and publicizing local music. Perhaps
Internet radio, by making the distant more commonplace, will help allow the
local to recover its value.

Live

Acoustic Café
Host: Rob Reinhart. A showcase for new acoustic music, featuring a
performance by, and interview with, a different singer/songwriter each week. A
syndicated, weekly, two-hour program. List of stations at **www.acafe.com**.
You can listen to the archives any time at **http://www.mlive.com/cafe**.

Bound for Glory
WVBR **www.wvbr.com**
Sunday 8–11pm Eastern. Host: Phil Shapiro. *Bound for Glory* recently
celebrated its 1,000th concert, which certainly gives weight to its claim to be
the longest-running folk concert program anywhere.

E-Town
www.etown.org
Hosts: Helen and Nick Forster. *E-Town* is a widely syndicated concert show
originating in Boulder, Colorado. Nick Forster is a former member of the string
band Hot Rize, and Helen is a veteran vocalist; the Forsters' musical ears make
the guest list for the program exceptional. It's not always what you'd call folk
music – it can range to Paul Winter or Rickie Lee Jones – but its range is a big

folk

part of its appeal. Musical guests on the show join together in fresh collaborations across genres, cultures, and distance – all part of the show's stated purpose of creating community and making us more aware of community. In addition to music, *E-Town* has commentary and environmental news, including the popular "E-chievement" awards to individuals who have made striking contributions in their communities. You can listen to the latest show any time from the website.

The Festival Tapes   WUMB **www.wumb.org**
Wednesday 8–9pm Eastern. Hosts: Dave Palmater and Sandy Sheehan. Recordings of live performances at festivals around New England.

Live at Noon   WUMB **www.wumb.org**
Weekdays noon–1pm Eastern. Studio visits to this Boston folk music institution. WUMB also hosts *Member Concerts* which are then broadcast on the station Sundays 11am–noon.

Mountain Stage   West Virginia Public Radio **www.wvpubcast.org**
Sunday 3–5pm Eastern. Host: Larry Groce. Widely syndicated, weekly, two-hour program (on the air for over 17 years) of traditional and contemporary music performed before a live audience in Charleston, West Virginia. The combinations themselves are often fascinating. One program, for example, mixed Odetta, The Cowboy Junkies, The Derailers, and Loudon Wainwright III.

The Songwriter Sessions   WPLN **www.wpln.org**
Saturday 7–8pm Eastern. Each week three songwriters come into the studio to talk and sing; the most recent show is also available on the website.

WoodSongs Old Time Radio Hour   WUKY **wuky.uky.edu**
Saturday 8–9pm Eastern. Host: Michael Johnathon. A live-audience performance show based in Kentucky and syndicated to over 200 stations. A live (video) Webcast can be found on the WoodSongs website (**www.woodsongs.com**) Monday 6:45–8:30pm Eastern. Also on the website are video outtakes from the Webcast.

folk

Gospel

Gospel favorites

| Gospel FM | see p.135 |
| KNON | see p.135 |

The Better Way Gospel Hour
KCSB www.kcsb.org
Sunday 6–9am Pacific. Host: Matthew Brown.

Black Gospel
WMUL www.marshall.edu/wmul
Saturday and Sunday 6am–noon Eastern.

Classical and Contemporary Gospel
KUCR www.kucr.org
Sunday 6–8pm Pacific. Host: George McClinton, Jr.

The Deniece Williams Show
BBC Radio 2
www.bbc.co.uk/radio2
Wednesday 9–10pm Greenwich. This program focuses on British gospel music, often with interviews.

Good News
WMBR wmbr.mit.edu
Sunday 8–10pm Eastern.

Gospel
WNUR www.wnur.org
Sunday 8–10am Central.

Gospel
WRTC www.wrtcfm.com
Saturday and Sunday 6–9am Eastern.

Gospel Chime
KGNU www.kgnu.org
Sunday 7–9am Mountain.

The Gospel Experience
www.kpfa.org
Saturday 6–9am Pacific. Host: Emmit Powell. Long-running Bay Area gospel show hosted by the leader of the group The Gospel Elites.

gospel

Gospel FM
www.gospelfm.com.br

This Brazilian stream brings you gospel music from around the world, all the time.

Gospel Grace
WEAA www.morgan.edu/geninfo/weaa.htm

Sunday 5am–5pm Eastern. *Twelve hours* of gospel every Sunday from this student station at Morgan State University in Baltimore, Maryland.

Gospel Music Machine
CIUT www.ciut.fm

Sunday 6–9am Eastern.

Gospel Reminiscence
KMUW www.kmuw.org

Sunday 6–8pm Central.

Gospel Train
www.gospeltrain.com

Host: Wally Robinson. Archived for listening any time.

Gospel Truth
WNCW www.wncw.org

Sunday 6–8am Eastern. Host: Dennis Jones. Gospel in a full range of traditions.

Harmony
5UV www.adelaide.edu.au/5UV

Friday 0330–0430 Greenwich. Host: Briar Eyers. This beautiful program from the University of Adelaide in Australia treats gospel and related singing styles.

KNON
www.knon.org

Even when a radio station has a gospel show, there is probably just one, usually on Sunday morning. KNON, on the other hand, has gospel music every day. Daily 4–7am Central, Saturday and Sunday until 9am.

Morning Glory
KCRW www.kcrw.org

Sunday 5–7am Pacific.

Old Ship of Zion
KAOS www.kaosradio.org

Sunday 3–4pm Pacific.

Psalm 150 Jamz
CJAM venus.uwindsor.ca/cjam

Sunday 6–8am Eastern. Urban gospel.

gospel

Sinner's Crossroads

WFMU **www.wfmu.org**

Saturday 9–10am Eastern. Host: Kevin Nutt. Scratchy vanity 45s, pilfered field recordings, muddy off-the-radio sounds, home-made congregational tapes and vintage commercial gospel throw-downs. Archived on the WFMU website so you can listen any time.

Songs of Praise

KFAI **www.kfai.org**

Sunday 6–9am Central. Host: Ernestine Gates.

Sounds of the Gospel

WLUW **www.wluw.org**

Sunday 2–6:30am Central.

Sunday Morning Gospel

WAER **www.waer.org**

Sunday 6–9am Eastern. Host: Cora Thomas. Features local (central New York State) and national gospel talent: everyone from Daryl Coley to the Brooklyn Tabernacle Choir to the Winans family.

Cora Thomas

gospel

Sunday Morning Gospel

WPFW **www.wpfw.org**

Sunday 6–9am Eastern.

Sunday Morning Gospel

WMUA **www.wmua.org**

Sunday 6–9am Eastern. Host: Rev. Bobby J. Wallace.

Wake Up with Gospel

Ampies Broadcasting Corporation (ABC)
www.abcsuriname.com

Sunday 0930–1100 Greenwich. Host: Yvonne Steeman. From Suriname, in Dutch. There is also a daily gospel program, 0800–0900.

Hip-Hop/Rap/Urban

Hip-Hop favorites

MAI FM	see p.137
StreetBeat	see p.137
TriniBase	see p.137

Hip-Hop Stations

KMEL
www.106kmel.com

Very enthusiastic commercial hip-hop station from the Bay Area.

MAI FM
www.maifm.co.nz

In addition to the live stream, this station from Auckland, New Zealand has several weeks worth of archived programs you can listen to at any time.

StreetBeat
WNUR **www.wnur.org**

WNUR streams four separate channels. One is *Streetbeat*, an excellent mix of dance and hip-hop. (*StreetBeat* is also live on WNUR weeknights 9:30pm–2am).

TriniBase
www.trinidad-online.org/Underwire

Hip-pop club beats from Trinidad.

hip-hop/rap/urban

Hip-Hop Programs

All Dawgs Go to Heaven
CHRW **www.usc.uwo.ca/chrw**
Thursday 2–6:30am Eastern.

Basementalism
KVCU **www.colorado.edu/StudentGroups/KVCU**
Saturday 3–7pm Mountain.

Chocolate City

KCRW **www.kcrw.org**
Weeknights 10pm–midnight Pacific. Host: Garth Trinidad. Urban rhythms with most of the edges smoothed off. Features interviews with invited guests. Recent programs archived on the KCRW website for listening any time. Similar is *The Drop*, Saturday 8–10pm, with Liza Richardson.

CM Fam-a-Lam Show
WKCR **www.wkcr.org**
Friday 1–5am Eastern. Hosts: Bobbito the Barber and Lord Sear. Bobbito used to co-host the *Stretch Armstrong Show* with Stretch Armstrong, which was voted the "best hip-hop show of all-time" by *The Source*. Bobbito's new show with rapper Lord Sear is just as good, but with even more emphasis on the New York underground.

Garth Trinidad

Droppin Dimez
CKLN **ckln.sac.ryerson.ca**
Monday 11pm–12:30am Eastern. An alternative twist on hip-hop, from an all-female crew.

God's Rhythmic Anointed Poetry
KCSB **www.kcsb.org**
Sunday 3–5pm. Pacific. This may be the only gospel-preaching hip-hop show on radio.

Half Time
WNYU **www.wnyu.org**
Wednesday 10:30pm–1am Eastern. DJs Eclipse and Riz present underground

hip-hop/rap/urban

hip-hop, with freestyles from both callers and guests like Method Man and Company Flow, and the annual *Ego Trip* night.

Hip-Hop

Australian Broadcasting Corporation Triple J
www.abc.net.au/triplej

Friday 1200–1500 Greenwich. Host: Nicole Foote.

Hip-Hop House Party

TNL Radio
www.lanka.net/tnl

Friday 1400–1600 Greenwich. Top hits countdown show from Colombo, Sri Lanka. Also check out *Bag o' Trix* Sunday 0700–1300.

Latin Hip-Hop

KNON
www.knon.org

Saturday noon–4pm Central.

Liquid Beat

KLCC
www.klcc.org

Saturday 11pm–2am Pacific. Host: Matt Nelkin. Independent and underground hip-hop.

Nicole Foote

Mass Appeal

KUGS www.kugs.org

Friday 8–10pm Pacific.

Maxima

www.maxima.org

Urban music from France.

Night Shift

CHKG www.fm961.com

Weeknights 1–6am Pacific. Bhangra-flavored grooves from Vancouver, British Columbia.

O-Dub

KALX kalx.berkeley.edu

Wednesday 9:30pm–midnight Pacific. Host: Oliver Wang. Journalist/DJ/crate digger Oliver Wang spins a hot mix of hip-hop and rare funk grooves for discerning beat heads. Playlists at www.o-dub.com.

hip-hop/rap/urban

Promised Land
CJSF **www.cjsf.bc.ca**

Thursday 8–10pm Pacific. Also tune in to *Straight No Chaser* at the same time Friday, and *Hip-Hop Collective*, which has news as well as music, Saturday 10pm–midnight.

Radio Campus Lille
www-radio-campus.univ-lille1.fr

Friday 1900–2300 Greenwich. Interesting go-go/rap program followed by hardcore hip-hop.

The Rhythm Selection
95B **www.95bfm.com**

Monday 0900–1100 Greenwich. From the University of Auckland, in New Zealand.

Roll Wit' It
KSHU **www.shsu.edu/~rtf_kshu**

Weeknights 6pm–midnight Central.

The Saturday Solution
WHRB **www.whrb.org**

Saturday 9–11pm Eastern. Hosts: Bobby Drake and Kasj. When one thinks of sources for the raw energy of hip-hop, Harvard University might not be the first place that comes to mind. Unless, that is, one has tuned into *The Saturday Solution*. *The Saturday Solution* offers live mixing of progressive underground hip-hop as well as guest performances and freestyles from many artists from the Boston hip-hop community. There's also more hip-hop later on in the evening, including a classics show on alternating weeks at 3am.

Seditious Beats
KPFK **www.kpfk.org**

Saturday midnight–3am Pacific. Fidel Rodriguez raps politics while two DJs spin music.

Street Beat
WMUL **www.marshall.edu/wmul**

Friday and Saturday 6pm–3am Eastern.

Thinking Man's Session
CFUV **cfuv.uvic.ca**

Thursday 9–10:30pm Pacific. Intelligent, funky hip-hop.

Thought Power
WRTC **www.wrtcfm.com**

A different hip-hop program every night from 10:30pm–6am Eastern.

Trip Hop
WMSE **www.wmse.org**

Friday 6–9am Central, but archived for listening any time.

Underground Railroad
WBAI **www.wbai.org**

Sunday midnight–2am Eastern. Host: Jay Smooth. The latest underground and independent hip-hop, with plenty of freestyles.

We Came From Beyond
KXLU **www.kxlu.com**

Sunday 11pm–2am Pacific. Host: Mike Nardone. One of the truly crucial underground hip-hop programs, with an emphasis on the left coast.

WERS
www.wers.org

Hip-hop weeknights 8–11pm Eastern.

Jazz

For Latin jazz, see the *Latin* section under *World Music*.

Jazz favorites	
Jazz from Lincoln Center	see p.148
KLON	see p.142
KMHD	see p.142
WBGO	see p.144
WNUR	see p.145
WWOZ	see p.145

Jazz Stations

CJRT
www.cjrt.fm

Solid all-jazz station from Toronto. Some good documentary programming (for example, "History of South African Jazz"). Limited archives available on the website.

CKLN
ckln.sac.ryerson.ca

Jazz weekdays 7–11am Eastern. Fresh jazz from Toronto, very contemporary, often avant-garde. Particularly interesting is Tuesday's program *Expandable*

jazz

Language, which "concerns itself with the variety of speech communities in jazz."

Jazz FM www.jazzfm.co.uk

This commercial station from London streams jazz around the clock, much of it groove-based and infectious.

KBEM www.jazz88fm.com

During school hours, this is a high school station, run by the Minnesota Public Schools. At other times, professionals take over. At any time, you can hear interesting jazz.

KBSU http://radio.boisestate.edu

KFAI www.kfai.org

Monday–Thursday 10:30pm–midnight Central.

KLON www.klon.org

On so many stations where jazz is heard, it is sandwiched in between folk music shows, or hours of public radio news, or in a mix of eclectic programming. That is one thing which makes KLON so valuable. KLON plays jazz and blues *all the time*. The other thing that makes it such a resource is that, because of its single focus, it has attracted programmers with a great deal of knowledge and love of the music. Tune in any time of the day or night and you'll hear something good. In addition to its airwave broadcast schedule, KLON streams the following specialty channels: *Mostly Bop*, *88 Greats*, and *Bossa Nova Samba*.

KMHD www.kmhd.org

If what you're looking for is a station you can put on for long stretches of time, without having to get up and change it because the news or something else came on, KMHD is what you need. There's blues on Friday nights, and some traffic reports during the morning and evening commutes (Pacific. time), but aside from that, it's really pretty much all jazz, with a good variety of artists and song selection, too.

KPLU www.kplu.org

KPLU is an interesting case study, one that could well serve as a model for other stations to follow. It is an NPR station carrying hours of news each day, and when not airing NPR talk, broadcasting jazz. While the NPR features are being broadcast over the airwaves, the Web version continues to stream jazz.

jazz

This makes a great deal of sense. The local listeners need the news, but the world doesn't need a thousand stations streaming *All Things Considered*. Why not use the extra time for more original programming? Speaking of original programming, the highlight of KPLU is the work of Jim Wilke. His *Jazz After Hours* from midnight to 5am Pacific, Saturday and Sunday mornings, is produced locally and syndicated via PRI. Wilke also produces *Jazz Northwest* Sundays 4–5pm Pacific, featuring local music including club performances taped by Wilke. While KPLU does not post playlists on its website, it does have an interesting "What Was That Song?" feature, allowing listeners to find out about particular songs. There is also an active jazz discussion board.

KSBR
www.ksbr.net

KSDS
www.ksds-fm.org

This station from San Diego has scads of interesting specialty shows. For example (all times Pacific):

▶▶ Percussion Monday 3–4pm
▶▶ Instrumental Women Wednesday 1–2pm
▶▶ New releases Thursday 6–9pm and Fridays 3–4pm
▶▶ World Jazz Saturday 1–2pm
▶▶ Local Jazz Corner Saturday 4–5pm
▶▶ Live local performance Second Tuesday of the month 8–10pm

KUNV
http://kunvjazz91.org/

Variety shows on the weekends, but weekdays it's pretty much all jazz.

KUSP
www.kusp.org

A different jazz program Monday–Thursday 9pm–midnight Pacific.

KUVO
www.kuvo.org

Jazz almost all the time.

Radio Campus Lille
www-radio-campus.univ-lille1.fr

Interesting jazz programming with a French flavor. Monday 1000–1200 Greenwich, Tuesday 1800–1900, Friday 1700–1800 (Eastern jazz show).

WAER
www.waer.org

Morning and evening news, and some specialty shows on weekends, but the rest is jazz. Specifically, you can always get jazz weekdays 9am–4 pm and 7 pm–5am Eastern.

jazz

WBEZ
www.wbez.org

Jazz from 8pm–4am Central.

WBFO
www.wbfo.org

Jazz weekdays 10am–2pm Eastern, every night 8pm, Saturday and Sunday midnight–6am. Make a particular effort to catch *Jazz Favorites Hour*, Sunday 9–10pm, to which host Macy Favor invites a guest to bring and discuss favorite recordings.

WBGO
www.wbgo.org

Houston Person and
Etta Jones play for WBGO

Great jazz station from Newark, New Jersey. Except for half an hour at 6:30pm Eastern, you can count on hearing an excellent jazz program whenever you tune in. The station produces many top-notch specialty shows, including superb Latin shows. (It is the home of NPR's *Jazz Set*.) In addition to its regular programming, WBGO hosts many live special broadcasts from New York and New Jersey jazz clubs, as well as over 100 live interviews per year.

WDUQ
www.wduq.org

In addition to jazz most of the day weekdays, WDUQ also has an all-jazz stream on its website.

WGMC
www.greeceny.org

Some specialty shows on the weekend, but the rest of the time it's all jazz. And in addition to the livecast stream, there's another that's all jazz.

WKCR
www.wkcr.org

The station from Columbia University devotes roughly 35 percent of its schedule to jazz, including weekdays 5–9:30am, noon–3pm, and 6–9pm Eastern. In addition, there are the station's traditional birthday broadcasts, which celebrate the music of a jazz legend (Charles Mingus, Ornette Coleman,

jazz

Coleman Hawkins, etc.) for 24 hours on his or her birthday, and the centennial broadcasts (Duke Ellington, Louis Armstrong) which devote a week or more to the work of a jazz legend.

WNUR
www.wnur.org

In addition to its variety of live programming, "Chicago's Sound Experiment" has a stream on the website devoted to non-stop jazz. WNUR features a wide variety of jazz artists and styles past and present, with special emphasis on new releases, independent labels, Chicago artists, and free jazz. The definition of jazz also occasionally spills over into creative contemporary composition, electronic music, world music, blues, rock, soul, and funk. There are frequent interviews and live performances by visiting musicians. A regular feature at 11am Central is a lengthy look at individual albums, artist, or theme.

WPFW
www.wpfw.org

Weekdays 6–9am, 4–10pm midnight–5am Eastern.

WRTI
www.wrti.org

Jazz weekdays 6pm–6am Eastern.

WUCF
http://wucf.ucf.edu

WWOZ
www.wwoz.org

The station from the "cradle of jazz" plays jazz midnight–11am and 4–7pm Central.

Jazz Programs

Alternate Takes
WYSO www.wyso.org

Wednesday and Thursday 7–10pm Eastern.

Jazz Alley
Lyric FM www.lyricfm.ie

Friday and Saturday 1900–2000 Greenwich. Host: Donald Helme. This interesting program from Ireland always has fresh new material.

Jazz Anthologie
Africa 1 www.africa1.com

Weeknights 2230–0000 Greenwich. Host: Solo Samuel. This program from Gabon presents jazz with an African flavor.

jazz

Jazz and Beyond
KGNU **www.kgnu.org**

Daily 9pm–midnight Mountain. Lively, wide-ranging, very progressive program. On second and fourth Fridays, from 11pm–midnight Mountain, the music of John Zorn is featured.

Jazz Beat
CBC Radio One **www.cbc.ca**

Sunday 11:05pm–1am Eastern. Host: Katie Malloch. Concert recordings, studio recordings, and interviews.

Jazz Classics
WPKN **www.wpkn.org**

Monday 10am–2pm Eastern. Host: Victor Pachera.

Jazz File
BBC Radio 3 **www.bbc.co.uk/radio3**

Saturday 1800–1830 Greenwich. *Jazz File* is a documentary feature that goes into depth on a particular topic. Individual programs are often part of a series. In 2001, for example, listeners got to hear a five-part series produced and hosted by cartoonist R. Crumb, who shared his collection of 78s from the 1920s and '30s. Another series reviewed the entire recorded output of Ornette Coleman.

Jazz Forms
WVTF **www.wvtf.org**

Weeknights 8pm–midnight Eastern. Host: Charlie Perkinson. Perkinson is a jazz bassist who has been on radio with jazz programming for a quarter century.

Jazz Legends
BBC Radio 3 **www.bbc.co.uk radio3**

Friday 1600–1700 Greenwich. Host: Julian Joseph. Each episode of *Jazz Legends* focuses on the work of an individual jazz musician.

Julian Joseph

Jazz Nonstop

Radio Television Hong Kong (RTHK) Radio 3
www.rthk.org.hk

Sunday 1500–1600 Greenwich. This program is archived for a year after broadcast, so there are 52 episodes on the RTHK website at any time.

Jazz Profiles

NPR **www.npr.org**

Host: Nancy Wilson. Each instance of this program weaves together something like a career retrospective of a jazz artist, using archival recordings, interviews and narration. The honorees are often fairly unknown to the general listener – bebop tenor saxophonist Johnny Griffin, trombonist Melba Liston, musical theorist George Russell – so the program makes a generous contribution towards one's jazz education. Heard on over 200 NPR stations, including WBGO **www.wbgo.org** Tuesday 7–8pm Eastern.

The Jazz Show

CITR **www.ams.ubc.ca/citr**

Monday 9pm–midnight Pacific. Host: Gavin Walker. Vancouver's longest-running jazz program.

Jazz Spectrum

WHRB **www.whrb.org**

Monday–Thursday 5am–1pm, Friday 5–11am, Saturday 5–9am Eastern. Strong jazz programming each morning from Harvard University.

Jazztrack

Australian Broadcasting Corporation Classic FM
www.abc.net.au/classic

Saturday and Sunday 0700–0900 Greenwich. Host: Jim McLeod. This is the national jazz program of Australia, including current and historical recordings and *Jazztrack*'s own recordings in studios and at festivals. The program also offers a monthly live-to-air segment with a studio audience. Not only complete playlists but also archives of the most recent shows are available on the website.

Panorama del Jazz

Radio UNAM FM
www.unam.mx/radiounam

Monday 7–8pm Central. Host: Roberto Aymes. From the Universidad Nacional Autónoma de México. Note that Radio UNAM has two streams. This program is on the FM stream.

Live

EBU Jazz Concert

Eesti Raadio Klassikaraadio
Saturday 1700–1900 Greenwich.
www.er.ee/eng/klassik

jazz

Jazz at the Kennedy Center
NPR **www.npr.org**

Host: Billy Taylor. Each week, Taylor invites a prominent jazz musician to perform with his trio onstage at the Kennedy Center in Washington, D.C. Available on many NPR stations; one is KUVO **www.kuvo.org** Tuesday 6–7pm Mountain.

Jazz from Lincoln Center
www.jazzradio.org

Jazz from Lincoln Center is an excellent one-hour show carried by NPR. This site has an archive of five years of the show, all available for streaming. It's a wonderful resource. Want to hear an hour of Chucho Valdes live right now? Hank Jones solo piano? A program of Cassandra Wilson singing Miles Davis? All there for the clicking.

Billy Taylor

Jazz on 3
BBC Radio 3 **www.bbc.co.uk/radio3**

Friday 2330–0100 Greenwich. This program offers some truly superb live performances, featuring top-notch talent.

Jazz Originals
KBEM **www.jazz88fm.com**

Sunday 6–7pm and Tuesday 11pm–midnight Central. Host: Butch Thompson. Yes, that Butch Thompson, the pianist (and clarinet player) on *Prairie Home Companion*. *Jazz Originals* is an ongoing tour of the early jazz tradition, recorded live at the Artists jazz club in downtown St. Paul. It features live piano music and commentary by Thompson, vintage recordings of Louis Armstrong, Jelly Roll Morton, Fats Waller, and other inventors of the music, his reviews of CDs, books, and other artifacts of the current traditional jazz scene, and incidental piano music by his laconic cousin, Buster Thompson.

Jazz Set
WBGO **www.wbgo.org**

Sunday 6–7pm Eastern, repeated Wednesday 7–8pm. Host: Dee Dee Bridgewater. This weekly, one-hour program offers recent performances each

jazz

week from venues around the world. The guest list is top drawer. Vocalist Bridgewater has recently taken over the program from long-time host Branford Marsalis. Syndicated on NPR stations; you can also hear it directly from the NPR website **www.npr.org**.

Riverwalk: Live from the Landing

Jim Cullum

A weekly syndicated show originating at Jim Cullum's jazz club, The Landing in San Antonio, Texas. It is hosted by Cullum and storyteller David Holt, and features the Jim Cullum Jazz Band (along with famous guests), usually performing a tribute to an early American jazz great. To illustrate, the spring of 2001 saw shows on Fats Waller, jazz photographer William Gottlieb, and Jabbo Smith. Guest artists included Lionel Hampton, John Cocuzzi, Clark Terry and Nicholas Payton, and Vernel Bangeris. Syndicated on over 200 PRI stations. You can catch it on KBEM **www.jazz88fm. com/** Sunday 4–5pm Central.

Guitar

Guitar Hour
Sunday 8–9pm Pacific.

KSDS **www.ksds-fm.org**

Guitar Jazz
Sunday 2–3:30pm Pacific. Host: Joe Scafone.

CFUV **cfuv.uvic.ca**

jazz

Organ

The Organist Entertains
BBC Radio 2
www.bbc.co.uk/radio2

Tuesday 2000–2100 Greenwich. Host: Nigel Ogden. Music and news from the popular (not exclusively, not even primarily, jazz) organ and keyboard world. This program has been running on the BBC for over 30 years.

Marian McPartland

Piano

88 Greats
KLON
www.klon.org

88 Greats is a KLON channel available for listening any time.

Marian McPartland's Piano Jazz

Weekly on most NPR stations. You can hear it on KANU **kanu.ukans.edu** Wednesday 9–10pm Central.

Vocals

Jazz Singers
WBGO **www.wbgo.org**

Monday 7–8pm Eastern. A documentary exploration of jazz through its singers.

Singers Unlimited
WBGO **www.wbgo.org**

Sunday 10am–2pm Eastern. Host: Michael Bourne.

Voices in Jazz
CKUA **www.ckua.org**

Saturday 8–9pm Mountain. Host: Dianne Donovan.

Ragtime

Ragtime America
KGNU **www.kgnu.org**

Thursday 8–9pm Mountain. Host: Jack Rummel.

jazz

Dixieland

At the Jazz Band Ball
WBFO **www.wbfo.org**
Saturday 9–10pm Eastern. Host: Ted Howes. Vintage, mostly Dixieland.

Dixieland Hour
KSDS **www.ksds-fm.org**
Sunday 3–4pm Pacific. Host: Al Adams.

The Story of Jazz
WVXU **www.wvxu.org**
Thursday 9–10pm Eastern. Host: Charley Carey. Frequently includes performances before a live audience in the WVXU studios. Archived on the website for listening any time.

Hot Jazz

Hot Jazz Saturday Night
WAMU **www.wamu.org**
Saturday 7–10pm Eastern. Host: Rob Bamberger. Rob Bamberger's day job is senior policy analyst for the Congressional Research Service. He has been collecting jazz records since 1963, and says he spends about twelve hours a week poring over them making selections for this program, which basically covers the years 1920–1950. (It has aired on WAMU for over 20 years.) Extensive notes on the musical sources are printed on the WAMU website.

Stompin' at the Cranium
KAOS **www.kaosradio.org**
Monday 3–4pm Pacific. Host: Sean Savage. Hot jazz from the 1920s and '30s and its tangents.

Swing

It Don't Mean a Thing
WNCW **www.wncw.org**
Saturday 10am–noon Eastern. Host: Charles Benedict.

The Malcolm Laycock Show
BBC Radio 2 **www.bbc.co.uk**
Sunday 2200–2300 Greenwich. Laycock's show celebrates the age of swing, particularly emphasizing British and American music from the 1930s.

The Old–Disc Jockey
CKUA **www.ckua.org**
Sunday 1-2pm Mountain. Host: John Worthington.

jazz

Saturday Swing
WVBR **www.wvbr.com**

Saturday 1–3pm Eastern. Jitterbug, shag, Lindy hop, and West Coast swing.

Swing That Music
WQNA **www.wqna.org**

Sunday 7am–noon Central. Host: Bill Hickerson.

The Swing Years and Beyond
KUOW **www.kuow.org**

Saturday 7pm–midnight Pacific. Host: Cynthia Doyon. Doyon's program has been on the radio in Seattle for 25 years. A sentimental saunter through times gone by, it sometimes has special tributes or themes.

When Swing Was King
WVXU **www.wvxu.org**

Sunday 2–4pm Eastern, archived for listening on demand.

Big Band

Big Band/Classic Jazz
WOJB **www.wojb.org**

Saturday and Sunday 5–8am Central.

Big Band Jive
Jazz FM **www.jazzfm.co.uk**

Sunday 1700–1800 Greenwich. Host: Alan Sykes.

Big Band Scene
KBEM **http://www.jazz88fm.com/**

Saturday 5–6pm and 11pm–midnight Central. Host: Jerry Swanberg. Playlists available on the website.

The Big Band Show
WHFR **whfr.hfcc.net**

Friday 10am–noon Central. Host: Dick Alfonsi.

Big Band Show
WMSE **www.wmse.org**

Sunday 9am–noon Central, but archives available for listening any time.

Big Band Sounds
WNYC **www.wnyc.org**

Saturday 8–10pm Eastern. Host: Danny Stiles.

Big Band Special
BBC Radio 2 **www.bbc.co.uk/radio2**

Monday 2000–2030 Greenwich. Host: Stacey Kent. *Big Band Special* has been on the air for over 20 years. The program often includes present-day big bands recorded in concert in the UK.

jazz

The Big Bands CJRT
www.cjrt.fm
Sunday 7pm–midnight Eastern.
Host: Glen Woodcock.

The DeSoto Hour WREK
www.wrek.org
Saturday 7–8:30pm Eastern – but available any time on WREK's website. Host: Fred Runde.

Saturday Night Bandstand 702
www.702.co.za
Saturday 1700–2200 Greenwich. Host: Thabo Modisane. This program from South Africa has its center in big band jazz, but it can range to blues, African music or other points as well.

Stacey Kent

Tuxedo Junction
KUMR **www.kumr.org**
Sunday 5–6pm Central. Hosts: Norm Movitz and Ray Lockhart. Archives available for listening any time.

Bop

Bebop and Beyond
WBFO **www.wbfo.org**
Sunday 8–9pm Eastern. Host: Dick Judelsohn. Often features a single artist.

Bird Flight
WKCR **www.wkcr.org**
Weekdays 8:20-9:30am Eastern. Host: Phil Schaap. An hour plus of Charlie Parker to start your day.

The Bop Connection
WVXU **www.wvxu.org**
Sunday 5–6pm Eastern. Host: Bob Nave. The particularly well-informed Nave, who is a working Hammond B3 player himself, and who has been hosting this show for nearly 20 years, elucidates the roots of bebop. The current program is archived on the WVXU website for listening any time.

jazz

Mostly Bop
KLON **www.klon.org**

Mostly Bop is a KLON channel available for listening any time.

Avant-Garde / Free Jazz

Avant Garage
KVMR **www.kvmr.org**

Friday 2–4pm Pacific. Host: Alice McAllister.

Waves
WREK **www.wrek.org**

8:30–10pm Eastern (but available any time on WREK's website). Host: Al Smith. *Waves* is a specialty program that features jazz, avant-garde jazz, New Music and black music from the 1950s–80s. *Waves* also features live recordings from avant-garde jazz artists who have performed in Atlanta over the past few years.

Zero Hour
Radio Active **www.radioactive.co.nz**

Sunday 1200–1400 Greenwich. Avant-garde from New Zealand.

Third Wave

The Third Wave
Lyric FM **www.lyricfm.ie**

Saturday and Sunday 2230–0100 Greenwich. Host: Carl Corcoran.

Lounge

Jimmy Twilight's Lonesome Lounge
CFUV
cfuv.uvic.ca

Tuesday 1–3am Pacific.

The Other Side
KVMR **www.kvmr.org**

Tuesday 10pm–midnight Pacific. Host: Mikail Graham. Lounge, exotica, space age, bachelor pad and film music.

The Retro Cocktail Hour
KANU **kanu.ukans.edu**

Saturday 7–9pm Central. Host: Darrell Brogdon. The instrumental pop of the 1950s and '60s: bachelor pad music, exotica, cocktail jazz, and lounge music. Archives on the Web for listening any time.

lounge

Royal Midnight Maitais
Radio Active www.radioactive.co.nz
Sunday 1000–1200 Greenwich. Groovy loungy schmooze from New Zealand.

Swanktown Radio
KBEM www.jazz88fm.com
Saturday 11pm–midnight Central. Host: Greg Wolfe. The website has an archive of past shows you can listen to any time. The playlists are there, as well, and they're well worth mining. (Note that individual shows can spend more time in Swing territory than Lounge land.)

Polka

Barney Tomas Polka Show
WVXA www.wvxa.org
Saturday 8–11am Eastern. Archived on the website so you can listen to it any time.

N. Texas Polka Show
KNON www.knon.org
Sunday 2–3pm Central. There's polka, then there's *Texas* polka. This is *Texas* polka.

Oh Johnny/The Polka Zone
WHUS www.whus.org
Saturday 5–9am Eastern. These two successive programs from the student station at the University of Connecticut are full of lively energy, presenting polkas old and new, and extending to other Polish, Slovenian, Bavarian, German and Italian music.

Polka
WRTC www.wrtcfm.com
Saturday 11:30am–2:30pm Eastern.

Polka Bandstand
WGMC wgmc.greeceny.org
Saturday 10am–noon Eastern. Host: Ray Serafin with Al Meilutis. On March 17, 2001, Serafin celebrated his 1,000[th] polka show on WGMC. Every show includes "Polka Memory Time," a tribute to a polka band from the past, and "The Polka Spotlight," during which Serafin and Meilutis feature a recent polka release. The program also sometimes features live interviews with polka giants such as eleven-time Grammy Award winner Jimmy Sturr, Gus Guzevich from the Polka Family, Happy Louie, Ania Piwowarczyk, and Kevin Adams.

Polka Country USA
WUSB www.wusb.org
Sunday 5:30–8:30pm Eastern. Host: Teresa Zapolska.

polka

part two

Polka Hop
WTMD **saber.towson.edu/wtmd**
Sunday 9–11am Eastern.

Saturday Polka Party
WRTC **www.wrtcfm.com**
Saturday 11:30am–2:30pm Eastern. Host: John Jeski. An archive of past shows is also available any time at **www.johnjeski.com/internetpolka party.htm**.

Sunday Polka Party
WFBO **www.wbfo.buffalo.edu**
Sunday 6–9pm Eastern. Host: Jeff Pieczynski.

WATJ
www.watj.com
Polkas start at 8am Eastern and, with slight detours through Germany (11am–noon) and Italy (1–2pm), go all day.

WMUA
www.wmua.org
Nine hours of polka every weekend: Saturday 6am–noon and Sunday 9am–noon Eastern.

Reggae/Dub/Ska

Air Jamaica
KLCC **www.klcc.org**
Friday 10pm–2am Pacific. Host: Frank Cataldo.

Alive and Dread
CFUV **cfuv.uvic.ca**
Saturday 6–9pm Pacific.

Downbeat
95B **www.95bfm.com**
Sunday 0600–0700 Greenwich. From the University of Auckland, in New Zealand.

Get Smart
WNYU **www.wnyu.org**
Friday 8–10:30pm Eastern. Host: Phillip Smart. On the air for 15 years.

The Irie Feeling Show
WPKN **www.wpkn.org**
Tuesday 6–10am Eastern. Roots reggae, from the foundations right up to this week's releases.

reggae/dub/ska

Ital Sunday
KUGS **www.kugs.org**

Sunday 8–10pm Pacific.

Ithaska
WVBR **www.wvbr.com**

Saturday 9pm–midnight Eastern. Rocksteady and ska.

KCSB
www.kcsb.org

This station from the University of California at Santa Barbara has several reggae programs. (All times Pacific.):

- ⟩⟩ *Ital Soundz* Sunday 9–11am. Host: Bernhard Hitz. Uplifting African sounds and roots reggae, with interviews, spoken word, and poetry mixed in.
- ⟩⟩ *Fire Pon Rome* Sunday 1–3pm. Roots reggae, dancehall, and dub, with an intense flame for social justice.
- ⟩⟩ *Champion Sounds* Monday 8–10pm. Pure consciousness rockers, dancehall, and roots reggae.
- ⟩⟩ *Return of the Dread* Saturday noon–2pm. Host: Danny Hoy. Vintage roots, conscious dancehall, and lots of dubwise.
- ⟩⟩ *Heart Beat Reggae* Saturday 6–8pm. Dancehall, roots reggae, and African.

KNON
www.knon.org

Two hours every night. Weeknights 10pm–midnight Central.

On the Wire
BBC Radio Lancashire
www.bbc.co.uk/england/radiolancashire/index.shtml

Saturday 2100–2300 Greenwich. Host: Steve Barker. Steve Barker's legendary radio program explores the breadth of the dub spectrum, from Lee "Scratch" Perry and Big Youth to Omni Trio and Techno Animal. A selected archive, plus a 24-hour dub loop, is available at **www.onthewire.f9.co.uk**.

One Drop Rhythms
CKUA **www.ckua.org**

Saturday 11pm–midnight Mountain.

Radio 1 Reggae Dancehall Nite
BBC Radio 1
www.bbc.co.uk/radio1

Saturday 2300–0100 Greenwich.

Reggae
WNUR **www.wnur.org**

Sunday 1–4pm Central.

Reggae Bloodlines
KGNU **www.kgnu.org**

Saturday 1–4pm Mountain.

reggae/dub/ska

Reggaemania
CKLN **ckln.sac.ryerson.ca**

Friday 9pm–midnight Eastern. Host: Ron Nelson.

Reggae Mix
KNBA **www.knba.org**

Sunday 3–6pm Alaska.

Reggae Schoolroom
WFMU **www.wfmu.org**

Sunday 9am–noon Eastern. Past programs are archived on the website so you can listen any time.

Reggae Sound
Radio Campus Lille
www-radio-campus.univ-lille1.fr

1900–2000 Greenwich. A mix of reggae, oldies, salsa, Jamaican jazz, ska, Latino, and rocksteady, from a student station in France.

Reggae Vibes
WLUW **www.wluw.org**

Friday 6:30–10pm Central.

Reggafrica
Africa 1 **www.africa1.com**

Saturday 2010–2110 Greenwich. Host: Nina Karine. An African reggae program from Gabon.

Reggea Fever
Ampies Broadcasting Corporation (ABC)
www.abcsuriname.com

Saturday 0000–0300 Greenwich. From Suriname. The announcing is in Dutch. And, yes, that's the way they spell "reggae."

Rockers
WERS **www.wers.org**

Weekdays 5–8pm Eastern. Three hours of reggae every day.

Rocket Ship Ska Trip
KFAI **www.kfai.org**

Wednesday 2–5am Central.

Saturday's a Party
WUSB **www.wusb.org**

Saturday noon–3pm Eastern. Host: Lister Hewan-Lowe. This program claims to be the longest-running reggae-politics mix (RPM) show in the USA.

Ska/Fast'n Loud
WNUR **www.wnur.org**

Sunday midnight–3am Central.

reggae/dub/ska

Skankster's Paradise
CFUV **cfuv.uvic.ca**
Saturday 3–4pm Pacific. Victoria, British Columbia might be a long way from Jamaica, but this is undiluted ska.

Thursday Night Reggae House Party
WMSE
www.wmse.org
Thursday 9pm–midnight Central, but archived for listening any time.

Tropical Storm
KVMR **www.kvmr.org**
Friday 7–9pm Pacific.

Soul/R&B

Soul favorites	
Fame FM	see p.160
The Groove	see p.160

Across 110th Street
WKCR **www.wkcr.org**
Saturday 1–4pm Eastern (except during football season, September–November). Funk classics and rarities from James Brown, Lee Fields, Gene Ammons and The St. Vincent Latinaires.

Bullet-Proof Soul
CKLN **ckln.sac.ryerson.ca**
Tuesday 12:30–2am Eastern.

Café Groove
KCSB **www.kcsb.org**
Friday 4–6am Pacific. Host: Angel Craig.

Classic Soul Friday
KNBA **www.knba.org**
Friday 8–10pm Alaska. Host: Martsy Sammartino.

DJ Zik Presents
WHRB **www.whrb.org**
Sunday midnight–2am Eastern. This mix of classic and contemporary R&B has been satisfying Boston for over a decade. (Followed by *R&B Classic Soul*.)

Downtown Soulville
WFMU **www.wfmu.org**
Friday 7–8pm Eastern. Archives available on the website for listening any time.

soul/r&b

part two

Dynaflow Diner
KUSP **www.kusp.org**

Saturday 8–10pm Pacific. Host: Orin Hutchinson.

Fame FM
www.radiojamaica.com/famefm

This station is way smoother and gentler than you would think given that it streams from Jamaica, verging on (some might say falling splat into) the sappy.

Filet of Soul
WBGO **www.wbgo.org**

Saturday 10am–2pm Eastern. Host: Walter Wade.

Filet of Soul and Waffles
KGNU **www.kgnu.org**

Saturday 8–9pm Mountain.

Funky Bag
KAOS **www.kaosradio.org**

Monday 6–8pm Pacific. Host: Paul Johnson.

The Good, the Bad, and the Funky
KCSB **www.kcsb.org**

Wednesday 10am–noon Pacific.

The Groove
www.catch thegroove.com

This digital radio station from London plays classic soul music, mostly hits from the 1960s and '70s.

Walter Wade

Leaders of the Old School
KUGS **www.kugs.org**

Saturday 2–4pm Pacific.

Let the Good Times Roll
CFUV **cfuv.uvic.ca**

Wednesday 8–9pm Pacific.

Metro
TNL Radio **www.lanka.net/tnl**

Monday 1500–1800 Greenwich. 1970s funk and soul in this program from Sri Lanka.

soul/r&b

160

Night Train ABC Coast FM **local.abc.net.au/goldcoast/radio**
Saturday 0600–1000 Greenwich. Host: Mac Cocker.

Night Train WKCR **www.wkcr.org**
Thursday 1–5am Eastern. Everything from Eddie Bo to Jimmy McGriff to Fela Kuti.

Paul Jones BBC Radio 2 **www.bbc.co.uk/radio2**
Thursday 2000–2100 Greenwich. This program is of interest for its inclusion of British material one does not hear on American stations. (Its definition of R&B is pretty loose, and includes way more blues than rhythm.)

R&B Classic Soul WHRB **www.whrb.org**
Sunday 2–3am Eastern. Hosts: TLove and Monique Bell.

R&B Flashback WNUR **www.wnur.org**
Sunday 6–8pm Central.

R&B Jukebox WMBR **wmbr.mit.edu**
Sunday 6–8pm Eastern. Host: Al Franklin.

R&B Oldies WRTC **www.wrtcfm.com**
Saturday 10:30pm–midnight Eastern.

Rhapsody in Black KPFK **www.kpfk.org**
Wednesday 8–10pm Pacific. Host: Bill Gardner. Classic R&B 1940–1969.

Rhythm and Blues Review CKUA **www.ckua.org**
Saturday 7–8pm Mountain. Host: Lionel Rault.

Rhythm and Blues Review KVMR **www.kvmr.org**
Saturday 6–8pm Pacific. Host: Brian Lee. 1950s–'60s R&B, doo-wop, and a cappella.

Rhythm Lounge WERS **www.wers.org**
Saturday 8–11pm Eastern.

Soul Express WHUS **www.whus.org**
Saturday 7–9pm Eastern. Host: Dean Farrell.

Soul Kitchen KAOS **www.kaosradio.org**
Tuesday 6–8pm Pacific. Host: Shannon Wiberg. All flavors of soul music.

soul/r&b

Soul on Sundays
KUCR **www.kucr.org**

This soul marathon, which extends from midnight Saturday night straight through to 6am Monday (Pacific), has a distinctly hip-hop flavor from 10am to 3pm, and touches on gospel from 6 to 8pm; the later you go on into the evening, the purer the soul becomes.

Soul Serenade
WQNA **www.wqna.org**

Sunday 2–5pm Central. Host: Dennis Clark.

Soulsville
CFRU **www.uoguelph.ca/~cfru-fm**

Thursday 9–10pm Eastern. 1945-75.

Straight Street
KLCC **www.klcc.org**

Friday 6:30–8:30pm Pacific. Host: John Glassburner. Soul, Gospel, and R&B, since 1981.

Twine Time
KUT **www.kut.org**

Saturday 7–10pm Central. Host Paul Ray. "Every R&B hit and miss from World War II to Watergate."

2 Groove
www.groovefm.net/2Groove.asp

2 Groove is the R&B stream of Groove FM, a community station in Brisbane, Australia. 2 Groove specializes in "early sounds of R&B, ballads, funk, soul, disco and house."

soul/r&b

Experimental Music

Bruit Blanc

Radio Campus Lille
www-radio-campus.univ-lille1.fr

Friday 1400–1500 Greenwich.

Carl Stone

KPFA **www.kpfa.org**

Sunday 9–11pm Pacific. Carl Stone is a brilliant composer whose primary instrument is a Macintosh. His compositions are often built from samples of other music, altered and reorganized into utterly original new shapes. Stone is therefore the perfect host for an exploration of experimental music. Each of his shows tends to focus on a single composer, and it often features an extremely

Carl Stone

experimental music

interesting conversation with that composer. Archives available at **www.sukothai.com**. (Side note: Stone's compositions are often named for small ethnic restaurants in Los Angeles, and his home page contains a great L.A. restaurant guide)

DFM RTV INT   **basis.Desk.nl/~dfm/**

Weird audio experiments, obscure electronics, home taping, field recordings, etc. 24 hours a day from The Netherlands.

Electronic Experiments   WMBR **wmbr.mit.edu**

Thursday 10pm–midnight Eastern. This is a live electronic show, hosted by students at MIT, offering an opportunity for a variety of electronic musicians to experiment on the air. *Electronic Experiments* is part of Boston's Tek Fu project. For more information, see **www.tekfumusic.com**.

Electronic Landscapes   CFRC **www.queensu.ca/cfrc**

Thursday noon–2pm Eastern (rebroadcast Friday 6–8am). Each week features a look at one artist or theme within the genre of electronic music.

Ex-perimento   Radio UNAM FM **www.unam.mx/radiounam**

Saturday 7–8pm Central. Host: Aldo Altamirano Aldana. In addition to experimental music, this program also features alternative literature (in Spanish). From the Universidad Nacional Autónoma de México. Note that Radio UNAM has two streams. This program is on the FM stream.

Mappings   **www.antennaradio.com/avant/mappings**

Host: Herb Levy. Weekly program focusing on contemporary composition and improvisation, featuring artists like Alvin Lucier, Pauline Oliveros, Ikue More and Olga Neuwirth. There is also an archive of all past shows.

Mixing It   BBC Radio 3 **www.bbc.co.uk/radio3**

Sunday 2200–2305 Greenwich. Hosts: Mark Russell and Robert Sandall. The BBC's flagship experimental music program features everyone from Karlheinz Stockhausen to Aphex Twin to Tuvan throat singers.

Le Navire   **radio-canada.ca/radio/navire**

Sunday 10pm–midnight Eastern. Weekly experimental spotlight from Radio Canada featuring anything from Oren Ambarchi and Axel Dörner to Merzbow and Robert Ashley.

Robert Sandall

New Dreamers
KLCC
www.klcc.org

Monday and Tuesday 11pm–1am Pacific. Host: Chris Owen (Monday), Kent Willocks (Tuesday). Everything from classical to progressive rock, avant-garde to space music.

ORF Kunstradio
thing.at/orfkunstradio

A continuous stream devoted to sound art and experimental sonic architecture from the likes of Brandon LaBelle and Scanner. Special series, like one on sound art in the '70s, are fully archived on the website.

Soma and Charm
CFUV cfuv.uvic.ca

Thursday 8:30–10:30pm Pacific. Electronic, experimental, and electroacoustic music.

Something Else
WLUW www.wluw.org

Sunday 10pm–2am Central. Host: Philip VonZweck. Experimental and avant-garde music, both live and recorded.

Tabula Non Rasa
KAOS www.kaosradio.org

Monday 2–4am Pacific. Host: Stuart Greene. In this unusual and interesting program, Greene layers a live mix of multiple songs played at the same time.

Unfortunate Sonic Casualties
CKLN ckln.sac.ryerson.ca

Thursday midnight–2am Eastern. Host: Gerald Balanger. This program explores the forward edge of techno, the point where contemporary meets avant-garde.

Le Vide
www.antennaradio.com/avant/levide

Host: Davey Schmitt. Avant-garde composition and electroacoustic music. Shows stay on the site for a week.

experimental music

World Music

For all the problems with the term "world music," invented as a music industry marketing vehicle in the 1980s, it will have to do here. Although the term tries to make a single category out of a vast variety of musics which are very different – as if pop dance tunes from Senegal belonged in the same bin as the classical music of India – and marginalizes those musics, making them *other*, Internet radio is largely organized along these lines. Below are a few shows that try to offer a sampling of all the music the world provides. Following are categories broken down by region.

World Music Programs

Andy Kershaw

Andy Kershaw   BBC Radio 3
www.bbc.co.uk/radio3
Friday 2230–2330 Greenwich. Kershaw gets to do his world music program from out in the world. A given week might find him in Scotland, Haiti, or Iraq.

Audible World   95B
www.95bfm.com
Sunday 0400–0500 Greenwich. Hosts: Ross Clark & Pim Gorter. A program of music from all around the world, from the radio station of University of Auckland, New Zealand.

World music favorites

Afropop Worldwide	see p.172
All India Radio	see p.177
BalkanMedia.Com	see p.188
Ceolnet	see p.187
China Radio International	see p.174
Radio Caraibes International	see p.184
Radio Casablanca	see p.207
Rádio Morena	see p.197
RDP Africa	see p.172
Salsoul	see p.200
Secret Museum of the Air	see p.170
Sikh Net	see p.178
Tropicana FM	see p.201
Village 900	see p.171

Aural Tapestry
Radio Nederland **www.rnw.nl**

Available any time from the "Sound Library" on the website. Host: David Swatling. Each episode of this program examines one stream of music from somewhere in the world, which might be the disco revival in the Netherlands. We hear not just the music, but quite a bit of interesting background information, in English.

Continental Drift
WNUR **www.wnur.org**

Weekdays 12:30–2pm Central. World, roots, and folk music.

Echoes
www.echoes.org

Host: John Diliberto. New instrumental, world fusion, acoustic, jazz, and vocal music from around the world. Each daily program highlights one artist or one new development in contemporary music. One of the best features is a monthly Living Room Concert, an intimate performance in the musician's home. The program is widely syndicated on PRI. You can hear archives any time from a link on the *Echoes* website.

world music

Global Beat
KFAI **www.kfai.org**

Wednesday 1–3pm Central. Hosts: Doug Cain and Deah Cain. KFAI schedules a world music show every weekday afternoon at one. On Wednesday it's this eclectic blend of new and old music from everywhere.

Global Pulse
Radio Active **www.radioactive.co.nz**

Saturday 1900–2200 Greenwich. Music with a beat from around the world, collected in Wellington, New Zealand, and then streamed to speakers near you.

Global Village
CBC Radio One **www.cbc.ca**

Saturday 7:05–8pm Eastern. Host: Jowi Taylor.

Global Village
KUSP **www.kusp.org**

Weekdays 1–4pm Pacific.

Gyroscope
WERS **www.wers.org**

Weekdays 10am–2pm Eastern.

In All Languages
WKCR **www.wkcr.org**

Sunday 11pm–2am Eastern. Each week this show explores a different musical tradition, for example, conch shell music of Tonga, Peruvian mountain music, or Iranian classical music.

International
WHPK **whpk.uchicago.edu**

Tuesday and Thursday 4–6:30pm Central, Friday noon–7pm, Saturday 2–7pm. Interesting mix of international music from this student station at the University of Chicago.

Krusa Kaya
Radio Nederland **www.rnw.nl**

Each episode of this program bores in on the music of somewhere, and it's almost always music you probably don't know: swing from the Netherlands Antilles and Suriname, say, or new blends from Indonesia.

Music 52-15
Radio Nederland **www.rnw.nl**

Tuesday 1000 Greenwich.; rebroadcast several times Tuesday, and archived on the website for 24 hours. Host: Martha Hawley. This half-hour program is organized around a theme each week, but the music is truly eclectic: "acoustic guitar, big band, Celtic fusion, dangdut, funk, Galician ballads, Hispanic rap, Italian opera, jazz, klezmer, Lusitanian love songs, Malagasy moods, no holds barred, Om Kalthoum, presidential pomp, Quebec riffs, rocksteady, slack-key,

world music

Tang dynasty, ugric undulations, vindaloo calypso, West African blues, Xhosa, Yaounde yellers and even zydeco." Much educational background information, delivered in English.

Música del Mundo

Radio UNAM FM
www.unam.mx/radiounam

Saturday 3–4pm Central. Interesting and well-produced world music show from the Universidad Nacional Autónoma de México. Note that Radio UNAM has two streams. This program is on the FM stream.

Music of One World

KGNU **www.kgnu.org**.

Sunday 10pm–midnight. Mountain.

The Planet

Australian Broadcasting Corporation Radio National
www.abc.net.au/rn/music/planet

Tuesday 0500–0600 Greenwich. Host: Lucky Oceans. Interesting music from around the world, with one artist featured each week. (Archived on the website for listening later.)

Planetary Folkways

KUT **www.kut.org**

Saturday 5–7am Central. Host: Howie Richey. Since 1982, covering indigenous folk musics of the world.

Lucky Oceans

Pop Secret

KCRW **www.kcrw.org**

Saturday (that is Friday night) midnight–3am Pacific. Host: Cathy Tamkin. International pop, emphasizing the absolute latest.

Putumayo World Music Hour

Hosts: Dan Storper and Rosalie Howarth. Syndicated show that emphasizes a theme each week. A recent show, "Surfin' Safari," for example, featured a variety of Hawaiian and beach styles. As you might expect, offerings from the Putumayo record label are prominently featured. There's a list of stations that air the program, and a schedule of when, at **www.putumayo.com**, along with playlists. You can listen to an archive of the program any time on WMSE (**www.wmse.org**).

world music

part two

RFI Musique
Radio France Internationale **www.rfimusique.com**

RFI Musique sports several great on-demand streams, including *Couleurs Tropicales*, *Musiques du Monde*, and *Eklektic*. The playlists are available in advance on the website, which you can choose to see in English.

Secret Museum of the Air
WFMU **www.wfmu.org**.

Tuesday 6–7pm Eastern. Hosts: Citizen Kafka and Pat Conte. This exceptional program is devoted to international music as preserved on 78 RPM recordings. Each episode treats a single theme. Recent programs have included: Al Oud, Son House, European recordings of the 1920s, Spanish strings, country music of Puerto Rico. You can listen to the extensive archives any time at **www.secretmuseum.net**.

Shake and Bake
KFAI **www.kfai.org**

Monday 1–3pm Central. Hosts: Tony Paul and Pablo Miranda. On the air in Minneapolis for 20 years, this program asks the question "Isn't *all* music world music?"

Sounds of a Planet
KUGS **www.kugs.org**

Sunday 5–8pm Pacific. "Everything new and interesting from everywhere but here."

Spin the Globe
Radio Singapore International **www.rsi.com.sg**

Wednesday and Saturday 1305–1330 Greenwich. A world music show from Singapore.

Third Stone
CHRW **www.usc.uwo.ca/chrw**

Thursday 6:30–8:30 Eastern.

Village 900
www.village900.ca

This community radio station at Camosun College in Victoria, British Columbia, has a music format of "global roots" programming. There are numerous specialty programs (college courses by radio 6–7pm weekdays, documentaries and talk on Saturday) but essentially this is a world music radio station. Various interviews with musicians are archived on the website for listening any time.

Wo' Pop
KEXP **www.kexp.org**

Tuesday 6–9pm Pacific. Host: Derek Mazzone. Extremely lively program of current sounds from all over.

world music

World Beat

WMBR **wmbr.mit.edu**

Sunday 10am–noon Eastern. Host: Brutus Leaderson.

World Beat Music

JOY **joy.org.au**

Saturday 2100–2300 Greenwich. Fun program from a volunteer-operated community gay and lesbian radio station in Melbourne, Australia.

Africa

Africa Kabisa

WMBR **wmbr.mit.edu**

Sunday 4–6pm Eastern. Hosts: Julia Goldrosen and Ethan Bloomberg. Classic and contemporary popular music from Africa and the Afro-Caribbean world. Soukous, ndombolo, rumba, zouk, mapouka, makossa, kompa, highlife, and even a bit of salsa.

African Rhythms

KFAI **www.kfai.org**

Thursday 1–3pm Central. Hosts: Rhoda Ohito and Salif Keita. Ohito is from Kenya, Keita from Mali. They play music from all over Africa.

African Roots

KGNU **www.kgnu.org**

Saturday 4–6pm Mountain.

The African Show

WKCR **www.wkcr.org**

Thursday 9:30–11:30pm Eastern. Host: Lawrence Nii Nartey. Originally founded by percussionist Babatunde Olatunji in the '70s, this is one of the oldest African music programs in the U.S.

AfricMusic

www.africmusic.com

This Internet-only station offers three streams of live programming all the time, plus on-demand cuts from featured albums.

Afrobeat World

CHKG **www.fm961.com**

Saturday 11am–1pm Pacific. Hosts: Ezeadi Patrick Onukwulu and Kemit-Soul Jallow.

Afropop Worldwide

Host: Georges Collinet. Since 1988, *Afropop* has been spreading the virus of African music across the world. It has probably done more than any other single force to familiarize Americans in particular with the amazing variety of

world music

part two

popular music always percolating out of Africa. Syndicated via PRI to over 100 stations. Several past shows and other radio resources for lovers of African music are available on the Afropop website (**www.afropop.org**).

Best Ambiance
KEXP **www.kexp.org**

Monday 6–9pm Pacific. Host: Jon Kertzer. In June, 1984, Jon Kertzer started one of the first feature programs of African music in the U.S. with his two-hour weekly show, *The Best Ambiance*, which is still running today and still excellent. Kertzer is head of Rakumi Arts, a non-profit organization which has done much to promote African music in the United States, and particularly in the Pacific Northwest: **www.rakumi.org**.

Kan Ya Makan
CKLN **ckln.sac.ryerson.ca**

Tuesday 8–10pm Eastern. All kinds of music from North Africa.

Pêlemêle Afro-Variétés
Radio Campus Lille
www-radio-campus.univ-lille1.fr

1630–1800 Greenwich.

RDP Africa
www.rdp.pt/africa

The African channel of Radiofusão Portuguesa (in Portuguese). Extremely varied mix of programming, sometimes including great music. (One nice feature is that they let you know what you're listening to as you listen to it.)

Sounds of Africa
CKLN **ckln.sac.ryerson.ca**

Saturday 6–8pm Eastern. This musical program is seasoned with news, interviews, and panel discussions on African issues.

Angola

Radio Luanda
www.rna.ao

The National Radio of Angola's website is in Portuguese, but the button for its Radio Luanda says "On-Line Real-Time." Click on that button, and you'll be glad you did. Radio Luanda plays a mix of African popular dance music more effective than any anti-depressant.

Benin

Radio Golfe   www.eit.bj
The stream can be frustratingly unsteady. The music is anything but.

Gabon

Africa 1   www.africa1.com
Africa 1 has a mix of programming, including quite a bit of news and public information, but also a good dose of music. The music is concentrated in the evenings Greenwich time; you can hear music weeknights from 1710 until signoff at midnight; Saturday from 1610; Sunday from 2230. The site also has clips from the recordings of well-known musicians such as Manu Dibango and Toups Bebey. The programming and the website are in French. If you have problems receiving the stream from the Africa 1 website, try ComFM (**www.comfm.com/live/radio/africa/africa.asx**).

Uganda

Radio Simba   www.simba.fm
Especially try to catch the program *Music Africa* starting every day at 2100 Greenwich and running until 0300 or so.

Central Asia

China

Chinese Music Circle   CHSR **www.unb.ca/chsr**
Sunday 9:45am–1pm Atlantic (one hour ahead of Eastern). This program, assembled by the Overseas Chinese Students Association at the University of New Brunswick, features some news of China in Chinese, but also large amounts of cool new Chinese music.

world music

China Radio International

web12.cri.com.cn/english

This website (presented in English) offers extensive archives of a variety of Chinese musical styles, from classical to folk to popular. One nice feature is English translations of the lyrics, along with educational background information about the region, instruments, etc.

China Radio International Crew

Hit FM

www.hitfm.com.tw

Contemporary popular music from Taiwan.

Jade Bells and Bamboo Pipes

Radio Taipei International–
Central Broadcasting System www.cbs.org.tw

Sunday 1615–1645 Greenwich. (On Channel A.) Also check out *Groove Zone* at the same time Friday for a look at what's popular in Taiwan today.

M Radio

www.taichungnet.com.tw

Several streams of music, mostly popular music in Chinese and English, although on the third stream you can hear tangos followed by Dixieland. (The streams are marked by "E Radio" and "MP3.")

world music

Public Radio System
www.prs.gov.tw

The Taiwanese Public Radio System delivers three streams on which you can find a variety of music and public service broadcasting, plus various archived snippets. All announcing is in Chinese, as is the website.

Sounds of China
WKCR **www.wkcr.org**

Saturday 10am–1pm Eastern. Presented in a variety of Chinese dialects, this program explores both traditional and the latest popular music from China.

Nepal

Lok Bhaka
HBC **www.hbc.com.np**

Sunday 0715–0745 Greenwich. Host: Dilip Kumar Jyoti. This program of Nepalese folk music comes to you in Nepali from Nepal.

East Asia

Full Moon
CKLN **ckln.sac.ryerson.ca**

Tuesday 10–11pm Eastern. An extremely eclectic blend of East Asian music, from a student station in Toronto.

Japan

FM Champla
www.fm-champla.co.jp

This commercial station from Okinawa plays a mix of musical styles, including quite a bit of traditional or the Japanese equivalent of "oldies."

Listening to the VOICES
KCSB **www.kcsb.org**

Thursday 12:30–2pm Pacific. Anime, J-pop, and other Japanese music.

Nippon Radio
KUGS **www.kugs.org**

Saturday 10pm–midnight Pacific. A showcase of many Japanese musical styles.

world music

Korea

Korean Broadcasting System FM 2
www.kbs.co.kr

KBS FM 2 plays a variety of popular music.

Korean World Music
CFUV cfuv.uvic.ca

Tuesday 4–5pm Pacific.

Munhwa Broadcasting Corporation (MBC)
www.imbc.com

MBC is an odd hybrid of public and commercial. Its charter is to a public foundation with a mandate to promote Korean culture ("Munwha" means "culture"), but it receives no public funding and supports itself as a commercial enterprise. A dispassionate observer would probably conclude that it has succeeded in the latter at the expense of the former. MBC streams two FM signals (and a TV station). Both radio streams carry pop music most of the time; FM 2 is mostly mainstream corporate pop in English you could get at home. FM 1 is mostly Korean music, and is sometimes interesting. Both pop up their own player, which will ask if you want to install some software; the station will still play if you decline.

Radio Korea International
http://rki.kbs.co.kr/

Top 10 pop songs.

Worldbeat: Korean Sounds of Chicago
WLUW www.wluw.org

Tuesday 10pm–2am Central. A variety of Korean pop, rock, and dance music.

South Asia

Garam Masala
WKCR www.wkcr.org

Sunday 7–8:30pm Eastern. Host: Anastasia Tsioulcas. An exploration of the subcontinent's folk, classical, and devotional music, with guests like Ravi Shankar and Zakir Hussain.

Masala Mix
CKLN ckln.sac.ryerson.ca

Saturday 4–6pm Eastern. Mostly bhangra, along with some classic and contemporary Hindi and Pakistani music, and even some Caribbean as well.

world music

Mehfil-e-sangeet
CJSW **www.cjsw.com**

Saturday 7–8am Mountain.

Mehil
CHSR **www.unb.ca/chsr**

Sunday 7:30–9pm Atlantic. Poetry and music from the South Asian subcontinent, sponsored by the University of New Brunswick South Asian Society.

Mystic Music of the East
CKDU **is2.dal.ca/~ckdufm**

Sunday 3:30–5pm Atlantic. Host: Anjou Sharma. Music from India and Pakistan. Including qawwaalis, ghazals, traditional Punjabi geets, bhangra, classical and instrumental music, filmi songs and remixes.

Swaraj
CHKG **www.fm961.com**

Weekdays 2–3pm Pacific. This program from a multicultural radio station in Vancouver, B.C. is devoted to music of "the South Asian invasion." It also includes quite a bit of news and commentary, with frequent interviews. And if you like this program, you will certainly enjoy *Planet Aaj Roots*, Saturday 1–3pm, Michael Sunner's mix of traditional and contemporary bhangra.

Bangladesh

Jalsha
CHSR **www.unb.ca/chsr**

Sunday 1–3pm Atlantic. Music from and information about Bangladesh, from the student station at the University of New Brunswick.

India

All India Radio
air.kode.net

AIR provides a powerful digital jukebox. From several categories – tunes, film music, Indian pop, light music, classical music, poetry, and devotional music – you can choose hundreds of musical selections to play on demand. Under the classical category, for example, you can choose by instrument – flute, sitar, sarod, violin, shenai, tabla, veena. Or pick a vocal selection from Tamil, karnatak, or Hindi. Or listen to orchestral music.

Bhangra Fever
CHRW **www.usc.uwo.ca/chrw**

Saturday 4–5pm Eastern. Host: Bindu Gahir.

world music

Geetanjali
CITR **www.ams.ubc.ca/citr**
Sunday 8–10pm Pacific. A wide range of music from India, including classical music – both Hindustani and karnatak – and popular music like ghazals, bhajans, and qawwaalis.

Glimpses of India
WRSU **www.wrsu.org**
Sunday 4–5pm Eastern. Indian music and news from the student station at Rutgers University.

India Show
KCSB **www.kcsb.org**
Saturday 2–4pm Pacific. Contemporary as well as classical Indian and Pakistani music.

Morning Ragas
WKCR **www.wkcr.org**
Sunday 6–8am Eastern. As the title suggests, two hours of ragas.

Raag Raagini
HBC **www.hbc.com.np**
Thursday 1100–1145 Greenwich. Host: Dilip Kumar Jyoti. Nepali program on Eastern classical music, particularly ragas.

Sabrang Music Sensation
CHKF **www.fm947.com**
Thursday and Friday 8–9pm Mountain, Sunday 1–3pm. Host: Gurdeep Dhaliwal. All kinds of Indian music, announced in a mix of English, Punjabi, and Hindi, from a commercial radio station in Calgary, Alberta. Dhaliwal takes requests, and each program includes a top hit countdown.

Sangam
CHRW **www.usc.uwo.ca/chrw**
Saturday 5–6pm Eastern.

Sikh Net
www.sikhnet.com
Click on "Multimedia Archive" for a well-stocked jukebox. "Gurbani by musician" alone has several weeks' worth of music in it, even if you were to

world music

forgo sleep while working your way through it. Which the quality of the music might tempt you to do.

Pakistan

Radio Pakistan
radio.gov.pk

If you click on the "Live Radio" button on this page, there is about a 50 percent chance you'll hear a news or information program in a language you probably don't know. The rest of the time, you'll hear incredible music: classical, folk, qawwaalis, pop, and instrumental.

Sadaa-E-Pakistan
WRSU www.wrsu.org

Sunday 3–4pm Eastern. Pakistani music and news from the student station at Rutgers University.

Sri Lanka

Sirasa FM
www.sirasa.com

Sirasa FM intersperses talk programming (in several languages) with music (of many kinds) throughout the day. There's a one-hour program of music with a beat from 0600 to 0700 Greenwich. daily. Hindi hits play from 0900 to 1000, and it's mostly popular music from 1200 to 1800. Sunday 0400 to 0600 is the best of Hindi hits and 0600–0730 is top Sinhala hits.

Southeast Asia

Burma

Burma Song
users.imagiware.com/wtongue/songbook.html

Archives of music from Burma.

Democratic Voice of Burma
www.communique.no/dvb

This site in Norway archives the transmissions of the Democratic Voice of Burma. Primarily public affairs programming (in Burmese), they also include quite a bit of music. They are organized on the website for listening any time.

world music

Radio Free Burma   **www.onedr.net/RFB/rfb.html**

Weekly radio program (announced in Burmese) of *wonderful* music.

Cambodia

Cambodian   CHKG **www.fm961.com**

Saturday 6–7am Pacific. This is the Cambodian hour on a multicultural station in Vancouver, B.C.

Cambodian   Fairchild Radio Toronto **www.fairchildradio.com**

Sunday 8–10am Eastern. Music and information of interest to Toronto's Cambodian community, in Cambodian.

Indonesia

Radio Salvatore   **www.radiosalvatore.co.id/**

Radio Salvatore carries informational programming which is not very informational to speakers of English and also quite a bit of pop music in English, which is also not very rewarding. (There are easier ways to hear "Here Comes the Sun" than to squeeze it through the narrow pipes to Indonesia.) But blended in the mix, if you wait patiently or come back later, is also some local music that repays the wait.

Laos

Laotian   Fairchild Radio Toronto **www.fairchildradio.com**

Saturday 10–11am Eastern. Music and information of interest to Toronto's Laotian community, in Laotian.

Malaysia

Malay   Fairchild Radio Toronto **www.fairchildradio.com**

Sunday 6–8am Eastern. Malay-language programming, including substantial amounts of music, from a commercial station in Toronto.

world music

Radio Malaysia Melaka

media.mmu.edu.my/rmm

A variety of traditional music (and some of the apparently inevitable Western hits). In addition to listening to the live stream, click on "Song Selection" to access a jukebox of music for your on-demand pleasure.

Singapore

FM 88.3 (Dongli)

www.fm883.com.sg

A mix of news and popular music.

Oli

oli.mediacorpradio.com

Oli's programming is a mix of talk and music designed for an audience of Indian heritage in Singapore. Some of the music is amazing. The block from 0200–0500 Greenwich each day is devoted to a variety of music programs, everything from folk music to movie music to music with a rock beat. The block from 1000 to 1300 is targeted at youth.

Radio Singapore International

www.rsi.com.sg

Radio Singapore International's stream is primarily devoted to public affairs programming, but there is some music on it. Of particular interest are *Singa-Pop* Tuesday and Thursday 1305–1330 Greenwich, and *Hot Trax* (new releases in Singapore) at the same time on Friday. (In case you're wondering, at the same hour Wednesday and Saturday is a world music show, and on Sunday is Latin music.)

Thailand

A-Time Media

www.atimemedia.com

This site puts out four streams of popular music from Thailand. *Hot Wave* offers the most consistent accessibility and sound quality, although the music is considerably less rhythmic than the name might suggest.

Ikazz

www.ikazz.com

There is a handy tuner across the top of the website, allowing you push-button access to some eleven Thai stations. Most of these stations play popular music, and it's not all just imported commercial pop. The music from *Luktung FM* seems to have the most grounding in local traditions.

world music

Thai   Fairchild Radio Toronto**www.fairchildradio.com**
Saturday 10pm–midnight Eastern. Music and information of interest to Toronto's Thai community.

Vietnam

Am Nhac Viet   CJSF **www.cjsf.bc.ca**
Friday 2–3pm Pacific. Vietnamese pop music and news.

Calgary Vietnamese Radio   CJSW **www.cjsw.com**
Saturday 11am–noon Mountain.

Vietnamese   Fairchild Radio Toronto**www.fairchildradio.com**
Saturday 8–10am Eastern. Music and informational programming in Vietnamese.

West Asia

Afghanistan

Afghanistan   Fairchild Radio Toronto **www.fairchildradio.com**
Weeknights 10pm–midnight Eastern. Music and information of interest to Toronto's Afghan community.

Kazakstan

Kazak Radio   **www.radio.kz**
This station from the Republic of Kazakstan offers a variety of programming, including some music. The stream is hard to get.

world music

Australia/New Zealand

Deadly Sounds
www.vibe.com.au

Host: Rhoda Roberts. *Deadly Sounds* is a weekly one-hour Australian Aboriginal and Torres Strait Islander music program. Broadcast on the Aboriginal owned and controlled Broadcasting for Remote Areas Communities Scheme (BRACS) to remote communities across Australia, which lamentably does not yet stream, *Deadly Sounds* is available on the website listed above for listening any time.

Kokoi
95B www.95bfm.com

Saturday 0200–0400 Greenwich. Maori music and issues, from the University of Aukland, in New Zealand.

Caribbean

Calypso Fusion
CKLN ckln.sac.ryerson.ca

Saturday midnight–2am Eastern. Host: Barry Johnson. This program from Toronto, which tries to include all the islands in the Caribbean as one nation, includes a healthy serving of zouk from the French Antilles.

Caribbean Affair
WEAA www.morgan.edu/geninfo/weaa.htm

Sunday noon–7pm Eastern. Host: Neil Mattel.

Caribbean Anthology
CFRU www.uoguelph.ca/~cfru-fm

Monday 7–9pm Eastern. Host: John W. Leacock. A historical approach to Caribbean music.

world music

Caribbean Cavalcade
WHPK **whpk.uchicago.edu**

Saturday 2–4:30pm Central. Host: Mike Sears. Particularly good for music of Trinidad.

Caribbean Express
CHKG **www.fm961.com**

Monday–Friday 9–11am Pacific. Host: Wayne Vernon. The daily Caribbean program on this multicultural station from Vancouver, B.C. is a consistent joy. Full of calypso, soca, and reggae. You should also listen in to the *Tropical Rhythms* show at the same time Saturday.

Caribbean Jam
KFAI **www.kfai.org**

Saturday 4–5:30pm Central.

Caribbean Pepperpot
CHRW **www.usc.uwo.ca/chrw**

Thursday 8:30–10pm Eastern.

Caribbean Show
CJSF **www.cjsf.bc.ca**

Saturday 6–8pm Pacific.

Caribbeana
WPFW **www.wpfw.org**

Saturday 7–10pm Eastern. Host: Von Martin.

Caribwave
CKDU **is2.dal.ca/~ckdufm**

Saturday 7:30–9pm Atlantic. Host: Lorraine Ferguson. Music, news, features, and recipes from different Caribbean Islands.

Jam Session
WMBR **wmbr.mit.edu**

Sunday 2–4pm Eastern. Host: Pam Spencer. Music from all over the Caribbean and interviews with musicians.

Radio Caraibes International
www.rci.gp

RCI has three radio commercial stations – from Guadeloupe, Martinique, Guyana – all of which you can hear from this page all in French, all with strong streams, all carrying lively music unlike any you'll hear elsewhere.

WRTC
www.wrtcfm.com

Various Caribbean shows:
▸▸Monday, Thursday, Friday noon–3pm Eastern.
▸▸Saturday 2:30–4pm Eastern.
▸▸Sunday 1:30–3:30pm Eastern. (This is a student station with a schedule that changes; check the schedule on the website for current hours.)

world music

Antigua

The Antigua and Barbuda Broadcasting Service (ABS)
www.cmattcomm.com/abs.htm

News and music. It's hard to sit down while listening to the music.

Barbados

Voice of Barbados
www.nationnews.com

Curaçao

Radio Korsou
www.korsou.com

Engaging mix of Latin and Caribbean music from the Dutch Antilles. Announcing in Portuguese. (Click on "Skucha nos.")

Haiti

Compas Sur FM
WMBR wmbr.mit.edu

Sunday 6–8am Eastern. Host: Emmanuel Rene. If you have not met Haitian compas music, this program will introduce you.

Haitian
WNUR www.wnur.org

Sunday 5–9am Central.

Radio L'Union
WLUW www.wluw.org

Saturday 4–6pm Central. Two hours of conversation on the politics and culture, plus music, of Haiti (in Creole, French, and English).

Radio Vwa Lakay
WHPK whpk.uchicago.edu

Saturday 4:30–7pm Central.

Serge Petit-Homme
WPKN www.wpkn.org

Sunday 5–7am Eastern. Haitian language, music and information show.

world music

St. Kitts

ZIZ **www.skbee.com/zizlive.html**
A mix of contemporary popular music.

St. Thomas

WWJZ **www.wvjz.net/kqswvjz.htm**
R&B, hip-hop, and a little bit of Caribbean music from this commercial station in the Virgin Islands.

Trinidad and Tobago

TriniRadio **www.nvo.com/triniradio**
Soca, calypso, steel drums, and chutney.

Underwire **www.trinidad-online.org/Underwire**
Music hotter than boiling point. Dance tracks up to the second, fed by all the tributaries that make up the sound of the Caribbean.

Celtic

Celtic Cadences KVMR **www.kvmr.org**
Wednesday 8–10pm Pacific. Host: Anne O'Dea Hestbeck.

Celtic Dawn WMFO **www.wmfo.org**
Monday 8am–noon Eastern. Host: Laura Davidson. "Ireland, Scotland, Cape Breton, Brittany, Galicia, the Scandinavian countries, and what came before and after."

Celtic Experience CFUV **cfuv.uvic.ca**
Saturday noon–1pm Pacific. Host: Desmond Linch.

Celtic Voices CHKG **www.fm961.com**
Saturday 8–9am Pacific. Hosts: Dave Abbott and Nessa Doyle. In addition to the music, this program from a multicultural station in Vancouver, B.C. includes

features, sports, and interviews.

Ceolnet
www.rte.ie/radio/ceolnet

RTE, the national radio service of Ireland, offers an incredible non-stop stream of traditional Irish music from its vast collection of recordings. In addition, it makes this collection available on demand, creating not just the largest jukebox of Celtic music in the world, but perhaps the largest Internet jukebox of any kind. The site is also an incredibly rich source of information about the music.

Clan Na Gael
CFRU **www.uoguelph.ca/~cfru-fm**

Sunday noon–2pm Eastern. Host: Terry Van Dreumel.

Continental Drift
KUSP **www.kusp.org**

Saturday 11am–1pm Pacific. Host: Cindy Odom.

The Long Note
CKLN **ckln.sac.ryerson.ca**

Sunday 8–9pm Eastern. Host: Colm O'Brien.

Mist-Covered Mountain
KLCC **www.klcc.org**

Sunday 10am–noon Pacific (archives on the website). Host: Leslie Hildreth.

Sounds of Scotland
CFUV **cfuv.uvic.ca**

Saturday 2–3pm Pacific Host: Wally Cunningham. Pipes and drums, country dance, fiddle music, and folk.

Thistle and Shamrock

Fiona Ritchie's weekly show *Thistle and Shamrock* is the only Celtic music millions of radios can receive. Good thing it's such a good show. Now in its 20th year, *Thistle and Shamrock* presents something new and interesting every week, often featuring new, young bands just heading out onto the road. Ritchie also has one of the world's greatest radio voices. If she played no music at all, a substantial audience would tune in just to hear her talk. *Thistle and Shamrock* is available on nearly every NPR station. You can find a list of the stations that stream the program, with times, at **www.npr.org/programs/thistle**.

Wheels of the World
KAOS **www.kaosradio.org**

Wednesday 10am–noon Pacific. Host: Burt Meyer. An exceptionally wide variety of Celtic music.

Whisky In the Jar
KVNF **www.kvnf.org**

Thursday 7-9:30pm Mountain. Host: Kele Lampe.

world music

Eastern European

BalkanMedia.Com   **http://www.balkanmedia.com/magazin/ radio/index.shtml**

This site has a wealth of interesting streams, including *Folk Express*, *Sarajevo Folk*, and *Balkan Folk Gold*, all available any time, as well as links to the five live streams from Bosnia, seven from Serbia, nine each from Slovenia and Croatia, and three from Macedonia.

Bosnia

Bosnian   Fairchild Radio Toronto **www.fairchildradio.com**

Sunday 11:30am–noon Eastern. Music and information of interest to Toronto's Bosnian community, in Bosnian.

Radio Mostar   **www.rtvmo.ba/rtvmo/live_frm.htm**

In addition to the live stream, extensive archives of interesting music.

Bulgaria

Folklore Concert   Bulgarian National Radio **www.nationalradio.bg**

Daily at 0300–0400 and 1600–1700 Greenwich on the *Hristo Botev* stream.

Croatia

Croatian   Fairchild Radio Toronto **www.fairchildradio.com**

Sunday 10–11:30am Eastern. Music and information of interest to Toronto's Croatian community, in Croatian.

Hrvatska Radio   **www.hrt.hr/streams/index.html**

Seven streams, plus archives. HR1 (**www.hrt.hr/streams/hr1.ram**) has a wonderful eclectic mix, unhesitant to juxtapose classical piano with funk bass dance riffs.

world music

Czech Republic

Cesky Rozhlas 2   **www.rozhlas.cz/praha/**

A variety of cultural programs, with many archived on the website for listening any time.

Hungary

Hungarian   CHKF **www.fm947.com**

Sunday 11am–noon Mountain. Music and information of interest to Alberta's Hungarian community, in Hungarian.

Hungary   WRSU **www.wrsu.org**

Sunday 7–8pm Eastern. Hungarian music and news from the student station at Rutgers University.

Macedonia

Macedonian   Fairchild Radio Toronto **www.fairchildradio.com**

Saturday 9–10am Eastern. Music and information of interest to Toronto's Macedonian community, in Macedonian.

Poland

Polish Hour   WRSU **www.wrsu.org**

Sunday 5–6pm Eastern. Polish music and news from the student station at Rutgers University.

Pryzmat   CFRU **www.uoguelph.ca/~cfru-fm**

Sunday 2–4pm Eastern. Host: Robert Byckiewicz. Polish language show featuring music, news and commentary from the station at the University of Guelph in Ontario.

world music

Romania

Radio Romania International Channel 2   **www.rr.ro**

This Radio Romania International stream is devoted almost entirely to news, but a two-hour music program streams Saturday and Sunday at 0000 and 0500 Greenwich.

Russia

Russian Internet Radio   **www.101.ru**

Russian Internet Radio has two channels streaming around the clock. One is *Russian Rock*. The other is *Russian Songs*, which contains primarily folk material. The website is available in English, but if you have trouble navigating it, where you want to be is **eng101.ru/live-pln.htm**.

Serbia

Srpskiradiokalgari   CJSW **www.cjsw.com**

Sunday 7–8am Mountain. Host: Dejan Ristic. A wide mix of musical styles with the lyrics in Serbian. For more information, see the program website (**www.srpskiradiokalgari.com**).

Turkey

Strolling Through Anatolia   CFRU **www.uoguelph.ca/~cfru-fm**

Sunday 2–4pm Eastern.

TRGT FM   **www.tgrt-fm.com.tr**

This Turkish station plays contemporary music saturated with tradition. Some of it has a fast dance beat laid underneath it, some of it is old style. All of it is hypnotic, captivating, and strong.

world music

Northern European

New Scandinavian Cultural Hour KFAI **www.kfai.org**
Wednesday 9:30–10:30pm Central. Host: Dick Rees. A wide range of music from Scandinavia, both old and new.

Latvia

SWH **www.radioswh.lv**
Most of the music you will hear on SWH is pop hits in English. But the local flavor occasionally seeps through. One particularly enjoyable program is *Tonight's Party* (weeknights 1800–2000 Greenwich), featuring "singing, dancing, congratulations and presents, toasts and rhymes."

Sweden

Sveriges Radio **www.sr.se**
The national radio service of Sweden is a treasure house containing not only several live streams, but also a huge archive. To open, click on "Lyssna."

Western European

Austria

Radio Burgenland **www.burgenland.orf.at**
A variety of popular music in German, from Eisenstadt, Austria, courtesy of ORF, the national public radio of Austria.

Radio Steiermark **steiermark.orf.at/stmk/on_demand/index.html**
Radio Steiermark, from ORF, has an extensive collection of archives for listening any time.

world music

Belgium

Music from Flanders

Radio Vlaanderen Internationaal
www.rvi.be

Saturday 0600–2300 Greenwich. Radio Vlaanderen Internationaal is the international radio station of VRT, the public broadcaster of the Flemish Community in Belgium. The station usually streams news and public affairs programming, but on Friday it is devoted to the music of Flanders. (Website available in English.)

Cyprus

Cyprus Broadcasting Corporation   **www.cybc.com.cy**
Three radio streams, including a mix of contemporary and traditional music.

Radio Proto   **www.radioproto.com.cy/**
Angelic vocal music.

France

Bonjour Minnesota   KFAI **www.kfai.org**
Wednesday 8:30–9:30pm Central. Hosts: Georgette Pfannkuch and Caryl Minnetti. Music and culture of France and francophone countries, in French with English translations.

French Music   CFUV **cfuv.uvic.ca**
Saturday 5–6pm Pacific.

French Toast   WMBR **wmbr.mit.edu**
Monday 6–8pm Eastern. Hosts: Yves Dehnel and Brian Thompson. This weekly bilingual program has entertained and educated Boston for over a decade with songs in French as well as reports on francophone culture.

Radio Campus Lille   **www-radio-campus.univ-lille1.fr**
This station plays music from all over the world, which includes some superb programs devoted to French songs:
▸▸*Les Echansons* Wednesday 1930–2030 Greenwich
▸▸*Ballade* Thursday 1100–1300

world music

▸▸ *Paradoxe* Thursday 1800–1900
▸▸ *Débits de Laids* Saturday 0900–1100

Germany

Bunte Welle
CJSW www.cjsw.com
Saturday 8–10am Mountain.

Greece

Aegean Waves
WREK www.wrek.org
Saturday 6–7pm Eastern (but available any time on WREK's website). *Aegean Waves* is a show featuring Greek music from all its phases and periods.

Annabouboula
CITR www.ams.ubc.ca/citr
Wednesday 8–9pm Pacific.

Dimotika
CHIR www.chir.com
Daily 3:30–4pm Eastern. Greek folk music.

E-Radio
www.e-radio.gr
Several channels of on-demand music, including dance tracks, world hits, and Greek ballads.

Greek
Fairchild Radio Toronto www.fairchildradio.com
Weekdays 11am–noon Eastern. Music and information of interest to Toronto's Greek community, in Greek.

The Greek Hour
CJSW www.cjsw.com
Saturday 10–11am Mountain. Greek music from rembetika of the 1960s to the hits of today, from Calgary, Alberta.

Melodia
www.melodia.gr
Jukebox of current Greek releases.

Mousiki Parelasi
CHIR www.chir.com
Every night 8–11pm Eastern. New releases and classic oldies, from this all-Greek station in Toronto. Sunday night is request night.

world music

Rendezvous With Greece

CHRW **www.usc.uwo.ca/chrw**

Sunday 1–3pm Eastern.

The Voice of Greece

WRSU **www.wrsu.org**

Sunday 2–3pm Eastern. An hour of Greek music, new and old, from the student station at Rutgers University.

Italy

Fantasia Musicala Italiana

CHRW
www.usc.uwo.ca/chrw.

Sunday 11am–1pm Eastern. Two hours of Italian music, news, and soccer scores.

Imagine Italia

CHKG **www.fm961.com**

Monday–Friday 1–2pm Pacific. Host: Maria Fierra. This program is the Italian hour on a multicultural station in Vancouver, B.C.

Radio Sorrento

www.sorrentoradio.com

This station plays songs in Italian, particularly emphasizing Neapolitan songs. The website is available in English as well as Italian.

Portugal

ESEC Radio

www.esec.pt

A wide range of music, from dance tracks to fado.

Sem Limit

CKLN **ckln.sac.ryerson.ca**

Sunday 7–9:30am Eastern. The music of Portugal flavors the music of the Portuguese-speaking world. This program from Toronto follows that taste all around the globe. And while traditional genres such as fado, goumbé, semba, morna, samba, and afoxé are featured, the emphasis is mainly on the contemporary music scenes of these varied regions and the contribution of Lusaphone artists to jazz, world beat, hip-hop, drum 'n' bass, electronica and dance.

world music

Spain

Canal Sur Radio

www.canalsur.es

This station from Andalusia carries many talk shows and sports programs, but it also has some excellent musical programming, particularly:

▸▸ *Riá Pitá* Saturday 0600–0700 and 0730–0800 Greenwich. Andalucian music
▸▸ *Quédate con el Cante* Saturday 2200–2300, Sunday 2100–2200. Flamenco

Radio Nacional de España

www.rtve.es/rne

Radio Exterior de España, a mix of music, including from jazz to Cuban dance music. *Radio 5 Todo Noticias* is all news and information.

Hawaiian and Pacific Islands

Hawaiian Hut

KTUH **ktuh.hawaii.edu**

Sunday 3–6pm Hawaii (Pacific -3, that is, Greenwich -11). You might think that the student station at the University of Hawaii would play a substantial amount of Hawaiian music, but you would be wrong. It's a diverse and free-form station with music from everywhere else on the planet. The one Hawaiian specialty show they do stream is notable for its contemporary cutting edge.

Island Style

KNBA **www.knba.org**

Sunday 9am–noon Alaska. Even for those whose sense of geography has already been thoroughly warped by the Internet, it may seem odd to get Hawaiian music from Alaska. But those who tune into this show once are on the way to becoming regulars.

Kani Ka Pila

KVMR **www.kvmr.org**

Sunday 9–11am Pacific. Host: Michael Keene. Hawaiian music and stories, with lots of slack-key guitar.

Na Mele O Hawaii

KAOS **www.kaosradio.org**

Thursday 10am–noon Pacific. Host: Sherry Bloxam.

Na Mele O Polynesia

KCSN **www.kcsn.org**

Tuesday 7–9pm Pacific. Host: Charles Kiaha. The music of Polynesia: slack-key guitar, cowboy music, Jawaiian, pop, and classic country, Hawaiian style. Also rap from Tonga and the Marshall Islands, jazz and hip-hop from Tahiti, and beyond.

world music

Samoan
2NUR **www.newcastle.edu.au/cwis/ra**

Sunday 1030–1130 Greenwich.

Tropical Rhythms
CHKG **www.fm961.com**

Saturday 9–11am Pacific. Music of Hawaii and the Pacific, also including Cuban and music of First Nations peoples.

Latin America

Brazilian Stations

Arapuan FM
www.arapuanfm.com.br/arapuan

Decidedly upbeat music.

Brazil Cast
www.visaonet.com/brazilcast

This Internet-only station from Uberaba, Brazil has three streams with a variety of popular Brazilian music.

FM O Dia
http://fmodia.ig.com.br/

A broad range of Brazilian music, from Rio de Janeiro.

JB FM
www.jbfm.com.br

Music and information station from Rio. The quality of the music varies greatly. You might hear a saccharine cover of "No Woman No Cry" buried in strings, and you might even hear Eric Clapton's latest, but you might also hear innovative Brazilian guitar. Click on "Agenda JBFM" for schedule of upcoming special events (in Portuguese). (Click on the picture of the headphones to listen.)

Rádio Amazonas
http://amazonasfm.portalamazonia.globo.com

Radio Amazonas has a great variety of specialty shows. Which means that if you don't like what you hear when you tune in, try sampling at another time of day or week. There's a schedule on the website in Portuguese.

Rádio Cidade Tropical
www.internext.com.br/cidade

Brazilian music of all kinds, sandwiched in between lots of talk.

Rádio Educadora
www.educadora.ba.gov.br

A smooth-as-glass mix of Brazilian classics, American pop, even some classical, from the Secretariat of Education in Bahia. Almost too easy to listen to. The program guide on the website will also direct you to a number of specialty shows covering genres such as jazz and blues.

Rádio Marano
www.infohouse.com.br/marano

Intensely commercial station with Brazilian music.

Rádio Morena
www.morena.com.br

Great multi-genre station: blues, jazz, classical, reggae, rock, along with regional and national pop music. (Hint: "Ao Vivo" means "Listen Live" in Portuguese. Click on the American flag to see the Web page in English.)

Rádio Nacional de Brasilia FM
www.radiobras.gov.br

This is the national public radio of Brazil. Its program grid moves from classical to jazz to pop music through the day, but there is a substantial amount of Brazilian content throughout.

Brazilian Programs

Brazilian Fantasy
KUVO www.kuvo.org

Sunday 6–8pm Mountain. Host: Cenir. *Brazilian Fantasy* always opens with "Girl from Ipanema," then explores a wide range of Brazilian music, from Flora Purim to Emilio Santiago, from Leila Pinheirre to Wanda Sa. Cenir, a native of Rio, brings a great radio voice to the program.

Brazilian Style
WMBR wmbr.mit.edu

Sunday noon–2pm Eastern. Host: Marion Catão.

Muito Prazer Brasil
Rádio Universitária
www.proex.ufu.br/links/radio.html

Wednesday 0030–0100 Greenwich. Host: Alexander Heilbuth. This program explores the music of diverse regions of Brazil.

Tudo Bem
WWOZ www.wwoz.org

Saturday 2–4pm Central. Host: Katrina Geenen.

world music

Cuba/Afro-Cuban/Salsa/Latin Jazz

Canto Tropical
KPFK **www.kpfk.org**

Saturday 8–10pm Pacific. Host: Hector Rodriguez.

Clave
CIUT **www.ciut.fm**

Saturday 10–11am Eastern.

Con Sabor
Radio K **www.radiok.net**

The *Con Sabor* stream (available any time) on Mexican station Radio K emphasizes salsa and merengue, frequently material you probably won't hear elsewhere, often intriguing, always hot.

Con Sabor Hispanico
WBRS **www.wbrs.org**

Saturday and Sunday 5–7pm Eastern.

Con Salsa

Hosts: Jose Masso, Peter Martinez and Greg Molina. Syndicated NPR show available on many stations; originates on WBUR **www.wbur.org** on Sunday night/Monday morning at midnight Eastern.

Cuban Connection
A channel on Afropop Worldwide's website: **www.afropop.org/**

(You can listen to it any time.)

Dimension Latina
WLUW **www.wluw.org**

Sunday 2–6pm Central.

Hurukan Caribe
KFAI **www.kfai.org**

Tuesday 1–3pm Central. Host: Marlon Ferrey. Mostly salsa, but you'll also hear some merengue, some cumbia, and possibly an African cut or two.

Jazz Latino
KCLU **www.kclu.org**

Tuesday 8–11:30pm Pacific.

Jazz on the Latin Side
KLON **www.klon.org**

Friday 7–11pm Pacific. Host: Jose Rizo.

Latin Connection

Host: Rae Arroyo. Rae Arroyo has as good an ear as anyone, a great sensibility, and a huge amount of knowledge. You can catch her show on

world music

several stations, for example, KUNV (**kunvjazz91.org**) Saturday noon–3pm Mountain.

Latin Jam
WQNA **www.wqna.org**
Wednesday 10:30pm–midnight Central. Host: Ron Sakolsky.

Latin Jazz Cruise
WBGO **www.wbgo.org**
Saturdays 9pm–midnight Eastern. Host: Awilda Rivera.

Latina del Swing
WGMC **wgmc.greeceny.org**
Saturday 3–6pm Eastern.

Latino Soy
CHKG **www.fm961.com**
Weekdays 11am–1pm Pacific. Host: Eduardo Olivares. This daily treat from a multicultural station in Vancouver, B.C. emphasizes salsa, samba, and merengue.

Radio Cadena
www.cadena3.com.ar
High energy music from Argentina with a hot dance beat.

Radio Mambo
www.mambo.it
This station is entirely devoted to Latin American music. Although their mix contains a touch too much sappy pop, there's also lots of very tasty salsa, interesting cumbia, and innovative Latin jazz. The station's real strength is the many strong specialty programs, including *Cubop*, a stellar program on Latin jazz. (Note that all the announcing, and the website, is in Italian.)

Ritmo Latino
KNBA **www.knba.org**
Sunday 6–7pm Alaska. Host: Zenia Nuez.

Ritmo y Mas
KAOS **www.kaosradio.org**
Wednesday 6–8pm Pacific. Hosts: Marcela Abadi and Jose Valadez. Salsa, merengue, bolero, and, as the program title says, more.

Sabor Latino
WNUR **www.wnur.org**
Sunday 10pm–midnight Central.

world music

Salsa Con Jazz
KUVO www.kuvo.org

Sunday 1–4pm Mountain. Host: Jimmy Trujillo. A great mix of modern and classic salsa, Latin jazz, traditional Afro-Cuban, as well as Puerto Rican music. Host Trujillo is a bass player in a Denver salsa conjunto.

Salsoul
www.salsoul.com

This station from San Juan, Puerto Rico, streams a seemingly infinite supply of tasty music. The following shows are of particular interest. (All times are Eastern.):

▶▶ *Salsa Dorada* Saturday 7–10pm. Hosts: Jimmy Rivera y Marvin Santiago. The "golden oldies" of salsa.

▶▶ *En Clave y Afinque* Sunday 7pm–midnight. Host: Hector Feliciano.

▶▶ *Los Mas Queridos* Tuesday and Thursday 7–8pm. The most requested songs.

▶▶ On Monday, Wednesday, and Friday, the hour from 7–8pm concentrates on the work of a single artist each night. Salsoul runs down the Top Ten Sunday evenings from 5–6pm.

Salsumbo
WVBR www.wvbr.com

Saturday 6–9am Eastern.

Saturday Night Salsa
KCLU www.kclu.org

Saturday 10pm–midnight Pacific.

El Son Caliente
Ampies Broadcasting Corporation (ABC)
www.abcsuriname.com

Tuesday 2130–2300 Greenwich. Host: Liliana Arias. From Suriname. Announcing is in Dutch. Arias also has another program, *Domingo Latino*, Sunday 2030–2100.

Tiene Sabor
WWOZ www.wwoz.org

Saturday 11:30am–2pm Central. Host: Yolanda Estrada. Features very fresh material. "If a record is played on a commercial station, I stop playing it. I want to play something new, something different," says Estrada.

WAEL
www.waelfm96.com

Hot music from Mayaguez, Puerto Rico.

world music

Colombia/Cumbia

Rumba Stereo
www.rcn.com.co

Rumba Stereo is a stream of perky music from Radio Cadena Nacional in Colombia.

Tropicana FM
www.tropicanafm.com

This station from Bogota, Colombia puts out an unending stream of phenomenal Latin dance music.

Univalle Estereo
uv-stereo.univalle.edu.co

From the Universidad del Valle in Meléndez, Colombia, a mix of Latin musical styles self-described as "adult contemporary," favoring the smooth and easily listenable.

La Vallenata
www.lavallenata.com

Absolutely wonderful stream of contemporary music from Colombia. This is your number one source for cumbia.

Mexico

En Alas de la Trova Yucateca
Radio UNAM AM
www.unam.mx/radiounam

Sunday 4–4:30pm Central. Host: Raul Esquivel. An exquisite sampling of trova music from the southeast of Mexico. (Note that Radio UNAM has two streams. This program is on the AM stream.)

El Fonógrafo
radiocentro.com.mx/elfonografo

This station brings you nostalgic Mexican music – gentle ballroom tunes from days gone by. It's a commercial station, with way too low a music-to-noise ratio, but the music is extremely pleasant.

Esta Noche Fiesta
Stereo 97.7 **radiocentro.com.mx/97.7**

Friday and Saturday 9pm–3am Central. Party music.

La Z
radiocentro.com.mx/laz

A variety of popular musical styles, from ranchero to cumbia. (Heavily commercial station.)

world music

Musica Mexicana

KVNF **www.kvnf.org**

Sunday 7–10pm Mountain. Host: Chilo Montes.

Peña Radio

Radio UNAM AM **www.unam.mx/radiounam**

Saturday 3–3:30pm Central. Host: Aída Luna. Folkloric music of Mexico. (Note that Radio UNAM has two streams. This program is on the AM stream.)

Radio K

www.radiok.net

This Mexican station offers several streams, including *Balades in Español*, *Pop Español*, *Rock en Español*, and *Trova,* in addition to their live signal.

Stereo Joya

radiocentro.com.mx/joya93.7

This commercial station plays popular hit music of Mexico, particularly romantic ballads with lush, soft orchestration. The program *In Concierto* (Monday–Saturday 7–8pm Central) concentrates on the music of one artist. *Joyas de Ayer* (Monday–Saturday 8–9pm) remembers the ballads of the 1960s–'90s.

Tango

Cien Años de Tango

Radio UNAM FM
www.unam.mx/radiounam

Sunday 2:30–3:30pm Central. Note that Radio UNAM has two streams. This program is on the AM stream.

Radio Tango

webs.satlink.com/usuarios/f/fm2000

All Tango, all the time.

Tangos y Recuerdos

LT24 **www.lt24online.com.ar**

Weekdays 1530–1700 Greenwich. If you care at all for tango, it's hard to get closer to the source than this without booking travel to Argentina. Also check out *SuperLatino* (Weekdays 1800–2200) and *Siempre A Tiempo* (0330–0900). (But don't be surprised if you're turned away for lack of server capacity.)

Other Latin American Music

This category comprises all the various kinds of Latin American music – from Andean pipes to sentimental ballads accompanied by guitar – which do not fall into one of the above categories. You will also find here stations and programs that combine the various categories.

Other Latin Stations

KQ-105
www.kq105fm.com

Top 40 hit music from Puerto Rico.

Radio Chiriqui
www.chiriqui.com/radiochiriqui

Radio Chiriqui is a commercial station in Panama playing contemporary hit music with complicated, fast rhythms.

Radio Corporation of Nicaragua
www.rc540.com.ni

You can find on Radio Corporation of Nicaragua's stream some music unlike any you will hear elsewhere: village choirs and bands, music of and for campesinos, old time canciones, and more. In addition to the live stream, you can click on *Nuestra Musica* for selections of various musical styles. *Misa Campesina* is mass sung to folk melodies accompanied by guitar.

Radioemisoras Universidad de Santiago de Chile
www.radio.usach.cl

This university station has extensive archives of its musical programming, from folkloric ballet to conjunto to mission music of the thirteenth century.

WYQE (Yunque 93)
www.yunque93.com

Popular music from Puerto Rico. *Domingo de Fiesta* Sunday noon–8pm Eastern. Top 20 countdown Saturday 4–6pm.

Other Latin Programs

Acordeones RPC
RPC Radio www.rpcradio.com

Saturday 9–11am Central. Host: Didia Gallardo. Two hours of accordion music from Panama.

Alegria Latina
CFRU www.uoguelph.ca/~cfru-fm

Friday 8–11pm Eastern. Host: Jose Fernando Mendoza. Spanish show with talk, music, information, interviews and old time music.

world music

Amanecer Jibaro

Radio Puerto Rico
www.radiopr740.com

Weekdays 4–5:30am Eastern. Host: Tito Rivera. The incomparable music of the Puerto Rican countryside.

Buenos Días País

FM Transformacion
www.pringles.com.ar/ fmradio

Weekdays 1000–1100 Greenwich and all day Saturday. Folkloric music program from Argentina.

Tito Rivera

Caminos de Ayer

Radio UNAM AM **www.unam.mx/radiounam**

Sunday noon–2:30pm Central. A collection of vintage popular and traditional music in Spanish, particularly from Mexico. Note that Radio UNAM has two streams. This program is on the AM stream.

De Lo Nuestro

CHKF **www.fm947.com**

Weekdays 3–5pm Mountain. Host: Raul P. San Martin. This is a program in Spanish on a commercial station in Calgary featuring music – primarily folk music – from Latin America, news, and information of particular interest to Alberta's Spanish-speaking population.

Global Village

KUSP **www.kusp.org**

Monday 1–3:30pm Pacific. Hosts: Brett Taylor and Mike Carballo. Global Village is KUSP's afternoon world music show; on Mondays the flavor of the day is Latin.

Hora Latina

WFHB **www.wfhb.org**

Friday 5:30–7:30pm Eastern. Host: Claudio Buchwald.

Horizontes

KUT **www.kut.org**

Friday 1–3:30pm Central. Host: Michael Crockett. Music of Latin America.

Hoy y Siempre

Radio Cadena 3 (LV3, Radio Córdoba)
www.lv3.com.ar

Weekdays 0000–0100 Greenwich. Folk music program from Argentina. The stream for Cadena 3 is just about the strongest of any you'll find coming out of Argentina, so it's worth dropping in on any time, and repays patience. If you wait through just a minute or two of talk, you will probably be rewarded with

world music

some music, and the music is drawn from a wide range of material, from the Argentine equivalent of bubble gum to unsurpassed cumbias.

La Invasora/El Pollivos
KUGS **www.kugs.org**

Sunday 8am–noon Pacific. Every kind of music you can think of that is sung in Spanish.

Onda Nueva
WUSB **www.wusb.org**

Saturday 3–5:30pm Eastern. Host: Felix Palacios. Latin American music from son to salsa, plena, Afro-Antillean, with interviews and live in-studio jams.

Our Latin Thing
KCSB **www.kcsb.org**

Sunday 6–8pm Pacific. Hosts: Ray and Josie Ramos. A variety of Latin music.

Radio Revolución
KCSB **www.kcsb.org**

Sunday 8–10pm Pacific. A variety of Latin music coming from Central and South America as well as Cuba and Puerto Rico.

Solo Latinos
FM Lider **www.mocovi.com.ar/fmlider**

Weekdays 1500–1700 Greenwich. FM Lider, from Argentina, seems to have limited bandwidth; not only the stream but also the website can sometimes be difficult to reach. Most of the time it plays pop hits from around the world. *Solo Latinos* concentrates on the local scene, and it's well worth trying to get.

Surcos Bolivianos
Radio Panamericana Bolivia
www.panamericana-bolivia.com

Weekdays 1815–1930 Greenwich.

Travel Tips for Aztlan
KPFK **www.kpfk.org**

Saturday 10pm–midnight Pacific. Host: Mark Torres. Music of all kinds from the Latin youth culture.

Ventana al Barrio
CKLN **ckln.sac.ryerson.ca**

Friday 7–9pm Eastern. Host: Maria Elena Escobar.

WRTC
www.wrtcfm.com

A different Latin show each weekday evening 6–7:30pm Eastern.

Yuca Stereo
CJSF **www.cjsf.bc.ca**

Friday noon–2pm Pacific. Latin American music and politics.

world music

Middle East

Middle East Station

Radio Méditerranée Internationale   **www.medi1.com**
Sufi and classic Arabian music. The website is in French. Click where it says "musique Soufi, Grands classiques Arabes."

Algeria

Radio Algeria   **www.algerian-radio.dz**
Great station with four streams, each a mix of talk and music. The music is first rate. Channels 1 and 2 are particularly rewarding. Web pages available in Arabic and French. ("Ecouter" means "listen" in French.) Programming is in Arabic.

Egypt

Egyptian Castle   **www.egyptiancastle.com**
An archive of classic programs from Radio Cairo, containing magnificent music.

Radio Cairo   **www.sis.gov.eg**
If you can get to the undependable stream, you will find informational programming in Arabic (English 0740–0840 Greenwich), interspersed with very good music programs, but the archives on *Egyptian Castle* may be your best bet.

Iran

Islamic Republic of Iran Broadcasting (IRIB)   **www.irib.com**
IRIB issues five live streams of informational and cultural programming. In addition, the website is a treasure trove of Persian music. If you just stick to the English version of the site, you'll miss a lot. Don't be afraid to jump into the Farsi pages and click on pictures of musical instruments.

Israel and the Jewish Diaspora

Arutz Sheva
www.israelnationalnews.com
Filed away under "Jukebox" on the Arutz Sheva site is lots of music, from children's holiday songs to Israeli dance sets.

The Israel Hour
WRSU **www.wrsu.org**
Sunday 1–2pm Eastern. An hour of Israeli music and news from the student station at Rutgers University.

L'Chayim
KCSN **www.kcsn.org**
Sunday 10am–noon Pacific. Host: Michael Russ. On this program, Russ, a cantor, plays everything from Ashkenzaic, Yiddish, Ladino, and Modern-American Jewish music to music for children.

Mah Hadash
CFUV **cfuv.uvic.ca**
Sunday 5-6pm Pacific. Hosts: Noam Sturmwind and Daniel Gordon. Music from Jewish people around the world.

Kuwait

FM 103.7
www.fm1037.net
Beautiful, hypnotic music, and lots of it. This website is in Arabic, but the button to push is pretty clear. If you'd prefer an English way there, use **www.q80.net**.

Q80 Main Channel
www.q80.net
The Q80 page lets you select amongst several streams, most of which never seem to provide sound. The Main Channel consistently provides the hauntingly melodious sound of an unaccompanied male voice presumably chanting prayers.

Morocco

Radio Casablanca
www.maroc.net/rc
Click on "Sound Bank" for a dazzling array of music you can listen to any time: rai, the two-stringed sharki, pop, etc. Or check out the live recordings under the heading "In Concert." Or just click on the live feed. You might never leave this site.

world music

Tunis

National Radio of Tunis   **www.radiotunis.com**
Under "Music" on this website is an incredible jukebox.

United Arab Emirates

Emarat FM   **emi.co.ae**
The tuner at the right side of this page allows you to select any one of six streams. On *Emarat FM* is a mix of spoken word and musical programming. *Emirates FM 1* is hit music, *Emirates FM 2* "smooth sounds." The next-to-last one in the list is *Sound of Music*, an all-music channel (**www.emi.co.ae/radio/sof.ram**) that is not to be missed.

Free-Form and Eclectic

At a truly free-form station, you could play the following set list and no one would bat an eye: Hindemith, Frank Zappa, Ralph Stanley, Tuvan throat singing, Thelonius Monk, Meredith Monk, Carl Stone, Radiohead, found sounds, Kate and Anna McGarrigle, Rickie Lee Jones, Wagner.

The number of stations this free-form is limited, and, what is sadder is that on many free-form stations you *could* play this playlist and get away with it, but no one does. The vast

Free-Form Favorites

New Sounds	see p.214
The Nixon Tapes	see p.214
WFMU	see p.212

preponderance of music played on free-form stations is contemporary popular music, albeit of an independent, alternative variety. It's unfortunate that the audience open to free-form radio does not cohere. It breaks off into smaller camps. People who become the most serious about music often become serious about a small subset – jazz, opera, folk – and their passion grows deeper rather than broader – late '40s West Coast hard bop, bel canto coloratura, Old Time fiddle. The bulk of this guide documents specialty shows that feed these interests. While being grateful that these specialty programs are out there, one can nonetheless feel a deeper affection for a radio program without the narrow walls, where the host can (and does) reach further into the distance to pull back something you never would have thought to juxtapose to what you just heard, but once the two are put together, create a third thing, a context that did not exist before, a new space.

According to a history of free-form radio on the website of the outstanding free-form station WFMU, the first free-form show was John Leonard's *Nightsounds* on the Pacifica Foundation's KPFA in Berkeley, soon followed by Bob Fass's *Radio Unnameable* on Pacifica's WBAI in New York. Lorenzo Milam, who founded Seattle's KRAB in 1962, was an influential free-form pioneer. Milam went on to help build several similar, free-form oriented community stations around the country during the '60s. In its heyday in the 1960s, free-form could be found even on commercial radio stations; now it has receded to a few noncommercial stations. Below are some of the best free-form stations available on the Net today. If you listen to the stations and programs below, you will hear a broad range of music, sometimes challeng-

free-form and eclectic

ing, always interesting. If more people listen to free-form radio, appreciate it, support it, and ask for more, perhaps the art form will become more widespread.

Free-Form Stations

CKLN   ckln.sac.ryerson.ca
CKLN regularly wins polls as "The Best Radio Station in Toronto." If you leave it running out of your speakers for a day or two, it is easy to see why. About half the programs on the station are devoted to a genre; the other half are wide open. All are good.

CKUA   www.ckua.org
With more than a dozen transmitters across Alberta, CKUA can be thought of as a community radio station for a very widespread community. For over 75 years it has served as the unifying force of "Wild Rose Country." CKUA has many excellent specialty programs, but for the bulk of the day it streams an easy mix of folk, jazz, pop and world music. The flagship program of the network is *The Listening Room* (Weekdays 9am–noon Mountain, hosted by Cathy Ennis). It often features studio guests. The afternoon programs are similarly diverse and also make for good listening.

KGNU   www.kgnu.org
This Boulder, Colorado station is a great radio station. It has numerous excellent specialty shows and great public affairs programs. But what keeps it high on a radio fan's list of favorites is that the bulk of its schedule is made up of free-form programming. Weekday mornings (9am–noon Mountain), afternoons (1–4pm Mountain) and late night (midnight–6am) is given over to wide-ranging, chewy, tasty music.

KLCC   www.klcc.org
From Lane Community College in Eugene, Oregon. For most of the day, KLCC broadcasts *Fresh Tracks*, which could include anything in the world. All of it interesting. Evenings and weekends have specialty shows, but many of them are wonderfully eclectic as well. One example is Cina Kraft's show *Heartwood Hotel*, which airs Tuesday 7:30–10pm Pacific., and has been doing so since 1988. It wanders widely – and well. A recent playlist includes Cesaria Evora, Chick Corea, and Tom Waits.

KNBA
www.knba.org

See if you can tell by listening to *Commercial-Free Music* (weekdays 11am–5pm Alaska), that KNBA is licensed to Koahnic Broadcast Corporation (KBC) a nonprofit, Alaska Native corporation in Anchorage, Alaska.

KPIG
www.kpig.com

If KPIG is not the last remaining commercial free-form station in America, it's in the running. Broadcasting from Freedom, California (near Santa Cruz), KPIG is the spiritual successor to legendary station KFAT. Its programming is fresh, inventive, and lively, and in addition to the live stream, the website is always loaded with lots of extras, such as concert recordings and additional channels.

Orange
www.orange.or.at

This non-commercial radio from Vienna, Austria streams specialty programs featuring everything from African music to feminist news updates, but the majority of its programming is free-form radio of the best kind.

Radio Campus Lille
www-radio-campus.univ-lille1.fr

This station features many specialty shows on subjects from jazz to French ballads. It also features shows that slip smoothly from Leonard Cohen to Andean flute music.

Radio Centro
www.radiocenter.com.ar

If you drop in at random on this Argentine station, you might hear (in order) an experimental cut with a strong dance bass track, a simple folk song on guitar, "Ain't She Sweet," Donna Summer, some carnivale music, and then a little Delta blues.

WCBN
www.wcbn.org

This station from the University of Michigan in Ann Arbor understands free-form radio. There's jazz programming in the morning, but pretty much the rest of the time the DJs mix jazz, reggae, blues, hip-hop, country, rock together in an intelligent fashion that shows the essential connections between these genres.

WFHB
www.wfhb.org

WFHB is community radio for Bloomington, Indiana. Its free-form format is loose enough to allow a wide range of interests, while still retaining a distinctive sound, one more folk than rock, more country than urban, more world than pop. The 80 most-played CDs of the past weeks are listed on the website to give you an idea. In August of 2001, the most-played CD was Gillian Welch's *Time (The Revelator)*, with Del McCoury close behind, but The Beta Band,

free-form and eclectic

Lo'Jo, Saffire, Brian Eno, and Radiohead were in there too. Good public service programming that is assertive without being strident.

WFMU
www.wfmu.org

WFMU has its share of specialty programs (and they're good specialty programs), but far and away the bulk of its programming is free-form. The program hosts seem to draw from particularly wide musical experiences and an unusually well-stocked music library. Best of all, most of WFMU's programming is archived on the web (usually with playlists as well) so that you can listen to it any time. If you're looking for a place to make your first acquaintance with free-form radio, this is a good one.

WPKN
www.wpkn.org

Much of WPKN's programming is specialty shows. If you tune in at a random hour, you might find a solid roots reggae, vintage blues, or folk music show. And the station has a serious commitment to public affairs programming. But chances are about 50-50 that you might instead hit an eclectic program. And the eclectic programs are truly eclectic, unafraid to follow Brahms with whale sounds with hardanger fiddle.

WREK
http://cyberbuzz.gatech.edu/wrek/

(Note: individual shows all directly available at any time: just click on the program name on the WREK schedule grid.)

Free-Form Programs

The Edge
TNL Radio www.lanka.net/tnl/

Sunday 1500–1900 Greenwich. TNL Radio in Sri Lanka plays primarily alternative and dance music. This program reaches out into opera, poetry, Tom Waits. If you find yourself wanting to hear more of the presenter, a woman identified only as Liana, she also has a less wide-ranging, more upbeat program weekdays 0300–0500. Another show on TNL somewhat like *The Edge* is *Breakfast in Bed*, Sunday 0000–0600.

Eklektikos
KUT www.kut.org

Weekdays 9am–2pm Central (ends at 1pm on Friday). Host: John Aielli. What started as a classical program in the early 1970s has become one of the most truly eclectic shows on radio. Also check out Jeff McCord's *Left of the Dial* Fridays 11pm–4am Central.

Late Junction

BBC Radio 3 www.bbc.co.uk/radio3

Monday–Thursday 2215–0000 Greenwich. Hosts: Fiona Talkington and Verity Sharp. Music from across time, from across the planet.

Make It With Me

HBC www.hbc.com.np

Monday 0615–0715 Greenwich. Host: Binayek Das Shresta. Program in English from Nepal that includes jazz, blues, rock, and hip-hop.

Morning Becomes Eclectic

KCRW www.kcrw.org

Weekdays 9 am–noon Pacific; also archived for later listening. Host: Nic Harcourt. The great popularity of this program from Southern California monster station KCRW helped encourage eclectic programming on radio. *Morning Becomes Eclectic* is not free-form. And it leaves out a lot. You're not likely to hear anything loud, dissonant, or political. But it does cover a great deal of territory, from jazz to pop to world beat. The production values are unsurpassed, and KCRW's location in Southern California makes available an impressive lineup of studio guests. Listening to *Morning Becomes Eclectic* is an easy way to keep up with what's current and trendy. Also of interest are: *Metropolis*, a show with a bit more beat, Weeknights 7–10pm; *Café L.A.*, Sundays noon–2pm, with host Tom Schnabel,

Nic Harcourt

former *Morning Becomes Eclectic* host and the person still most associated with its success, now a record producer, spinning an interesting mix that includes a large dose of world and trance music; and Gary Calamar's theme show *The Open Road*, which could take on Dwight Yoakam, Rick Nelson, or Aimee Mann, Sunday 8–11pm.

free-form and eclectic

Musica Perdida

Radio UNAM **www.unam.mx/radiounam**

Tuesday and Thursday 9:30–10:30pm Central. Hosts: Manuel Zozaya and Javier Platas. This program weaves together music of all types, from all cultures, with the one common characteristic that none of it is listened to very much. (The program title translates as "lost music.") From the Universidad Nacional Autónoma de México.

New Sounds

WNYC **www.wnyc.org**

Every night 11pm–midnight Eastern. Host: John Schaefer. A given program might play variations on a theme, or feature a studio guest, or share recordings made live at this show's concert series. There is enough cutting edge music to justify categorizing this program under the "New Music" heading, but also Ry Cooder, African jazz, Elvis Costello, and music from Mali. Archived on the website for listening any time.

The Nixon Tapes

KPFK **www.kpfk.org**

Saturday 3–5pm Pacific. Host: Tom Nixon. Many people create eclectic mixes of music today, but no one has been doing it longer than Tom Nixon, and no one does it better. A recent playlist included The Missourians, Pilgrim Jubilee Singers, music from Northern Thailand, Caetano Vaeloso, Jo Lemaire, Bad Livers, John Bilezikjian, Salamat, and music from Laos. The program is particularly notable for including material from further back in time than most.

Other Worlds

Australian Broadcasting Corporation Radio National
www.abc.net.au/rn/audio.htm

Archived for listening any time. Host: Brent Clough. This weekly two-hour show could bring you Incan human-sacrifice music played by a woman from Germany, a Jew's Harp from the highlands of Papua New Guinea, an Italian bongo band recorded live in California in 1955, Jamaican space music made in Tokyo, or the sighs and whispers of a group of school children recorded in Helsinki. There is almost always spoken word material as well, which ranges equally widely.

Richardson's Roundup

CBC Radio One **www.cbc.ca**

Weekdays 2:04–4pm Eastern. Host: Bill Richardson. Richardson's music is drawn from all over to fit with the spoken material that makes up most of the roundup: storytellers from across Canada mixed with liberal doses of listeners' letters and calls. What makes this all much more interesting than a description of it sounds is Richardson himself: his voice, his wit, and most of all his expansive spirit.

Sarcastic Fringehead
KCSN **www.kcsn.org**

Saturday 10pm–5am Pacific. The sarcastic fringehead is "a bad-tempered, big-mouthed aggressive fish" found along the California coast, often living in man-made debris. The radio show named for it mixes "punk-rock, ancient chants, oratorio, death-rock, acid-rock, trance-music." Put together by the students of California State University Northridge under the direction of Tony Hanover.

College Stations

In many communities in the United States, the public radio station is licensed to the university. As described elsewhere in this guide, this station often plays classical music all day each weekday, broken only by news reports. Evenings and weekends are given over to specialty shows, mostly syndicated from NPR and PRI. That is *not* what is meant by a college station. At the same university as the public radio station, a license was often granted, usually for an extremely weak signal, for students to have their own radio station, staffed by student volunteers and designed to appeal to students, and listened to only on campus. In fact, the power to most of these stations was, and often still is, so weak that their coverage is described in such terms as "the lower floors of Centennial Towers and the Eastern half of Johnson-McFarlane hall."

What these stations carry can be extremely uneven. With no sponsors to worry about, no program director to satisfy (and sometimes almost no audience to annoy), individual DJs have great latitude to play music that interests them. This can allow self-indulgence – long unfocused talks and narrow, self-absorbed tastes – occasionally seasoned with technical ineptitude. But the freedom can also allow some very hot radio. Insulated from the concerns of a commercial environment, student stations need not make programming decisions based on demographics, market research, or sponsor demands. A programmer with an avid interest in one thin slice of the musical pie can create a show around it unlike anything you can hear anywhere else in the world. College radio stations can also be very hip, right up to the very second in their understanding of what is most alive right *now*.

The schedules of college radio stations can vary frequently as their volunteer hosts come and go, as college terms change. (Some small stations even go off the air entirely during summer break.) When college stations have some fairly well-established specialty programs, they are sometimes referenced elsewhere in this guide. But, as a rule, this guide does not try to map these shifting sands. Schedules are posted on the stations' websites. But what you find there may well not illuminate very much: the name of a person you've never encountered, and perhaps an entertaining program name as witty as that of the neighborhood rock band, but unlikely to let you know very much about what music will be played during the program.

Perhaps the best way to experience college radio stations is to just spin the dial at random. Pick a station, drop in, eavesdrop, and if you like what you hear, hang around for a while; if not, move on down the line. There are scores of these stations. On one of them, a volunteer programmer is doing something that will entertain, educate, challenge, and stimulate you. Over the years, some of one's most memorable listening experiences can be serendipitous encounters with a young person alone in a control booth on the opposite end of the continent, playing music they love passionately.

Although they are included in the list below, many campus stations have also set down roots in their surrounding community.

college stations

These stations include non-students as volunteers, which can create more continuity over longer periods of time, and can help pass along a culture to incoming programmers, creating some of the best radio stations anywhere. This community connection is particularly common in Canadian student stations.

Note: If you find yourself interested in college radio stations, you may also be interested in *The College Music Journal* (CMJ), which has reviews and features of new music and tracks the college radio scene. See **www.cmj.com**.

Favorite College Stations	
CITR	see p.218
CIUT	see p.218
CJSF	see p.219
CKUT	see p.219
ITU Radyosu	see p.233
KALX	see p.220
KVRX	see p.222
Rádio Universidade Marão	see p.233
Student Broadcast Network	see p.230

College Stations of the U.S. and Canada

CFRC
www.queensu.ca/cfrc/

CFRC, from Queen's University in Kingston, Ontario, has been broadcasting for 75 years. It currently streams a wide variety of music. The website has a program guide color coded to make it easy to find: pop/rock, jazz/blues/folk, eclectic, and world beat.

college stations

CFRU

www.uoguelph.ca/~cfru-fm

Robust radio from the University of Guelph in Ontario.

CHMA

www.mta.ca/chma

From Mount Allison University, in New Brunswick, a wide variety of music.

CHMR

www.mun.ca/munsu/chmr

The program grid at this student station from the Memorial University of Newfoundland is arranged in consistent stripes to create some order. The weekday highlights are listed below. (All times are Atlantic.):

➡ 11am–3pm. Spoken Word.

➡ 5–6pm. Jazz and Blues.

➡ 9–10pm. Spoken Word.

➡ 10pm. Rock.

Weekends are all rock except a dance and hip-hop block Saturday 9pm–2am.

CHRW

www.usc.uwo.ca/chrw

From the University of Western Ontario in London, with a variety of music, including numerous multicultural programs and a commendable number of highly eclectic shows.

CHSR

www.unb.ca/chsr

Excellent programming, with particularly good specialty shows on Sunday. From the University of New Brunswick.

CIOI

www.mohawkc.on.ca/msa/cioi

From Mohawk College in Hamilton, Ontario.

CITR

www.ams.ubc.ca/citr

Captivating student station from the University of British Columbia.

CIUT

www.ciut.fm

Toronto is one of the most cosmopolitan cities on earth, and this station from the University of Toronto is appropriately programmed for its environment. CIUT's multiculturalism is not reflected, as at so many Canadian stations, by a weekend block of the Italian hour followed by the Portuguese hour; instead it permeates the hip offerings of the program grid, which comfortably holds an *Opera Zone*, *Dhantal Radio*, *Black Roots Radio*, and *Gaywire*. The programming is arranged into stripes to allow each day to make some predictable sense. (All times Eastern.):

▸▸6–9am. Urban.
▸▸9–10am. Rockish.
▸▸10–11am. Specialty shows.
▸▸11am–3pm. Spoken word.
▸▸3pm–8pm. Folk / World.
▸▸8pm–10pm. Urban.
▸▸10pm–midnight. Rockish.
▸▸midnight–6am. Global Groove Network.

CJAM
venus.uwindsor.ca/cjam

From the University of Windsor, acting as a community radio station for the Windsor/Detroit area, providing a broad variety of music programs.

CJSF
www.cjsf.bc.ca

CJSF, from Simon Fraser University in British Columbia, is more than a student station. It has a paid staff, and its volunteer programmers are drawn from the community as well as the student body. But it has all the liveliness of the best student stations, and a bang-up roster of specialty programming.

CJSW
www.cjsw.com

Absolutely excellent station from The University of Calgary in Alberta, which functions as much as a community station as a student station.

CJUM
www.cjum.com

Most programs on this student station from the University of Manitoba in Winnipeg offer eclectic music. There are also numerous specialty shows, everything from indie rock to bebop to Celtic.

CKDU
is2.dal.ca/~ckdufm

Solid station from Dalhousie University in Halifax, Nova Scotia, with many interesting specialty programs and good multicultural programming.

CKUT
www.ckut.ca

From McGill University, CKUT functions as an excellent community radio station for Montreal. There are numerous community programs (for the Filipino, Korean, Muslim, and Caribbean communities, for example), and a great deal of lively public affairs programming. But there is also music programming worth visiting for: more New Music programming than probably any radio station on earth, blues, bluegrass, quite a bit of Francophone music, no shortage of rock and dance music, and several extremely eclectic shows.

college stations

part two

KALX
kalx.berkeley.edu
Particularly vivacious programming from the University of California, Berkeley. One of the very best college stations.

KAMP
kamp.arizona.edu
From the University of Arizona in Tucson.

KCOU
kcou.mu.org
From the University of Missouri.

KCSB
www.kcsb.org
This station from the University of California at Santa Barbara, which mixes student with community programmers, has scads of fresh programs, covering every musical genre you could think of plus excellent public affairs coverage.

KDVS
www.kdvs.org
This extremely varied station from the University of California at Davis has a convenient color-coded program grid to help you see at a glance whether it's playing punk, blues, techno, or public affairs.

KEPC
www.ppcc.cccoes.edu/dept/kepc/
This station from Pikes Peak Community College, in Colorado Springs, Colorado follows an "Adult Album Alternative" format: Ani DiFranco, Cowboy Junkies, Dave Matthews Band, David Byrne, Delbert McClinton, Black Crowes, Eric Clapton.

KJHK
kjhk.ukans.edu
The student station of the University of Kansas color-codes its program grid to make it easy to find what you're looking for. Most of the grid is coded "new rock music." There are interesting specialty shows on the weekend.

KLPI
www.techrome.latech.edu/tech/orgs/klpi/
From Louisiana Tech University, a fairly mainstream rock station.

KPSU
www.kpsu.org
KPSU, from Portland State University in Oregon, only streams from 5pm to 2am Pacific time. (Its airwave signal is a time-share arrangement with another station.) Although completely student-run, KPSU also serves many of the functions of a community radio station for Portland, with a wider variety of programming than most student stations, from *Philly Kid's Guitar Shop* through the interesting program *Father Issues, Family Issues*, which sometimes features

studio guests discussing aspects of parenting, and sometimes features live music. (Thursday 6–7pm Pacific.)

KRLX
www.krlx.carleton.edu

From Carleton College in Minnesota.

KRUA
www.uaa.alaska.edu/krua

From the University of Alaska Anchorage.

KSDB
wildcatradio.ksu.edu

From Kansas State University, KSDB plays rock in the daytime, hip-hop at night.

KSDT
www.ksdt.org

Extremely varied programming from the University of California at San Diego.

KSHU
www.shsu.edu/~rtf_kshu

"The Kat," streaming from the Dan Rather Communications Building at Sam Houston State University in Huntsville, Texas. A broad mix of music in consistent blocks. Modern rock on weeknights, 6pm–midnight Central. Of particular interest is a program on Wednesday 6–8pm devoted to new music found on MP3.com.

KSLU
www.selu.edu/kslu www.shsu.edu/~rtf_kshu

From Southern Louisiana State University in Hammond, purveyor of syndicated NPR content by day, college rock station by night.

KSUN
www.sonoma.edu/ksun

From Sonoma State University in Rohnert Park, California.

KTUH
ktuh.hawaii.edu

From the University of Hawaii. KTUH has organized its diverse programming into a daily grid, giving its stream much more predictability than most college stations. (Hawaii time is 3 hours earlier than Pacific – that is, Greenwich -11.):

➤➤ midnight–6am. Free-form.
➤➤ 6am–9am. Specialty shows.
➤➤ 9am–noon. Jazz.
➤➤ noon–3pm. Rock.
➤➤ 3pm–6pm. Specialty shows.
➤➤ 6pm–9pm. Jazz and blues.
➤➤ 9pm–midnight. Rock.

Many of the specialty shows are particularly strong.

college stations

KUCI
www.kuci.uci.edu
From the University of California, Irvine. Each volunteer on the station gets a two-hour block in which to do something interesting, and the resulting variety is impressive.

KUOI
kuoi.asui.uidaho.edu
KUOI has been broadcasting from the University of Idaho in Moscow for over 50 years. Currently it streams (via a nice, fat stream) primarily alternative rock, with respectable public affairs programming.

KUOM
www.cee.umn.edu/radiok
This station from the University of Minnesota provides an example of how the Internet has expanded the opportunity for college stations. The broadcast signal goes off the air at sunset, owing to FCC restrictions. But the Internet stream continues round the clock.

KUSF
www.kusf.org
From the University of San Francisco in California. Emphasizes new music and community service.

KUTE
www.kute.org
From the University of Utah.

KVCU
www.colorado.edu/StudentGroups/KVCU
This station from the University of Colorado in Boulder leans heavily to independent music. Favorite bands in 2001 were: Hefner, Belle and Sebastian, Pavement, Autechre, Anticon and Thievery Corporation.

KVRX
www.kvrx.org
Excellent station from the University of Texas, in Austin, streaming a broad range of music.

KVSC
www.kvsc.org
From St. Cloud State University in Minnesota. More a community radio station than just an outlet for students: Good specialty shows, syndicated programs.

KWVA
gladstone.uoregon.edu/~kwva
From the University of Oregon in Eugene.

KXMS
www.kxms.org
From Missouri Southern State College.

college stations

KXUL
www.kxul.com

If you like everything about conventional "Modern Rock" radio except the commercials, you will like this station from The University of Louisiana Monroe.

KZSU
kzsu.stanford.edu

You might imagine that the student station of Stanford might be particularly inventive and interesting. You'd be right.

S@y Radio
csca.senecac.on.ca

The Student Station of Seneca College of Applied Arts and Technology at York, Ontario.

Trent Radio
www.trentu.ca/trentradio

From Trent University in Peterborough, Ontario.

WAMH
www.amherst.edu/~wamh

From Amherst College in Massachusetts, WAMH offers an extremely easy to read color-coded program guide that all other stations should look at.

WCCS
wccs.wheatonma.edu

From Wheaton College, near Boston, Massachusetts.

WCDB
www.albany.edu/~wcdb

From the State University of New York at Albany.

WCLH
www.wclh.net

From Wilkes University in Pennsylvania. Specialty shows can include jazz, classic rock, contemporary and traditional religious music, blues, hip-hop, R&B, classical, world music, gothic, hardcore, death metal, black metal, industrial, heavy metal, doom, reggae, and Americana.

WCWM
www.wm.edu/SO/WCWM

From the College of William and Mary, near Williamsburg, Virginia. In addition to a variety of music, features quite a bit of talk and news.

WDCR
www.dartmouth.edu/~brdcast/

Dartmouth College has two student stations. The FM one acts very much like a commercial rock station. This is the AM one, which carries more of the alternative fare and loose programming you expect from a college station. (At some points of the day, the AM station carries the FM station's programming.)

college stations

WEAA
www.morgan.edu/geninfo/weaa.htm

This unique and very professional station from Morgan State University in Baltimore plays jazz weekdays, with some innovative talk shows 7–9pm Eastern week nights, specialty shows on Saturday, and twelve hours of gospel Sunday.

WFAL
www.wfal.org

Modern rock and metal from Bowling Green State University, in Ohio.

WFDU
www.wfdu.fm

WFDU, from Farleigh Dickinson University in New Jersey, devotes most of its air time to a "Music America" format, primarily acoustic music in traditional forms. Each weekday has a dose of R&B, and there is alternative on the weekends.

WFNP
www.wfnp.org

From the State University of New York, New Paltz, "The Edge" streams a variety of programs: alternative, hip-hop, punk, electronic, Latin, and a little talk.

WGDR
www.goddard.edu/wgdr

WGDR is a community radio station for Plainfield, Vermont, as well as the student station at Goddard College. It is bubbling with energy and has scads of specialty shows that are like the proverbial potato chip: it's hard to stop after just one.

WHFR
whfr.hfcc.net

Classical, blues, hip-hop, progressive, lo-fi, avant-garde, free-form, hardcore, metal, industrial, space rock, and lots of jazz programs on this station from Henry Ford Community College in Dearborn, Michigan.

WHRW
www.whrwfm.org

Pop, folk, jazz, rhythm and blues, hip-hop, reggae, rap, soul, music from the Caribbean, Latin America and the African Diaspora, space music, original radio theater, and more, from Binghamton University in New York. Some programs archived for listening any time.

WHUS
www.whus.org

A sparkling array of original and intriguing specialty shows from this station at the University of Connecticut.

WIIT
www.iit.edu/~wiit

One of the oldest student stations in the U.S., at Illinois Institute of Technology. Many interesting specialty shows.

WIUS
www.indiana.edu/~wius

From the University of Indiana.

WJUL
wjul.cs.uml.edu

From the University of Massachusetts in Lowell. Great mix of specialty shows. Color-coded program guide to make it easier to find the kind of music you're interested in.

WKCR
www.wkcr.org

A mix of seasoned broadcasters and students from Columbia. Jazz and New Music during the day on weekdays, specialty programs at night and during the weekends.

WKDU
www.wkdu.org

From Drexel University in Philadelphia, Pennsylvania.

WKNC
www.wknc.org

From North Carolina State University, in Raleigh. The website has an active forum engaging WKNC listeners and DJs in extended conversations.

WLJS
www.jsu.edu/92j

From Jacksonville State University in Alabama, this station includes lots of NPR programming, a Sunday morning of Christian rock, a Latin Saturday, and a stiff dose of alternative rock.

WMBH
www.colby.edu/wmhb

From Colby College in central Maine. Each two-hour show mines a different genre, which means that WMBH offers much more folk, jazz, bluegrass, and world music than most college stations.

WMBR
wmbr.mit.edu

Captivating station from the Massachusetts Institute of Technology (MIT). Every day's schedule is made up of one intriguing specialty show after another. One could start listing to WMBR and just never stop. Raucous political programs weekdays 6:30–8pm Eastern.

college stations

WMFO

www.wmfo.org

Brims with specialty programs and free-form at its core, staffed as much by community volunteers from Medford, Massachusetts as from students at Tufts University.

WMPG

www.wmpg.org

From the University of Maine at Portland, a station with high production values and a wide variety of programs, from alt-country to hip-hop.

WMTU

www.wmtu.mtu.edu

From Michigan Technological University.

WMUA

www.wmua.org

From the University of Massachusetts, WMUA organizes its shows in a block format, so that you can count on hearing the same kind of program at the same time (Eastern) every day.

➼ 6–9am. Eclectic.
➼ 9am–noon. Jazz.
➼ noon–2:30pm. World.
➼ 2:30–5:30pm. Blues.
➼ 5:30–6pm. Public Affairs.
➼ 6–9pm. Rock.
➼ 9pm–midnight. Urban Contemporary.

Specialty shows on the weekends.

WMUC

wmuc.umd.edu

Vigorous and free programming, leaning heavily to the indie, from the University of Maryland.

WMUL

www.marshall.edu/wmul

This station from Marshall University in West Virginia has a simple program grid. Mornings are jazz, noon to midnight alternative, with heavy metal after midnight and street beat on Friday and Saturday nights.

WMUR

www.marquette.edu/stumedia/wmur

From Marquette University in Milwaukee, Wisconsin. One nice feature is a button on the website to Instant Message the DJ.

WMWM

wmwm.star.net

Primarily progressive/alternative rock station from Salem State College in

college stations

Massachusetts, with specialty shows on the weekend.

WNEC
www.wnec.org

This station from New England College in New Hampshire has particularly good folk music programming.

WNTI
www.wnti.org

From Centenary College, in Hackettstown, New Jersey. An extremely broad and adventurous blend of programming.

WNYU
www.wnyu.edu

From New York University.

WOWL
wowl.fau.edu

From Florida Atlantic University in Boca Raton. A bit more mainstream than most college stations.

WPRK
www.rollins.edu/wprk/

Rollins College, in Winter Park (Orlando), Florida. Much more varied than most student stations, lots of classical, 16 kinds of rock, hip-hop, dance, world, and jazz.

WPTS
www.wpts.pitt.edu

From the University of Pittsburgh.

WQFS
www.guilford.edu/wqfs

From Guilford College in North Carolina. The website includes an archive of guest performances and interviews.

WRBC
www.bates.edu/wrbc

Free-form station from Bates College in Maine has excellent archives that let you listen to any program from the past ten days.

WRCT
www.wrct.org

Free-form radio with lots of variety, from Carnegie Mellon University in Pittsburgh, Pennsylvania. Good public affairs. A noise/ambient program called *Dead Air* every morning; the time varies, but usually 2–9am Eastern.

WRSU
www.wrsu.org

From Rutgers University in New Jersey. Great variety of music. Community shows on Sunday afternoon.

college stations

WRUR
wrur.rochester.edu

Interesting and extremely varied (from experimental music to all-Russian) throughout the week and especially on the weekend. From the University of Rochester in New York.

WRVU
www.wrvu.org

From Vanderbilt University in Nashville, Tennessee, WRVU also operates as an alternative station for non-country Nashville.

WSBF
wsbf.clemson.edu

From Clemson University in South Carolina. The program guide lights up to show you what is on right now. The Web page has a picture (refreshed every few seconds) of the DJ at the controls, a count of how many people are listening, a chance to rate the program, and a graph of others' ratings.

WSHL
www.stonehill.edu/wshl

From Stonehill College in Easton, Massachusetts.

WSIA
wsia.csi.cuny.edu

From the College of Staten Island, part of City University of New York.

WSRN
wsrn.swarthmore.edu

From Swarthmore College in Pennsylvania.

WTMD
saber.towson.edu/wtmd

This station from Towson University in Maryland differs from most college stations in that it is neither free-form nor rock. The program director selects the music, and the music is what program directors call "New Adult Contemporary," a primarily acoustic mix of new age, light pop, contemporary jazz and soft male and female vocals. Sunday offers some specialty programs.

WTPL
wtpl.tusculum.edu

From Tusculum College in Greeneville, Tennessee.

WUNH
www.wunh.org

From the University of New Hampshire Specialty shows from 6pm–midnight Eastern weeknights and most of the weekends, wonderful eclectic programming the rest of the time.

WUSC
wusc.sc.edu

From the University of South Carolina.

WUTK
www.sunsite.utk.edu/newrock

From the University of Tennessee in Knoxville.

WUTM
www.utm.edu/~wutm

From the University of Tennessee at Martin.

WUVT
www.wuvt.vt.edu

An extremely broad spectrum of music, from Virginia Tech.

WVKR
www.wvkr.org

A mixed-format station created by DJs from the Hudson Valley, New York community as well as from Vassar College. Jazz, classical, blues, hip-hop, metal, polka, techno and independent and underground rock.

WVUD
www.wvud.org

Two streams, WVUD and WVUD-2 from the University of Delaware in Newark. Diverse music and complete coverage of University of Delaware sports.

WVUM
www.wvum.org

University of Miami.

WVUR
www.valpo.edu/student/wvur

From Valparaiso University, in northwest Indiana.

WWPI
radio.wpi.edu

From Worcester Polytechnic Institute in Massachusetts.

WXCI
www.wcsu.ctstateu.edu/wxci

Rock station from Western Connecticut State University.

WXDU
www.wxdu.duke.edu/

Duke University, in Durham, North Carolina. Large number of free-form shows, based on a playlist; urban music late nights; jazz weekday evenings 5–8 Eastern.

WXYC
www.wxyc.org

WXYC, from the University of North Carolina, in Chapel Hill, claims to be the first radio station in the world to offer a live Internet simulcast of an airwave signal. The date to beat is November 7, 1994, using Streamworks technology. (Even before the emergence of Streamworks, WXYC was experimenting with delivering its stream via Cu-SeeMe.)

college stations

WYBC

This AM station from Yale University allows each programmer to fill a two-hour block with whatever they choose, and what they choose ranges way beyond the usual college station's currently popular groups. The schedule changes frequently, but if you drop in at any random time you might hit a program of Broadway show tunes, one devoted to folk rock, or two hours of angry metallic sounds of the 1990s.

WZBC

www.bc.edu/bc_org/svp/st_org/wzbc/

Boston College's student station has for fifteen years featured the show *No Commercial Potential* each evening 7pm–1am Eastern. Also many great specialty programs.

College Stations of the United Kingdom

Britain's many universities host a roster of vigorous student radio stations. The programming is primarily alternative, often with a large component of dance music. There are many more student stations in the UK than are listed below, as most stations are still somewhere in the course of finding their way onto the Net. Many have not begun streaming at all, some have experimented for brief periods before having their campus hosts inform them that the bandwidth involved in the experiment was too expensive to continue, and many of those that are currently trying to stream are inaccessible. One can hope that all of these conditions will ameliorate over time and that future editions of this guide will be able to include a longer roster of UK student stations.

Be advised that most UK student stations shut down completely for the summer, and that the summer lasts until October.

Unlike student stations in the rest of the world, student stations in the UK carry commercial advertising. The good news is that they have not succeeded in selling very much of it.

Student Broadcast Network

Most of the student stations of the UK belong to the Student Broadcast Network (SBN). The SBN offers its own stream – **www.sbn.co.uk** – put together from the best shows of its member stations. This stream is definitely the place to begin an exploration of British student station radio. (In turn, many of the member stations stream SBN programming at times, for example, overnight, when their station is not staffed.) On Monday from 1400 to 1600 Greenwich, SBN presents the *UK Student Radio Chart Show*, running down the current favorite music on UK campuses. (Repeated Sunday 1900–2100.) On Tuesday 1400–1500 (repeated Wednesday 1900–2000) is the *CMJ Countdown*, a survey of top hits from college stations in the United States, compiled by the *College Music Journal*.

Bailrigg FM
radio.lancs.ac.uk

From Lancaster University.

Burn FM
www.guild.bham.ac.uk/burnfm

An eclectic mix of music from the University of Birmingham.

CUR
www.cur.co.uk

From Cambridge University.

Demon FM
www.demonfm.com

In addition to an interesting program grid, this station from DeMonfort University has some archives of past programs on the website for listening any time.

Fusion FM
www.fusionradio.uklinux.net

From Glasgow Caledonian University and the University of Strathclyde, Fusion FM sticks a little closer to a playlist than one would choose to see at a student station.

IC Radio
icradio.com

A particularly strong station from Imperial College, London. One strength is a live venue, the Back Room, where DJs spin dance music.

Insanity 1287
http://134.219.88.26/insanity

From Royal Holloway.

Krisp FM
www.krispfm.com

A particularly lively station from Grimsby College.

LCR
www.lborosu.org.uk/lcr

From Loughborough University.

NSR
www.nsrfm.com

From Newcastle University.

Rare FM
www.rarefm.co.uk

From University College London. Good programming, but often seems to have problems with its stream.

Sub-City Radio
www.subcity.org

Particularly eclectic and lively station from Glasgow University.

URB
www.bath.ac.uk/~su9urb

From the University of Bath. On the air 0800–2300 Greenwich, Friday night until 0200.

URN
http://urn.nott.ac.uk/

From the University of Nottingham. Well-designed daily blocks, with quieter music in the morning, alternative rock most of the day, and dance tunes getting more vibrant as the evening progress.

Xpress Radio
www.xpressradio.co.uk

From Cardiff University.

Xtreme Radio
http://xtreme.swan.ac.uk/

From Swansea University.

College Stations of the World

Many of the stations scattered through the World Music section of this guide are college stations distinguished by the fact that their music is from, say, France. Below are some college stations that you might have a hard time telling do not originate from Upstate New York until the announcer comes on and begins speaking in, say, Dutch.

ITU Radyosu
http://radio.itu.edu.tr

This station from the Istanbul Technical University in Turkey streams a variety of programming: classical, rock, and ethnic. The website is available in English.

95B
Monday 0900–1100 Greenwich. From the University of Auckland, in New Zealand. A mix of popular music styles, including lots of dance music. Funny station promos either trying to be like, or mocking, commercial stations' style.

Rádio Universidade Marão
www.rumarao.pt
You could think you're listening to your favorite hip college station, until the announcer comes on and starts talking in Portuguese.

URGent
http://urgent.rug.ac.be
From the University of Ghent in Belgium. Good archives.

High School Stations

KEOM
www.keom.fm
This community station from the Mesquite Independent School District in Texas produces a fair amount of public service programming, but devotes the majority of its airtime to oldies.

KNHC
www.c895fm.com
Operated by students at Nathan Hale High School in Seattle, Washington, KNHC streams current soul hits, heating up to a strong dance beat in the evenings.

WBER
wber.monroe.edu
Alternative rock.

WBFH
www.wbfh.fm
Rock of all kinds from the Bloomfield Hills School District in Michigan.

WMPH
www.wmph.org
Dance station from Mount Pleasant High School in Delaware.

WQNA
www.wqna.org
From the Capital Area Career Center in Springfield, Illinois, WQNA has a few programs put together by students, but mostly offers a wide variety of specialty shows – blues, folk, 70s rock, ska, country, funk – produced by adult volunteers.

college stations

Foreign Language

Stations listed in this section are of primary interest to those wanting to practice listening to languages other than English. There is considerable crossover with two other sections of this book: *World Music*, which also contains many programs and stations broadcasting in languages other than English, but which emphasizes music, and *Ethnic Communities*, which also contains foreign-language shows, but primarily emphasizes news and features of interest to ethnic communities. So *World Music* is the first place to look for Italian music, *Ethnic Communities* is the first place to look for finding Italian-American events in Portland, Oregon, and this section is the first place to look for practicing your Italian listening skills.

Multilingual

It is sometimes of value, particularly when just trying to learn a language, to have access to the same information in more than one language. The international services of the great national broadcasting establishments, such as the BBC and Radio France, are invaluable in this regard. These services also sometimes supply streams in languages which are simply very hard to find elsewhere. Below are some of the largest multilingual resources.

Foreign Language Favorites

BBC World Service	see p.235
Deutsche Welle	see p.236
Eyou Dipajimoon	see p.242
National Radio of Tunis	see p.239
Nuntii Latini	see p.249
Radio Nederland	see p.242
Radio Österreich International	see p.245
Voice of Tibet	see p.256

All India Radio
air.kode.net

AIR has radio dramas archived for listening any time in several languages: Bengali, Gujarati, Hindi, Kannad, Malayam, Marathi, and Tamil.

BBC World Service
www.bbc.co.uk

Just as it is hard to imagine any dictionary ever rivaling the *Oxford English Dictionary*, it is hard to imagine anyone else on earth ever putting together a broadcast organization as impressive as the BBC. One respect in which this is true is its multilingual service, available in 43 languages: most languages have not only the basic news and analysis, but also several other streams of information, usually including sports. Languages: Albanian, Arabic, Azerbaijani, Bengali, Bulgarian, Burmese, Caribbean English, Chinese, Croatian, Czech, French, Greek, Hausa, Hindi, Hungarian, Indonesian, Kazakh, Kinyarwanda, Kirundi, Kyrgyz, Macedonian, Nepali, Pashto, Persian, Polish, Portuguese (two dialects), Romanian, Russian, Serbian, Sinhala, Slovene, Slovak, Somali, Spanish, Swahili, Tamil, Thai, Turkish, Ukrainian, Urdu, Uzbek, and Vietnamese.

CBC Radio Mackenzie
www.north.cbc.ca

CBC Radio Mackenzie serves the cultural variety of Canada's vast Northwest Territories with programming in six languages: Chipewyan, Dogrib, Gwich'in, Inuvialuktun, North and South Slavey. For a sample, tune in Saturday 5–6pm Eastern for a summary of the week's news in all six languages. (Click on the Yellowknife stream.)

foreign language

Channel Africa
www.channelafrica.org

Archived news in Chinyanja, English, French, Portuguese, Silozi, and Swahili.

Deutsche Welle
www.dwelle.de

The national broadcasting service of Germany offers news and a variety of on-demand audio in 29 languages: Albanian, Amharic, Arabic, Bengali, Bosnian, Bulgarian, Chinese, Croatian, Dari, English, French, Greek, Hausa, Hindi, Indonesian, Kiswahili, Macedonian, Pashto, Persian, Polish, Portuguese (two dialects), Romanian, Russian, Sanskrit, Serbian, Spanish, Turkish, Ukrainian, and Urdu.

Islamic Republic of Iran Broadcasting (IRIB) World Service
www.irib.com/worldservice

IRIB's World Service streams news and cultural information languages: Albanian, Arabic, Bangla, Bosnian, Chinese, English, French, German, Hindi, Hausa, Italian, Japanese, Kurdish, Melayu, Pashto, Russian, Spanish, Swahili, Turkish, and Urdu. There are also extensive multilingual archives containing the Qu'ran and other Islamic resources.

Kazak Radio
www.radio.kz

Programming in Azerbaijani, English, German, Kazakh, Korean, Russian, Tatar, Turkish, and Uygur. Thin stream.

Oli
oli.mediacorpradio.com

Singapore station Oli tries to reach Singapore's population of Indian ancestry. It broadcasts in six languages: Bengali, Hindi, Malayam, Punjabi, Tamil, and Telegu.

Radio Australia
www.abc.net.au/ra

This service of the Australian Broadcasting Corporation offers Asia-Pacific news in English, Tok Pisin, Indonesian, Chinese, Khmer, and Vietnamese.

Radio France Internationale
www.rfi.fr

Radio France Internationale is available in 19 languages: Albanian, Arabic, Bulgarian, Cambodian, Chinese, Creole, Croatian, English, German, Laotian, Persian, Polish, Portuguese, Romanian, Russian, Serbian, Spanish, Turkish, and Vietnamese.

Radio Free Europe
www.rferl.org

On the website of Radio Free Europe are archives of news programs in many languages: Albanian, Arabic, Armenian, Azerbaijani, Belarusian, Bosnian,

Bulgarian, Croatian, Czech, Estonian, Georgian, Kazakh, Kyrgyz, Latvian, Lithuanian, Moldovian, Persian, Romanian, Russian, Serbian, Slovak, Tajik, Tatar, Turkish, Ukrainian, and Uzbek. Some websites are in English, some in the native language, but even the native language pages say "On Demand Audio" and "Listen Now."

Radio Japan International
www.nhk.or.jp/rj

At the Radio Japan site you can listen to a short news program any time in the following languages: Arabic, Bengali, Burmese, Chinese, English, Farsi, French, German, Hindi, Indonesian, Italian, Japanese, Korean, Malay, Portuguese, Russian, Spanish, Swahili, Swedish, Thai, Urdu, and Vietnamese. The site also offers Japanese lessons for speakers of many of these languages.

Radio Taipei International–Central Broadcasting System
www.cbs.org.tw

Archived news and live streams in Arabic, Burmese, Chinese, English, German, Japanese, Korean, Russian, Spanish, Thai, and Vietnamese.

SBS Radio
www.sbs.com.au

SBS Radio was established in 1975 by the Commonwealth Government of Australia to "provide multilingual and multicultural radio and television services that inform, educate and entertain all Australians and, in doing so, reflect Australia's multicultural society." It broadcasts in 68 languages. Each language has its own website, and each has an extensive archive of programming in that language, available for listening any time. The languages include: Albanian, Armenian, Assyrian, Belarusian, Bengali, Bosnian, Bulgarian, Burmese, Cantonese, Cook Islands Maori, Croatian, Czech, Danish, Dari, Dutch, Estonian, Fijian, Filipino, French, German, Greek, Gujarati, Hebrew, Hindi, Hungarian, Indonesian, Gaelic, Italian, Japanese, Khmer, Korean, Kurdish, Macedonian, Maltese, Mandarin, Norwegian, Farsi, Polish, Portuguese, Punjabi, Russian, Samoan, Serbian, Slovene, Spanish, Swedish, Thai, Tongan, Turkish, Ukrainian, Urdu, Vietnamese, and Yiddish.

United Nations Radio
www.un.org/av/radio

One underutilized resource for those interested in languages is United Nations Radio. The UN Radio site is particularly valuable because, while the great imperial world services shape their programs differently for different audiences, the UN streams are as identical as the translators can make them. The languages other than English are: Arabic, Chinese, French, Spanish, and Russian. The website has audio material produced in other languages as well.

foreign language

Voice of America
www.voa.gov/divisin.cfm
The Voice of America website contains archives of short news broadcasts in many languages: Afan Oromo, Albanian, Amharic, Arabic, Armenian, Azerbaijani, Bangla, Bosnian, Bulgarian, Burmese, Chinese, Creole, Croatian, Czech, Dari, Estonian, Farsi, French, Georgian, Greek, Hausa, Hindi, Hungarian, Indonesian, Khmer, Kinyarwanda, Kirundi, Korean, Kurdish, Laotian, Latvian, Lithuanian, Macedonian, Pashto, Polish, Portuguese (two flavors), Romanian, Russian, Serbian, Slovak, Slovene, Spanish, Swahili, Thai, Tibetan, Tigrinya, Turkish, Ukrainian, Urdu, Uzbek, and Vietnamese.

Afrikaans

OFM
www.ofm.co.za

Amharic

Ethiopian Telecommunications Corporation
www.telecom.net.et/sunset.htm
This site has the live stream of Radio Ethiopia, which you probably won't be able to get to, and several archived programs which you will.

Arabic

Arabic Broadcasting System
www.absradio.com.au
This station is a service for the Arabic-speaking community of Australia. The website is in English.

Emarat FM
emi.co.ae
From the United Arab Emirates. From this website, you can also access several other streams. The top one, *Abu Dhabi Radio*, is primarily spoken word programming. The bottom one, *Alqu'ran Alkarim*, is for the Qu'ran.

foreign language

King Abdulaziz City for Science and Technology
www.kacst.edu.sa

On-demand reading of the Qu'ran.

National Radio of Tunis
www.radiotunis.com

Live stream and many recorded documentaries in Arabic.

Lily of the Valley
CHKF www.fm947.com

Thursday 7–7:30pm Mountain. This unique show is an outreach program of Christian churches in Alberta to the Arabic-speaking population there, featuring interviews, drama, and Middle-Eastern Christian songs.

OutLoud
home.birzeit.edu/outloud/

Students at Birzeit University in Palestine supposedly produce a half-hour Internet-only radio stream called *Outloud*, but during the time this guide was in preparation, the stream could not be accessed successfully.

Radio Cairo
www.sis.gov.eg

Radio Cairo carries news and information programming in Arabic from 0700 to 2100 Greenwich daily, but the stream is erratic.

Radio Kuwait
www.radiokuwait.org

Archived news updated twice daily.

Radio Méditerranée Internationale
www.medi1.com

The website is in French; programming is half French and half Arabic. Extensive archives.

Armenian

Armenia
WJUL wjul.cs.uml.edu

Sunday 11am–1pm Eastern.

Cyprus Broadcasting Corporation
www.cybc.com.cy/

Radio 2 has programs in Armenian from 1400–1500 Greenwich.

foreign language

Bosnian

Radio Mostar www.rtvmo.ba/rtvmo

Bulgarian

Bulgarian National Radio www.nationalradio.bg
Has several streams as well as extensive archives of news and information programs, including Radio Horizont and Radio Bulgaria. This is the English website.

Burmese

Democratic Voice
of Burma www.communique.no/dvb
This site in Norway archives the transmissions of the Democratic Voice of Burma. Primarily public affairs programming (in Burmese), they also include quite a bit of music. They are organized on the website for listening any time.

Radio Free Burma www.fast.net.au/rfb/
Via an archive in Australia, this stream provides dissenting voices from Burma.

Cambodian

Voice of the Cambodian Children WJUL wjul.cs.uml.edu
Friday 9am–noon Eastern.

Chinese

Broadcasting Corporation www.bcc.com.tw
of China (BCC)
Four channels from Taiwan: news, sports, and two music channels.

China National Radio 1

www.cnradio.com

Extensive archives of informational programming.

CHKF

www.fm947.com

This primarily Chinese-language station in Calgary offers Cantonese programming weekdays 7am–3pm Mountain and 9pm–5am. There is Mandarin on Saturday 7–10am.

CHKG

www.fm961.com

This Vancouver, B.C. station streams in Mandarin Monday through Saturday 3pm–midnight Pacific, and Cantonese throughout Sunday.

Chongging Commercial Radio

http://203.93.111.169/cqbs.ram

Mostly panel discussion programs.

Fairchild Radio Toronto

www.fairchildradio.com

Cantonese programming every day noon–8pm Eastern on the AM stream of this commercial station in Toronto, essentially all the time on the FM stream.

MediaCorp Radio

www.mediacorpradio.com

The MediaCorp website from Singapore streams three commercial stations in Chinese.

Public Radio System

www.prs.gov.tw

The Taiwanese Public Radio System delivers three streams on which you can find a variety of music and public service broadcasting, plus various archived snippets. All announcing is in Chinese, as is the website.

Radio Taipei International– Central Broadcasting System

www.cbs.org.tw

On-demand news and two live streams. Included on the live streams are several levels of Chinese lessons.

Radio Television Hong Kong (RTHK)

www.rthk.org.hk

RTHK offers six continuous streams, three of which are in Chinese, with amazingly deep archives.

foreign language

Cree

Eyou Dipajimoon
Noon–1pm Eastern.

CBC Nord Quebec **north.cbc.ca**

Croatian

Hrvatska Radio
Seven streams, with a variety of programming, plus archives.

www.hrt.hr/streams/index.html

Danish

Radio Danmark
Many archived news broadcasts.

www.dr.dk/rdk

Dutch

Ampies Broadcasting
Corporation
This station from Paramaribo, Suriname streams a mix of music and news. The daily news program is archived on the website for listening any time.

www.abcsuriname.com

Radio Apintie
From Suriname.

www.apintie.sr

Radio Nederland
Web information and stream are translated into several languages, so you can check your Dutch against the professional English translation. Radio Nederland produces many in-depth documentary programs archived in a "Sound Library" for listening any time.

www.rnw.nl

Radio Vlaanderen Internationaal
Radio Vlaanderen Internationaal is the international radio station of VRT, the

www.rvi.be

public broadcaster of the Flemish Community in Belgium. The station usually streams news and public affairs programming in Dutch daily (website available in English).

Esperanto

Radio Österreich International · roi.orf.at
This information service from Austria has web pages, streams, and on-demand in five languages, one of which is Esperanto.

Estonian

Eesti Raadio Vikerraadio · er.ee/eng/viker
Information, lifestyle programs, and Estonian music, from the national radio of Estonia.

Farsi

Islamic Republic News Agency (IRNA) Radio · www.irna.com/en/radio
The website includes a collection of speeches and entertainment programs available any time.

Krifarsi · www.radio-international.org
Talk radio from Tehran.

Persian · Fairchild Radio Toronto www.fairchildradio.com
Weekdays 9–10pm and Sunday 8–10pm Eastern. Music and information of interest to Toronto's Iranian community, in Farsi.

Finnish

Soitellaan
CFUV **cfuv.uvic.ca**

Saturday 9:30–11am Pacific. Host: Pirkko Kiansten. Features news, interviews, and poems in Finnish, along with Finnish music ranging from folk and classical to pop.

YLE
www.yle.fi

Finland's national radio service offers several streams of news and information in Finnish. There is also a set of audio courses for learning Finnish.

French

Africa 1
www.africa1.com

From Gabon, Africa 1 has a wealth of public affairs programming weekdays.

Cap Acadie
www.capacadie.com/capradio

Two streams of radio from Acadia, divided along age lines, both offering primarily music programming for Francophone Canadians.

Radio Campus Paris
www.radiocampusparis.org

A wealth of news and cultural programs, many archived for listening any time.

Radio Canada Première Chaîne
radio-canada.ca

Francophone Radio Canada offers two streams. The *Chaîne Culturelle* is primarily devoted to classical music. The *Première Chaîne* is a feast of talk: news, commentary, discussion, and particularly strong literary and cultural programming. (Becomes musical in the evenings.)

Radio France Internationale
www.rfi.fr

Extensive archives.

Radio Méditerranée Internationale
www.medi1.com

The website is in French; programming is half French and half Arabic. Extensive archives. Check out the program *Écrivans du Monde Francophone*.

Gaelic

BBC Radio Nan Gaidheal   **www.bbc.co.uk/scotland/alba**

German

Deutsche Welle   **www.dwelle.de**
The national broadcasting service of Germany offers deep archives. Pull down
the drop-down box on the main page, and you might not come out for years.
There is also a series of 26 audio lessons in German.

Orang   **www.orang.orang.org**
Excellent sampler of tons of German audio material.

Radio Österreich International   **roi.orf.at**
In-depth information service from the international service of Austria's national
broadcast system ORF, with many magazine format programs. There is an on-
demand feature that lets you hear news updates any time. Website information
available in five languages, including English.

Radio Steiermark   **steiermark.orf.at/stmk/on_demand/index.h**
Radio Steiermark, from ORF, the national public radio of Austria, has an
extensive collection of archives for listening any time.

Greek

CHIR   **www.chir.com**
Greek radio station from Toronto.

Cyprus Broadcasting Corporation   **www.cybc.com**
In addition to two stations that broadcast in Greek (Channels 1 and 3), this site
offers 105 Greek lessons by radio.

ERT   **http://ert.ntua.gr**
Five channels of news, music, folklore, tourist information, sports, etc.

foreign language

Icelandic

Ríkisútvarpid (RUV) Channel 2   **www.ruv.is**
The National Broadcasting Service of Iceland's Channel 2 mixes pop music and public affairs programming.

Inuktitut

CBC Radio Nunavut   **www.cbc.ca**
Throughout the day, CBC Radio Nunavut serves its listeners news, information and features in both English and Inuktitut. The program *Sinnaksautit* (Weekdays 10:30pm Eastern) is devoted to traditional Inuktitut storytelling.

Hebrew

Arutz Sheva   **www.israelnationalnews.com**
News and extensive audio archives in Hebrew and English (also Russian and French). There is also a daily news broadcast in "Easy Hebrew."

Israel Broadcasting Authority   **www.iba.org.il**
This official network, usually referred to as Kol Israel, ("Voice of Israel"), offers several stations: *Reshet Bet*, *Reshet Gimmel*, and *Reshet Dalet*, as well as an on-demand service. If you don't read Hebrew, the site is pretty hard to navigate. An unofficial guide through the network in English is available at **israelradio.org**.

Hindi

All India Radio   **air.kode.net**
AIR has several programs of news in Hindi, as well as numerous radio dramas, archived for listening any time.

Hungarian

Radio Budapest
www.wrn.org

Radio Budapest has several programs of news in Hungarian available on demand.

Indonesian

Radio Salvatore
www.radiosalvatore.co.id/

This commercial station carries a mix of music and informational programming in Indonesian.

Radio Surabaya
scfm.surabaya.indo.net.id

Commercial station with a mix of programming that emphasizes talk shows.

Italian

Radi-O-Espresso
CHKF www.fm947.com

Thursday 11:30am–1pm Mountain. Hosts: Giovanni Longhi, Mariangela Serpico. Music, news, sports, current affairs and interviews about and by Calgary's Italian Canadian community. Thirty minutes of the program hosted by Father Valentino of Our Lady of Grace Church.

Voice of Italy
WMSE www.wmse.org

Sunday 3–6pm Central – but the website has several weeks of archives you can listen to any time.

Japanese

Radio Japan International
www.nhk.or.jp/rj

Live and archived news.

Radio Tampa

Talk station with extensive archives.

www.tampa.co.jp

Kazakh

Kazak Radio

www.radio.kz

This station from the Republic of Kazakhstan offers a wide spectrum of programming in several languages, including Kazakh. The website is available in English. The stream, on the other hand, is often unavailable in any language.

Korean

Korean Broadcasting System (KBS)

www.kbs.co.kr

Unlike Radio Korea International (see below), this is a live stream of a radio signal, or, actually, several (all in Korean):

➡ KBS FM 1 – Classical music
➡ KBS FM 2 – Popular music
➡ KBS 1 – Culture, economy, news and information
➡ KBS 2 – Variety of formats, with a great deal of talk

Kyung-A Channel

http://www2d.biglobe.ne.jp/~kmlabs/k_chane.html

This is a site from Japan (in English) with links to two dozen Korean radio stations.

Radio Korea International

http://rki.kbs.co.kr/

RKI has a very well-developed Web presence, projected in ten languages, including English and Korean. Almost all the features are "on-demand" rather than time-streamed. That is, if you're interested in news, you need not wait for a news program, you can click on a headline and hear the story any time. Similarly, *Music Trap*, the section on Korean pop has a Top 10 list you can listen to any time, and an audio show on news in Korean pop (again, all in ten languages). You can also get breaking news, in Korean or the other nine languages, on your WAP-enabled cell phone.

Latin

Nuntii Latini
www.yle.fi/fbc/latini/summary.html

Nuntii Latini – "News in Latin" – is a weekly review of world news in classical Latin, produced by YLE, the Finnish Broadcasting Company.

Lithuanian

Dainos Aidas
WGMC **http://wgmc.greeceny.org/**

Sunday 9–9:30am Eastern. Lithuanian music and community news, in Lithuanian.

Lithuanian Radio
www.lrtv.lt/en_lr.htm

The English website will help you find the programming you want on this national network station from Vilnius. Lithuanian Radio broadcasts three channels, but only offers one – the news and information channel – on the Net.

Malay

MediaCorp Radio
www.mediacorpradio.com

From the MediaCorp website in Singapore you can access two commercial stations – Warna and Ria – that broadcast Malay.

Radio Malaysia Johor
www.rtmjb.net.my

News and a variety of talk shows.

Radio Singapore International
www.rsi.com.sg

Radio Singapore International streams informational programming in English, Malay, and Chinese.

foreign language

Nepali

HBC
www.hbc.com.np

A variety of programming from Kathmandu, Nepal, mostly in Nepali, with some English: market news, documentaries on Nepal's cultural diversity, and quite a bit on the subject of meditation.

Radio Nepal
www.catmando.com/news/
radio-nepal/radionp.htm

Archived news in Nepali.

Norwegian

NRK Alltid Nyheter
http://www3.nrk.no/alltidnyheter

Public non-stop news channel.

Oromo

Sagalee Oromiyaa
KFAI www.kfai.org

Sunday 8–9pm Central. A program of news, music, culture, and practical information of use to the Oromo people in Minnesota. The program is in the Oromo language, the most widely spoken language in the Horn of Africa.

Pijin

News in Solomon Island Pijin
Radio New Zealand
www.rnzi.com

Monday 2015–2030 Greenwich.

Polish

Polsaa Fala
CHKF **www.fm947.com**

Thursday 7–8pm Mountain. Host: Marek Domaradzki. News about the Polish community in Calgary; coming attractions addressed to members of the Polish community; Polish songs, melodies, poetry; interviews with famous Polish people; and cultural and political news service from Poland.

Portuguese

Asas de Portugal
CFRU **www.uoguelph.ca/~cfru-fm**

Sunday 7–9pm Eastern. Host: Jeronimo Mendez. Music, news, information, sports and more in Portuguese.

Noticiário Nacional
Rádio Nova de Cabo Verde
www.cabonet.cv

Thirty-nine minute news program archived on the website for listening any time.

Portuguese
WJUL **wjul.cs.uml.edu**

Sunday 9–11am Eastern.

Radio Jornal
www2.opopular.com.br

The Jaime Câmara organization in Brazil has four radio stations all accessible from this page: Executive, Araguaia, Anhanguera, and Jornal. All stream extensive news coverage in Portuguese.

Rádio Nacional de Brasilia AM
www.radiobras.gov.br

The national public radio of Brazil, which has its musical programming over on the FM band, carries a variety of news and talk programs here.

Rádio Universitária
www.proex.ufu.br/links/radio.html

A variety of educational and cultural programming from the Universidade Federal de Uberlandia in Brazil, including sports, ecology, market reports, human interest, and agricultural advice.

Rede Itatiaia
www.itatiaia.com.br

You can access multiple Itatiaia stations from Brazil here. Radio Extra, from the capital, has a particularly deep lineup of news and public affairs programs.

foreign language

part two

Punjabi

Punjabi
Fairchild Radio Toronto **www.fairchildradio.com**
Weekdays 10–11am Eastern. Music and informational programming in Punjabi
daily on this commercial station from Toronto.

Romanian

Radio Romania International
www.rr.ro
This is an International Service, so Channel 1 is devoted to languages other
than Romanian, but Channel 2 is Romanian all the time. There is a program
schedule on the website; essentially two hours of news alternates with the one-
hour Radio Romania International program of news, commentaries, features,
and cultural background on Romania.

Russian

Eesti Raadio Raadio 4
er.ee/eng/r4
This is the Russian language stream from the national radio of Estonia.

Sami

Sami Radio
www.yle.fi/samiradio
News and information in Sami, from YLE, the national radio of Finland.

Spanish

Colorín ColorRadio
www.colorincolorradio.com
For students at an early stage in their acquisition of Spanish, this Colombian
children's station could provide an easier introduction than some of the incredibly
fast-talking news announcers found on the other stations listed in this section.

foreign language

Domingo Especial
KUNV http://kunvjazz91.org/

Sunday 6–8am Mountain. Host: Marcelo Alcocer. International programming in Spanish.

El Espectador
www.espectador.com

Commercial news radio from Uruguay.

FM Transformacion
www.pringles.com.ar/fmradio

This station from Argentina streams public affairs programs weekdays 1100–1700 Greenwich.

Opine FM
www.opinefm.com

Informational programming from Costa Rica.

Radio Chilena
www.radiochilena.com

All-news station from Chile, with the top news stories available on the website for listening any time.

Radio Chiriqui
http://www.chiriqui.com/radiochiriqui/programacion.html

Weekends feature musical programs; weekdays are almost entirely devoted to informational programming. (From Panama.)

Radio Columbia
www.columbia.co.cr

Strong stream in multiple formats bringing news and sports from Costa Rica.

Radio Continental
www.continental.com.ar

Several current news stories from this Buenos Aires station are archived on the website for on-demand listening.

Radio Corporation of Nicaragua
www.rc540.com.ni

News and entertainment programming, live and archived. *The Archives of Pedro Madrigal* is a collection of tales you can listen to any time.

Radio Mitre
www.radiomitre.com.ar

News for the world, in Spanish, from Argentina.

Radio Monumental
www.monumental.co.cr

A variety of programming from Costa Rica, including news, sports, public affairs debate, and humor. There is a program grid on the website.

foreign language

Radio Panamericana Bolivia

www.panamericana-bolivia.com

News, sports, and music programming from Bolivia.

Radio Primero del Marzo

www.780am.com.py

Public affairs discussion programming from Paraguay.

Radio UNAM

www.unam.mx/radiounam

From the Universidad Nacional Autónoma de México, an extensive archive of lectures on subjects from cervical cancer to safety on local transport to the rights of indigenous groups, in addition to two live streams with a wide variety of informative programs.

RPP

www.rpp.com.pe

News and talk shows from Peru.

La Súper Kadena

www.spiderlink.net/superkadena

Informational programming designed to serve the population of Puerto Rico.

Union Radio

www.unionradio.com.ve

News radio from Venezuela.

Viva FM

www.vivacaracol.com/

The Caracol group in Colombia offers several excellent radio stations to the world, with great sound and consistent bandwidth. Their station Viva provides an educated mix of news and cultural programs.

Swedish

Sveriges Radio

www.sr.se

In addition to its several live streams, the national radio service of Sweden has a large archive containing news, sports, business, humor, and informational programming.

Swedish Radio Theatre in Finland

www.yle.fi/radioteatern/english/index.htm

Features the science fiction adventure *Particularly Primitive Ones* by Petri Salin, "probably the very first radio play written and produced expressly for the Internet," available on the Net since May 22, 1996.

YLE
www.yle.fi

Finland's national radio service offers several streams of news, information, and music in Swedish.

Tagalog

Bagong Pagasa
CJSW **www.cjsw.com**

Sunday 9:30–10am Mountain. Host: Lydia Viloria. Music, current news from the Philippines, movies, and community information.

Buhay Pilipino
CHKF **www.fm947.com**

Sunday 6–7pm Mountain. Current events in the Philippines; culture, traditions and family solidarity; music, drama, entertainment; and information of particular interest to Filipinos in Calgary. In Tagalog and English.

Tamil

Canadian Tamil Radio
www.ctbc.com

Oli
www.mediacorpradio.com/oli/

Broadcasting from Singapore, Oli also has an archive of past documentary programs on the website.

Tamil
Fairchild Radio Toronto **www.fairchildradio.com**

Daily midnight–6am Eastern. Music and information of interest to Toronto's Tamil-speaking community.

Thai

Sunshine Radio
www.sunshineradio.co.th

Two streams of news and information programming from Thailand.

foreign language

Tibetan

Voice of Tibet   **www.vot.org**
Every day Voice of Tibet broadcasts a 30-minute news service in the Tibetan language followed by fifteen minutes of news in Chinese. The programs are produced by Tibetan journalists stationed in several countries, with the main editorial office in India. Programs, divided into two parts, news of the day and a feature story, follow developments inside Tibet closely as well as the activities of exile institutions. There are several weeks' programs archived on the website.

Tongan

News in Tongan   Radio New Zealand **www.rnzi.com**
Sunday–Thursday 1940–1955 Greenwich.

Tongan   2NUR **www.newcastle.edu.au/cwis/ra**
Friday 0900–1000 Greenwich.

Turkish

Cyprus Broadcasting Corporation   **www.cybc.com.cy/**
Radio 2 has programs in Turkish most of the day (0300–1400 Greenwich).

The Turkish Language Show   WGMC
wgmc.greeceny.org

Saturday 11am–noon Eastern.

Ukrainian

Radio Ukraine   KFAI **www.kfai.org**
Thursday 8–8:30pm Central, archived for listening any time.

The Ukrainian Radio Show
CHKF www.fm947.com

Weekdays 6:45–7pm Mountain. Hosts: Halya Wilson, Slavko Chabrowsky. A program in Ukrainian on a commercial station in Calgary that offers community highlights, activities and interviews; music and information.

Urdu

Radio Pakistan
www.radio.gov.pk/urdu.html

This website of the Pakistan Broadcasting Corporation has news bulletins in Urdu you can play any time, as well as transcripts and news in English.

Vietnamese

Windy City Weekly Magazine
WLUW www.wluw.org

Sunday 9–10am Central. A one-hour program of news, interviews, and cultural reports in Vietnamese.

Welsh

BBC Radio Cymru
www.bbc.co.uk/cymru

Yiddish

The Yiddish Hour
WBRS www.wbrs.org

Sunday 11am–noon Eastern.

Yiddish Yiddish
Radio Judaïca www.judaica.be

Friday 1300–1400 Greenwich.

foreign language

News and Commentary

For a quick update on world news, an excellent source is one of the world services listed in this guide under the Multilingual section. Almost all of these sites have their most current summary of world news archived on a website for listening any time.

Simply because it is so very easy to become insular, and so difficult to see one's own filters, biases and preconceptions, it can be a particularly useful and broadening exercise to get one's news from another part of the world for an extended stretch of time. One need not even go so far as to try to see the world through the eyes of Islamic Republic of Iran Broadcasting; simply observing it from Australia for a while can give Northerners a fresh perspective. Since the world news in summary is fairly easily locatable, the listings below are selected primarily for offering fresh viewpoints.

All India Radio   air.kode.net
AIR has its English broadcasts archived for listening any time.

As It Happens   CBC Radio One **www.cbc.ca**
Weekdays 6:30–7:30pm Eastern. Hosts: Mary Lou Finlay and Barbara Budd. Listeners become hooked on this news and interview program, praising not only its choice of subjects and depth of coverage but also its guest list. Archives are available on the CBC website, about a day after the broadcast.

News and Commentary Favorites

Australian Broadcasting Corporation   www.abc.net.au

ABC has 15 stations online with a variety of local, national, and international coverage (as well as music and entertainment). Among the most interesting to a North American are two shows on Radio Australia – *Pacific Beat,* an excellent news magazine, and *Asia Pacific,* probably the best coverage you can get of Asia in English. ABC's Radio National service archives most of its most popular programs for listening any time, including its incisive and scrupulously researched documentary series *Background Briefings*.

Background Briefing   KPFK www.kpfk.org

Monday 3–4pm, Sunday 11am–noon Pacific. Host: Ian Masters.

Free Speech Radio News

Host: Verna Avery-Brown. Journalists on strike from the Pacifica Network News, led by Brown, an anchor with PNN for twelve years, present independent reporting from across the country and around the world. Available on several stations, for example KDVS (**www.kdvs.org**) weekdays 4:30–5pm Pacific. Archives available at **www.fsm.org**.

Latin American Journal   KCSB www.kcsb.org

Thursday 7–8pm Pacific. Hosts: Corey Dubin and Marcus Lopez.

Making Contact

A half-hour show produced by The National Radio Project which features voices and perspectives too infrequently heard in the media in an effort "to focus on the human realities of politics, the connections between local and global events, and creative possibilities for people to engage in hopeful democratic change." For example, for a recent show on women's health NRP correspondent Erica Bridgeman brought together Belma Gonzalez, Center for Collaborative Planning Women's Health Leadership, Sharon Levin of the National Women's Law Center, Diane Williams of the Native American Health Center, Ellen Leopold of the Women's Community Cancer Project, and Joy

Stephanie Welch/Making Contact

Moore of the Food Systems Project. Probably because The National Radio Project offers the show free of charge, it is heard on over 100 stations. See the list – with a schedule – on the NRP website: **www.radioproject.org**. The most current show, in MP3 format, is there as well.

Pacifica Network News   **www.pacifica.org**

Nightly half-hour broadcast available any time from the Pacifica website. In addition to owning the licenses for Berkeley station KPFA, KPFK in Los Angeles, KFPT in Houston, WBAI in New York, and WPFW in Washington, D.C, Pacifica acts as a national syndicate providing broadcasting, particularly this program, to many small community radio stations across America. In many communities it has long functioned as the only non-corporate news available. Pacifica and this news program have been devastated by a series of conflicts that raged through the 1990s and reached the flash point at the end of the millennium. At the heart of the controversy were two desires of Pacifica's national board: to increase listenership of the stations, and to

news and commentary

consolidate its power over them. As part of the latter, it removed the local stations' representatives from the board and appointed new station management. When this involved removing long-time and much-respected leaders, station employees and volunteers protested. Protesters in turn were fired. When programmers mentioned the conflict on the air, their programs were censored or canceled. (Even outside programs mentioning the conflict were censored.) At the same time, the new management was imposing program changes, which involved canceling programs that in some cases had run for years and whose audience was fiercely loyal. The program changes also had some of the flavor of an ideological purge, with political and community programming the first to be cut. Boycotts started. Donations to the stations dropped precipitously. The whole affair was conducted as badly as possible, with management of this famously progressive institution hiring union-busting lawyers and Pinkerton thugs, with the owners of these famously community-based stations discussing which community's frequency would be sold off against their will. Volunteers were hauled away from microphones screaming, stations boarded up and taken off the air. Streets filled with protest. More and more long-time programmers resigned their posts in protests, starting alternative institutions, including *Free Speech Radio News* (see p.259). Unfortunately, this uneasy situation still stands today. The institution of Pacifica and all of its stations have been severely damaged, and the quality of programming is much lower than it has been in years. Essentially everyone on the staff of *Pacifica Network News* has resigned or been fired. Many of the Pacifica Network's premier shows are shells of their former selves. All the parties involved are thoroughly polarized, and it is unclear how, or whether, Pacifica will ever recover.

Radio Nederland   www.rnw.nl
An excellent source of world news and in-depth current affairs documentaries, archived in a "Sound Library" for listening on demand any time. Web information and stream are translated into several languages, one of which is English.

Radio New Zealand   www.rnzi.co.nz and www.rnzi.com
and Radio New Zealand International
Several news and sports programs, a few of which are **archived for listening any time**.

Radio Österreich International   roi.orf.at
This service from Austria is a good source of European news in English (as well

news and commentary

as four other languages). There is an on-demand feature that lets you hear news updates any time.

Radio Television Hong Kong (RTHK) Radio 3

www.rthk.org.hk

RTHK offers four continuous streams. Radio 3 offers news and public affairs in English. Everything is archived on the website, so you can listen to it any time.

Third World News Review

KCSB **www.kcsb.org**

Tuesday 7–8pm Pacific.

Voice of Barbados

www.nationnews.com

News from the Caribbean.

A World in Your Ear

BBC Radio 4 **www.bbc.co.uk/radio4**

Sunday 2000–2030 Greenwich. Host: Emily Buchanan. This is an interesting sampler stitched together from English-language radio programs from around the world.

Underground

Clandestine Radio

www.clandestineradio.com

This site is a rich find for anyone interested in original source information from the participants in conflicts around the world. Clandestine Radio, as defined here, is usually the audio voice of an insurgent movement, broadcasting anti-government propaganda, guerrilla warfare news, and calls to revolution. The site has a deep archive containing, for example, five different partisan streams that came out of Afghanistan in the 1990s (as well as the last broadcast from the Taliban radio station as it was being bombed by Allied forces), live radio originating in the Falkland Islands in 1982, Radio Free Russia from the 1970s and white Southern secessionists from the United States. There are also links to currently active streams, for example, two (one rebel-controlled) from the Congo, the Voice of the Malayan Revolution, and Tamil Radio from Sri Lanka.

Interval Signals

www.intervalsignals.com

A collection of all kinds of radio snippets from around the world, including a large assortment of clandestine radio.

Public Affairs Discussion

The Commonwealth Club
KQED **www.kqed.org**

Saturday 2–3pm Pacific. The Commonwealth Club is a public affairs forum in San Francisco which among its other activities invites speakers to address contemporary issues; these speeches are then broadcast on KQED.

The Connection
WBUR **www.wbur.org**

Weekdays 10am–noon. Host: Dick Gordon. Each of two one-hour segments features a panel put together to discuss an issue which is not necessarily taken from today's headlines. (One recent show centered on Freemasonry the first hour, Eudora Welty the second.) Listeners can call in, as well as continuing the discussion in online forums at **www.theconnection.org**. Syndicated on NPR.

The Diane Rehm Show
WAMU **www.wamu.org**

Weekdays 10am–noon Eastern. Each morning, Rehm convenes a panel of distinguished guests (WAMU's studios are in Washington, D.C.) to discuss a single current event. The format allows for more depth than most programs, and the selection of guests usually generates more light than heat. Best of all, the program is archived on the website, so that you don't necessarily have to catch it during its live hours. The second hour of most programs features the author of a current book. Syndicated on NPR.

From Our Own Correspondent
BBC Radio 4

www.bbc.co.uk/radio4

Saturday 1130–1200 Greenwich; also archived. Host: Kate Adie. BBC correspondents around the world reflect on current events.

Me and Mario
WAMC **www.wamc.org**

Thursday 8:30–9pm Eastern, archived for listening any time. A weekly discussion of government, public policy, and America today, between former New York Governor Mario Cuomo and Dr. Alan Chartock.

Dr Alan Chartock and Mario Cuomo

news and commentary

Peace Waves
WLUW **www.wluw.org**

Friday 9–10am Central. Interviews, panels, and music addressing issues of peace.

To the Best of Our Knowledge
Wisconsin Public Radio
www.wpr.org

Sunday 9–11am Central. Host: Jim Flemming. Two hours of interviews with guests, often going more deeply into ideas than many radio programs. Syndicated on PRI.

United Nations Radio
www.un.org/av/radio

The United Nations produces several syndicated programs, in six different languages. In addition to special events, the UN offers:

▸▸ *Perspective* – an overview of human rights and development issues.

▸▸ *Scope* – recent issues addressed bridging the digital divide in developing nations, telecommunications for rural villages, and "The Cultural and Spiritual Values of Biodiversity."

▸▸ *Women* – covering global women's issues.

▸▸ Archives available for listening any time on the UN website.

WLUW
www.wluw.org

WLUW describes itself as a community-oriented, pro-social radio station, committed to the Jesuit philosophy of ethical action, and its schedule is full of community affairs programs (as well as excellent music). Among them: *Contact* Sunday 7–7:30am Central, a weekly Jesuit series which "builds bridges among those who struggle for a better life."

World of Ideas
WBUR **www.wbur.org**

Sunday 9–10pm Eastern. Host: Ted O'Brien. One-hour show, often featuring Boston University faculty, discussing issues such as current events, national and international politics, and public affairs.

Environment

Costing the Earth
BBC Radio 4 **www.bbc.co.uk/radio4**

Thursday 0900–0930 Greenwich. A documentary series examining humans' effect on the environment.

news and commentary

The Environment Show

Saturday 6–7am Eastern. Host: Peter A.A. Berle. Each week, Berle (former president of the Audubon Society) speaks with environmental activists and government decision makers about current issues. Archived on the website for listening any time.

Food Not Lawns

KUGS **www.kugs.org**

Monday 6–8pm Pacific. Talk show discussing current environmental issues.

Living on Earth

Host: Steve Curwood. A weekly, one-hour NPR program airing news, features, interviews and commentary on a broad range of ecological issues. You can listen to it any time at **www.loe.org**.

The Ocean Report

A one-minute update on the state of the seas. You can listen to the archives any time at **www.seaweb.org**.

Radio High Country News

www.hcn.org/radio

Host: Betsy Marston. *High Country News* is a newspaper devoted to news primarily of interest to those who care about the Mountain West of the United

Greg Hanscom (left) / Radio High Country News

news and commentary

265

States. Although actively environmentalist, *High Country News* is strongly differentiated from the likes of *Sierra* by being imbued with a lived sense of what existence is actually like in small communities of the West. This offers a perspective perhaps less polemical, probably more pragmatic, and definitely more deeply informed about the particularly local. *Radio High Country News* is a weekly half-hour radio show, produced out of Paonia, Colorado station KVNF, and widely syndicated. The program begins with a news broadcast from around the region, then proceeds into several thematically related interviews. Most shows are rounded out by short Op-Ed pieces read by the writer. Particularly amusing is the feature "Heard around the West," a collection of quirky news bits. You can listen to the show any time from the *High Country News* website.

Law

Justice Talking   www.justicetalking.org
Host: Margot Adler. Weekly, one-hour NPR show on issues currently before American courts. Each program is based on a pending lawsuit that raises substantial questions of constitutional law. Invited advocates argue the issues and take questions from Adler and from the live audience. You can listen to the archives any time.

The Law Show   WAMC www.wamc.org
Monday 8:30–9pm Eastern. Hosts: Jim Horne and Thomas H. Sponsler. Hosts and distinguished guests discuss new developments in the laws of the land. Archived on the website for listening any time.

Media

CounterSpin
Weekly show produced by Fairness and Accuracy in Reporting (FAIR). Syndicated widely; see list at **www.fair.org/counterspin/stations.html**.

The Media Project   WAMC www.wamc.org
Monday 3–3:30pm Eastern, archived for listening any time. Examines media coverage of current news stories.

news and commentary

The Media Report

Australian Broadcasting Corporation Radio National **www.abc.net.au/rn/audio.htm**
Archived for listening any time. Host: Mick O'Regan. The weekly half-hour program takes a critical look at the latest developments in the communications industry, including media ownership, industry regulation and new technology.

Media Talk

Wisconsin Public Radio **www.wpr.org**
Friday 5–6pm Central. Host: Dave Berkman.

On the Media

NPR show syndicated on many stations, for example WBUR **www.wbur.org**
Sunday 2–3pm Eastern.

Progressive

Alternative Radio

Host: David Barsamian. A weekly, one-hour program. Each program is usually devoted to an interview with a progressive thinker such as Edward Said, Bill McKibben, Peter Dale Scott, Michael Parenti, Barbara Ehrenreich, or Howard Zinn. And some you might not have expected, such as Ruben Blades. See the website (**www.alternativeradio.org**) for more information. The program is offered free to any radio station that will carry it. You can catch it any time on WREK (**www.wrek.org**).

Anti-Globalization Radio

CFRU **www.uoguelph.ca/~cfru-fm**
Monday 7–9pm Eastern. Weekly program produced by students at the University of Guelph in Ontario.

Between the Lines

WPKN **www.wpkn.org**
Tuesday 5:30–6pm Eastern, rebroadcast other times, and available any time from the WPKN website. Since 1991, this syndicated, half-hour program has offered a platform for individuals and spokespersons from progressive organizations generally ignored or marginalized by the mainstream media. Each program begins with a five-minute summary of some of the week's under-reported news stories gathered from the alternative press. This summary is followed by three five-minute interview segments.

news and commentary

part two

Culture of Protest
KCSB www.kcsb.org

Thursday 6–7pm Pacific. Host: Dick Flacks. Music and commentary on social struggle – past and present, local and global.

Democracy Now
KPFKwww.kpfk.org

Weekdays 6–7am Pacific, rebroadcast 9–10am. Host: Amy Goodman. *Democracy Now* offers daily commentary on the daily news, emphasizing stories the mainstream media usually does not even cover, such as a recent story about CBS's *Late Show with David Letterman* show canceling the appearance of singer/songwriter Ani DiFranco after DiFranco refused to substitute a more "upbeat" song for one about white fear and racism. The program is available any time at **www.democracynow.org**.

Grassroots
KCSB www.kcsb.org

Tuesday 8–9am Pacific. News, interviews and commentary on activism for social and environmental justice.

Guerrilla Radio
CFUV cfuv.uvic.ca

Monday 5–6pm Pacific. Host: Chris Cook. Social justice program from Victoria, British Columbia, usually with two invited guests each week.

Hightower Radio

Host: Jim Hightower. A daily two-minute dose of anti-fat-cat outrage and humor from the (sometimes almost too) folksy former Texas Commissioner of Agriculture. Available any time at Hightower's website (**www.junction-city.com/hightower**).

International Connection
CKLN ckln.sac.ryerson.ca

Sunday 9:30–10:30am Eastern. Host: Greg Duffell.

No Censorship Radio
WMBR wmbr.mit.edu

Friday 6:30–8pm Eastern.

No U-Turn Radio
WMFO www.wmfo.org

Thursday 8–9am Eastern. Host: Martin Voelker.

RadioNation
www.radionation.org

Available for listening any time. Host: Marc Cooper. Weekly, one-hour program. Each program consists of several segments, most consisting of an essay or speech by a progressive thinker. Particularly good are the ones by Harold

news and commentary

Meyerson, longtime *L.A. Weekly* editor, now Executive Editor of *The American Prospect*. A spin-off of the venerable progressive magazine *The Nation*, first produced on Los Angeles Pacifica station KPFK, now heard on more than 130 stations.

TUC Radio

Host: Maria Gilardin. Produced from Gilardin's loft in San Francisco's Mission District, TUC radio focuses issues such as "The Global Financial Casino," "The Hollow City," "Women of the '60s," and "Reclaiming Native American History," with the ongoing theme being globalization. Many programs are devoted to the ideas of a single person, recently Peter Dale Scott, Mike Davis, Lawrence Ferlinghetti, Ralph Nader, and Alexander Cockburn. Others are impressively detailed research documentaries. TUC stands for "Time of Useful Consciousness," a term from aviation, describing the amount of time a pilot has left, after experiencing oxygen deficiency, before he or she loses consciousness. "That's the time we're in right now," says Gilardin. The program is self-syndicated on several stations. You can catch it on KGNU **www.kgnu.org** Friday 4–4:30pm Mountain.

WebActive   **www.webactive.com**

A resource for progressive audio, including Jim Hightower, *Oyate Ta Olowan*, *Mom-bo*, *Democracy Now*, *Pacifica Network News*, *Free Speech Radio News*, *RadioNation*, and *The Environmental News Network*, all available any time.

Word of Mouth   CKLN **ckln.sac.ryerson.ca**

Weeknights 7–8pm Eastern. Long-running political program from Toronto. Each night of the week includes its own standing features. For example, Monday night features a report on the international anti-fascist movement, Wednesday a report on Ireland.

Right Wing

Almost all commercial media around the world present staunchly conservative viewpoints on the news. It should not surprise that huge corporations present positions that favor the interests of huge corporations. But it is impressive how successful they are creating an entire worldview, a complete and coherent closed system that encourages individuals to identify with the interests of huge corporations, to define freedom is primarily as freedom of capital, prosperity primarily as profitability for owners, to laugh off any alternative constructions as ridiculous radicalism. One does not need a list of particular conservative news and opinion programs: just tune in to the largest commercial stations. Listed below are stations and programs that go beyond the commercial consensus to present more individual viewpoints from the right.

American Freedom Network

www.americanewsnet.com/radio.htm

Round the clock roster of hour-long programs on faith, freedom, and health.

Beverly LaHaye Today

www.oneplace.com/Ministries/Beverly_LaHaye_Today

Daily, half-hour program sponsored by Concerned Women for America; current program and archives available from the website.

Family News in Focus

www.family.org/cforum/fnif

Daily radio news broadcast sponsored by James Dobson's huge Colorado Springs ministry, Focus on the Family, broadcast by more than 1500 stations in the U.S. You can listen any time from the website.

The Michael Savage Show

KSFO **www.ksfo560.com**

Weekdays 4–7pm Pacific. This passionate and articulate "compassionate conservative" is currently very popular in Northern California.

The Rush Limbaugh Show

www.rushlimbaugh.com

Weekdays noon–3pm Eastern. The current episode of this daily, three-hour call-in program is available live on the website; listening to archives requires registration.

Washington Watch

www.frc.org

Host: Janet Parshall. Daily program sponsored by the Family Research Council. Today's program and archives going way back are available for listening any time from the FRC website. Also available in Spanish.

Conspiracy

Art Bell
www.artbell.com

Weekdays 10pm–3am Pacific. The extremely popular Art Bell, whose late night program is carried on over 500 radio stations, is willing to listen to almost any hypothesis about the paranormal, alien encounters, and *X-Files*-like government conspiracies. But his guests also include hardcore theoretical physicists such as Michio Kaku. Recent shows included "actual recorded voices of ghosts," the Chandler Wobble in geology, remote viewing, interdisciplinary approaches to parapsychology, and the Center for the Study of Extraterrestrial Intelligence. The past 30 days of programming is archived on the website for listening any time.

For the Record
Found on several stations, including WFMU
www.wfmu.org

Monday 6–7pm Eastern. WFMU also has an archive of prior shows that you can listen to any time. Host: Dave Emory. Dave Emory is the king of conspiracy radio, reeling through detail after detail in a huge web of connections.

Arts and Culture

Art Talk
KCRW **www.kcrw.org**

Tuesday 3:55–4pm Pacific; archived for listening any time. Host: Edward Goldman. This little snippet of a show, five minutes in its entirety, is a quick update on the Los Angeles art scene.

Arts and Culture Favorites

Arts Today
Australian Broadcasting Corporation Radio National
www.abc.net.au/rn/audio.htm

Archived for listening any time. Host: Michael Cathcart. A daily arts and culture program specializing in literature, publishing, performance, theatre, visual arts, film, popular culture, and architecture. Includes commentary and opinion pieces.

Artzone
Lyric FM **www.lyricfm.ie**

Sunday 1900–2000 Greenwich. Host: Aedin Gormley. Cultural comment and key happenings from the arts world.

The Culture Bunker
95B **www.95bfm.com**

Saturday 2200–0000 Greenwich. Hosts: Peter McLennan and Adrienne Rikihana. Magazine-format show with theater reviews, film reviews, music, books, and the arts, from the University of Auckland, in New Zealand.

Desert Island Discs
BBC Radio 4 **www.bbc.co.uk/radio4**

Sunday 1115–1200 Greenwich, repeated Friday at 0900. Host: Sue Lawley. The format of this program was created in 1942. Each week, a guest is invited to choose eight records they would take to a desert island. The guest also gets to choose a book and an inanimate, impractical object. The discussion of the choices can lead to wider discussion of aesthetics and values.

Fresh Air
WHYY **www.whyy.org**

Weekdays 3–4pm Eastern. Host: Terry Gross. A magazine-format show on contemporary arts and issues, known for interviews with interesting guests from show biz or letters. You can listen to the current show any time at **http://freshair.npr.org/**.

arts and culture

Front Row
BBC Radio 4 **www.bbc.co.uk/radio4**

Friday 1915–1945 Greenwich. Host: John Wilson. Art interviews, news, and discussion of current books.

Saturday Review
BBC Radio 4 **www.bbc.co.uk/radio4**

Saturday 1900–1945 Greenwich. Host: Tom Morris. Morris and his guests review the week's cultural events.

Studio 360
WNYC **www.wnyc.org**

Saturday 10–11am Eastern. Host: Kurt Andersen. Weekly, one-hour program on arts and culture. The program begins with commentary by Andersen, a novelist, then goes into a sequence of regular features, such as "Design for the Real World," in which designers discuss why things are made as they are, or "How Art Works." You can listen to archived programs any time on the WNYC website.

Kurt Andersen

Books

A Good Read
BBC Radio 4 **www.bbc.co.uk/radio4**

Tuesday 1630–1700 Greenwich, repeated Sunday 1300, and accessible any time in the "Listen Again" section. Host: Louise Doughty. Guests discuss their favorite books.

Australia Talks Books
Australian Broadcasting Corporation Radio National **www.abc.net.au/rn/audio.htm**

Monthly program available on the website for listening on demand.

arts and culture

Booklet

Tuesday 8–8:30pm Pacific. Host: Jacquie Hunt. Reviews, interviews and readings.

Books and Writing

Australian Broadcasting Corporation Radio National **www.abc.net.au/rn/audio.htm**

Archived for listening any time. Host: Ramona Koval. Novelists, poets, biographers and critics from Australia and the world, discussing letters and ideas.

The Book Feature

702 **www.702.co.za**

Thursday 15:45–1600 Greenwich. Host: Kate Turkington. Turkington reviews a book each week.

The Book Report

Syndicated Canadian program featuring interviews with authors. You can hear it on CJSF **www.cjsf.bc.ca.** Tuesday 5–6pm Pacific.

The Book Show

WAMC **www.wamc.org**

Tuesday 3–3:30pm Eastern, archived for listening any time. Host: Gretchen Holbrook Gerzina. Interviews with authors.

Bookworm

WNYC **www.wnyc.org**

Sunday 4:30–5pm Eastern. Host: Michael Silverblatt. Each week the program invites a prominent novelist or poet to talk about a current book.

From the Bookshelf

KUSP **www.kusp.org**

Sunday 9–9:30pm Pacific. Host: Billie Harris.

Literary Discord

WPKN **www.wpkn.org**

Fourth Thursday noon–12:30pm Eastern. Host: Hans Konig. A program about book publishing.

Loose Leaf Book Company

WBGO **www.wbgo.org**

Monday 6:30–7pm Eastern. This program discusses children's literature for an audience of adults.

Open Book

BBC Radio 4 **www.bbc.co.uk/radio4**

Sunday 1600–1630 Greenwich. Host: Charlie Lee-Potter. Conversations with authors.

arts and culture

Charlie Lee-Potter

Open Books WLUW
www.wluw.org
Second and Fourth Sundays of the month 9–10pm Central. Host: Donna Seaman of the American Library Association.

Radiogram KUSP
www.kusp.org
Monday noon–1pm Pacific. Host: Eric Schoeck.

Shakespeare Lectures BBC Radio 3
www.bbc.co.uk/radio3
A series of lectures on Shakespeare by writers such as Germaine Greer is available on the website for listening any time. (There are also transcripts.)

What's the Word WBGO
www.wbgo.org
Wednesday 6:30–7pm Eastern. Host: Sally Placksin. A weekly, half-hour program about language and letters, taking on topics such as "Shakespeare in Performance," and "Famous First Sentences." Supported by the Modern Language Association, which archives past programs at **www.mla.org**.

Writers and Company CBC Radio One www.cbc.ca
Sunday 3–4pm Eastern. Host: Eleanor Wachtel.

arts and culture

275

Science Fiction

Destiny: The Voice of Science Fiction
WUSB
www.wusb.org

Saturday 11:30pm–midnight Eastern. Host: Howard Margolin. On the air for 20 years, this program features convention news and an audio book sampler.

Hi Sci-Fi
CJSF **www.cjsf.bc.ca**

Friday 5–6pm Pacific.

Hour 25
www.hour25online.com

Host: Warren W. James. Since 1972, when it was started by Mike Hodel, this program has brought listeners news from the world of science fiction. Often features interviews with authors. Great follow-up links for more information.

Shockwave
KFAI **www.kfai.org**

Saturday 3:30–4pm Central. Host: David E. Romm. Also includes quite a bit of science fact.

Poetry

Art Aloud
KGNU **www.kgnu.org**

Monday 8–9pm Mountain. Poetry, literature, drama and other spoken works, live and taped.

Fine Lines
BBC Radio 4 **www.bbc.co.uk/radio4**

An occasional series, Sundays 1630–1700 Greenwich. Host: Christopher Cook. Two guest poets read from their own work and the work of those they admire, then a conversation ensues.

HCC Southwest Radio
swc2.hccs.cc.tx.us/iradio

Although HCC Southwest Radio offers a wide variety of music and news programming, its heart is in English literature. It may be the only radio station started and run by an English professor. Douglas Rowlett, of Southwest Houston Community College has built an Internet radio station in his English department office. HCC Southwest Radio offers a mix of poetry readings, lectures, and readings. Rowlett encourages students to prepare radio programs as class projects, and offers air time to others in the department, including creative writing classes. Recent programs include:

▸▸ A tribute to poet Anne Sexton
▸▸ Literary Big Sur: A Celebration
▸▸ The Poetry of Langston Hughes and Adrienne Rich
▸▸ The Insider's Guide to Childhood, with Tricia DeGraff and her fifth grade creative writing class

Douglas Rowlett

Inspiration House

KPFK **www.kpfk.org**

Monday 10–11pm Pacific. Host: Peter Harris. Poets read live to recorded music background.

Poetry at the Pub

2NUR **www.newcastle.edu.au/cwis/ra**

Sunday 0800–0900 Greenwich. *Poetry at the Pub* gathers a majority of its material from local poetry readings at the Northern Star Hotel in Newcastle, New South Wales, Australia.

arts and culture

Poetry Please

BBC Radio 4 **www.bbc.co.uk/radio4**

Sunday 1630–1700 Greenwich (repeated Saturday at 2330). Host: Frank Delaney. This is a request show. Delaney selects from listeners' requests. Poems are read by well-known actors and poets.

Poetry Proms

BBC Radio 3 **www.bbc.co.uk/radio3**

During breaks of musical concerts Tuesday evenings, late July through mid-September. Each year the BBC hosts "The Proms," an impressive concert series. Interspersed throughout the Proms are "Poetry Proms," readings by top-flight British poets. In addition to appearing in the live stream, selected poems are available on the BBC web page for listening any time.

The Poetry Show

KUSP **www.kusp.org**

Sunday 8–9pm Pacific. Hosts: Morton Marcus, Dennis Morton, and Kim Nelson.

Radio Poets Society

KVMR **www.kvmr.org**

Monday 7–8pm Pacific. Host: Jenessa Peterson. Call-in poetry.

Why Poetry?

KPFK **www.kpfk.org**

Friday 2–2:30pm Pacific. Host: Paul Lieber. Mostly talk with poets about their work and lives.

Wordslingers

WLUW **www.wluw.org**

First and Third Sundays 9–10pm Central. Host: Michael C. Watson.

Write On Radio

KFAI **www.kfai.org**

Thursday 11am–noon Central. Hosts: Lynette Reini-Grandell and Julie Nyquist. Readings, recordings, interviews, and a calendar of literary events.

Language

Word for the Wise

This two-minute daily feature produced by Merriam-Webster does not always merely pick a word to define and discuss. More often it addresses questions of usage or language history. A few recent examples: "Malay words," "Naked or nude," "Words of 1966," and "Hunter S. Thompson." On many public radio stations. You can hear it on WUMB **www.wumb.org** weekdays at 9:40 and 11:40am Eastern. Transcripts available at **www.m-w.com/wftw**.

Word of Mouth   BBC Radio 4
www.bbc.co.uk/radio4
Friday 1600–1630 Greenwich, repeated Sunday 2030–2100. Host: Michael Rosen. A series about words and the way we speak.

Film

Back Row   BBC Radio 4
www.bbc.co.uk/radio4
Saturday 1730–1800 Greenwich. Host: Andrew Collins.

Michael Rosen

Film Close-Ups   KALX **kalx.berkeley.edu**
Saturday 5:30–6:30pm Pacific. Host: Peter Crimmins.

Movietrax   CFUV **cfuv.uvic.ca**
Tuesday 9–10:30pm Pacific. Features movie soundtracks, history, trivia, and reviews, from Victoria, British Columbia.

The Treatment   KCRW **www.kcrw.org**
Friday 2:30pm Pacific; archived for listening any time. Host: Elvis Mitchell. *New York Times* film critic Mitchell talks with an impressive roster of guests about movies.

arts and culture

Business

Australian Broadcasting Corporation NewsRadio
www.abc.net.au/newsradio/finance.htm

Host: Geoffry Hill. The radio source for news of the Asian Pacific economic world is the daily market wrap-up report of ABC newsradio. Updated at 0730 Greenwich, it is available on the website for listening any time.

Marketplace
www.marketplace.org

Host: David Brancaccio. Nightly wrap-up of financial news. You can hear the current program or past ones on the Marketplace website (which also allows you to jump straight to the segment of the program called "The Numbers").

Investments and Personal Finance

E*Trade on Air
www.etrade.com

Weekdays 9–10 Eastern. Live daily market analysis from the online brokerage.

Financially Speaking
KVNF **www.kvnf.org**

Saturday 11am–noon Mountain, but you can listen to the archives on the website any time. Host: Bill Tennison. A chatty, folksy look at the week's events on Wall Street, as seen from a small town in the Colorado Rockies.

On the Money
WVXU **www.wvxu.org**

Saturday 10–11am Eastern. Host: Chris DiSimio. About personal investing.

Sound Money
Minnesota Public Radio **www.mpr.org**

Hosts: Debra Baer and Chris Farrell. Each program contains several interviews with guests who address topics of interest to individual investors and consumers. The program is archived on the website for listening any time.

Upside Today
Upside.com

An audio feature of the investment-oriented website Upside, *Upside Today* offers live market commentary, especially interviews with analysts and strategists. You can select among various daily features on the website to listen to on your own schedule.

Labor

Free and Fair On the Air
KAOS **www.kaosradio.org**

Friday noon–1:30pm Pacific. Labor and social justice news, views, and music.

Labor Express
WLUW **www.wluw.org**

Sunday 7–8pm Central. Interviews, discussion, and music focusing on Chicago's working people.

Union Yes
KCSB **www.kcsb.org**

Monday 6–7pm Pacific. Hosts: Steven Weiner and Rey Ybarra. Labor news, politics, and workers' issues.

Working L.A.
KPFK **www.kpfk.org**

Sunday 5:30–6pm Pacific. Host: Henry Walton.

business

Human Interest Features

Human Interest Favorites

Basic Black
CBC Radio One **www.cbc.ca**

Saturday 10–11:30am Eastern, with all shows also archived on the website for later listening on demand. Host: Arthur Black. Arthur Black has an enviable job. Each week he talks to someone interesting. Maybe someone who has just released an album of lawnmower sounds, maybe a woman who, as a volunteer in a scientific research project, agreed to wear spectacles that turn her world upside down. Black also reminisces, opines, investigates etymologies, talks about food, and also plays a few records. The program is enriched by the contributions of a cast of regulars. One popular feature is the "Humline," which allows listeners to call in and hum a melody that has been driving them crazy so the tune can be identified and internal peace restored.

Letter from America
BBC Radio 4 **www.bbc.co.uk/radio4**
Friday 2045–2100 Greenwich, repeated Saturday 0545 and Sunday 0845, accessible any time from Radio 4's "Listen Again" page. Host: Alistair Cooke. Britons have long enjoyed Cooke's wry observations on their former colony, but until Internet radio, the colonials have not been able to overhear.

Profiles
WFIU
www.indiana.edu/~wfiu
Sunday 6–7pm Eastern. Host: Bob Willard. This program does a particularly good job of getting people to open up, of revealing "the person behind the persona." Perhaps the guest list helps. In 2001 it included Barbara Kingsolver, Steve Martin, Noel Paul Stookey, Jonathan Winters, and Michael Ondaatje. The profiles are archived on the website, so you can listen to any of them at any time.

Ramblings
BBC Radio 4
www.bbc.co.uk/radio4
Sunday 1430–1500 Greenwich. Host: Clare Balding. Each week, Balding takes a walk with a companion through the British countryside. Conversational topics include the landscape, the history, and the beneficent effects of walking. Archived on the website for listening any time.

Alistair Cooke

human interest features

The Satellite Sisters
WNYC **www.wnyc.org**

Saturday 4–5pm Eastern. Julie, Liz, Sheila, Monica, and Lian Dolan are five sisters spread around the globe, from Pasadena to Bangkok, who get together once a week on the radio to talk about life. You can listen to all their archives on the website any time.

Food

A Chef's Table
WHYY **www.whyy.org**

Saturday noon–1pm Eastern. Host: Jim Coleman. Each week, Coleman, a Philadelphia chef, interviews other chefs, reports on food news, and answers listeners' questions. Of course there are recipes.

Everybody's Cooking
WVXU **www.wvxu.org**

Wednesday noon–12:30pm Eastern, archived for listening any time. Hosts: Jimmy Gherardi and Kevin "Doc" Wolfe. Includes interviews with cookbook authors and other guests; a wine segment; food news and views; a travel segment; and standing features such as "Talk with a Master Chef." Often broadcast from unusual venues such as the Cincinnati Zoo or a Rolling Stones concert.

Good Food
KCRW **www.kcrw.org**

Saturday 11am–noon Pacific; archived for listening any time. Host: Evan Kleiman. Recipes, restaurants, techniques, and places to buy ingredients.

A Matter of Taste
www.talkamerica.com

Saturday 3–4pm Eastern. Hosts: Rachel and David Michael Cane. This program, which usually features interviews with restaurateurs and authors, benefits from the Canes' wide travels.

The Produce Pair
www.talkamerica.com

Saturday noon–1pm Eastern. Hosts: Dan Avakian and Mark Ferro. These people have spent their whole lives in produce. They know produce.

The Splendid Table
Minnesota Public Radio **www.mpr.org**

Host: Lynne Rossetto Kasper. Each week Kasper, who has several cookbooks to her credit, talks to invited guests, visits outstanding restaurants, gives recipes, and speaks on cooking techniques. Archives on the website for

human interest features

listening any time. Particularly valuable are the contributions of in-house food scientist Shirley Corriher.

Gardening

Gardeners' Question Time

BBC Radio 4
www.bbc.co.uk/radio4

Sunday 1400–1445 Greenwich. A panel of expert gardeners and horticulturalists travel around Britain answering questions from, and solving the problems of, gardeners without green thumbs.

Magic Garden

www.talkamerica.com

Saturday 9–10am Eastern. Host: Mort White.

Paul's Garden Club

www.talkamerica.com

Sunday 6–7am Eastern. Host: Paul Parent. Parent has been providing radio gardening advice to New England listeners for nearly 20 years.

Talking Dirt

NPR www.npr.org/programs/talkingplants/radio

Host: Ketzel Levine. Levine's gardening segments usually appear on NPR's *Morning Edition*, and often involve conversations with interesting people about

Ketzel Levine

garden-related topics. (One segment, for example, treated the subject of couples in the garden.) You can hear the archives any time on the NPR website.

You Bet Your Garden
WHYY **www.whyy.org**

Saturday 11am–noon Eastern. Host: Mike McGrath. A weekly, one-hour program offering a breezy, light-hearted approach to a wide variety of gardening topics, from an organic perspective.

Health

Apple a Day
KUMR **www.kumr.org**

Half-hour program about developing a healthy lifestyle, available any time on the KUMR website.

Ask the Doctor
www.talkamerica.com

Weekdays 10–11pm Eastern. Host: Derrick M. DeSilva, Jr.

Body and Soul
CBC Radio One **www.cbc.ca**

Monday 8–9pm Eastern. *Body and Soul* is a one-hour, weekly exploration of humans' relationships with their bodies, bringing together personal health issues, sexuality, the practice of medicine, spirituality, and popular culture.

Healing Spirit
WFHB **www.wfhb.org**

Tuesday 10:30–11pm Eastern.

The Health Report
Australian Broadcasting Corporation Radio National **www.abc.net.au/rn/audio.htm**

Archived for listening any time. Although about half the programs in this series focus on public health issues in Australia that may not interest the rest of the world, the other half are provocative examinations of health issues that concern us all. A recent program, for example, focused on the health effects of the popularity of caffeine drinks among the young.

The Health Show
WAMC **www.wamc.org**

Thursday 3–3:30pm Eastern, archived for listening any time. Host: Nina Sax.

human interest features

LifeWise

KAOS **www.kaosradio.org**

Monday 8–9pm Pacific. Hosts: John Ford and Sally Johns. Focuses on mental health and wellness.

Natural Alternatives

WUSB **www.wusb.org**

Friday 6–7pm Eastern. Hosts: Eugene Zampieron and Ellen Kamhi. Zampieron, a naturopath, and Kamhi, a holistic educator, explore topics in natural medicine and preventive health.

Natural Living

Host: Gary Null. Widely syndicated show exploring the nature and politics of medicine, health, nutrition and the environment. You can hear it on WPFW (**www.capcity.com/wpfwradio**) Monday–Thursday 2–3pm and Sunday 7–8pm Eastern. More information on Null's website (**www.garynull.com**).

The People's Pharmacy

Hosted by pharmacologist Joe Graedon and medical anthropologist Terry Graedon, this hour-long, weekly show covers a wide variety of topics. Recent shows have included: the Omega diet, sexual addiction, plaque, longevity, diabetes, and akido. List of stations at **www.healthCentral.com/peoples pharmacy**. One is Wisconsin Public Radio **www.wpr.org** Saturday 6–7am and Sunday 11am–noon Central.

Sound Medicine

This hour-long weekly show from WFYI, featuring physicians from the Indiana University School of Medicine, includes interviews with medical researchers, education on health topics, and listener call-ins. Shows are archived at **soundmedicine.iu.edu** for listening any time.

Zorba Paster on Your Health

Wisconsin Public Radio
www.wpr.org

Ideas Network Saturdays 8–9am and 1–2pm Central. Weekly show carried on many stations. Family doctor Zorba Paster and co-host Tom Clark talk to callers from around the country about health, fitness, and healthy living, with a strong emphasis on attitudes, values, and spirit (Paster's most recent book has an introduction by the Dalai Lama).

human interest features

Tom Clark and Zorba Paster

Sex

Speaking of Sex
KCSB www.kcsb.org

Wednesday 6–7pm Pacific. Host: Lorena Guzman. Covers issues of reproductive health and human sexuality, in English and Spanish.

The Real Deal: Sexuality 101
Trent Radio
www.trentu.ca/trentradio

Thursday 10–11pm Eastern. Host: Jenny Scott. A "no bull low-down on the risks, myths, and politics of sex and sexuality in the 21st century."

AIDS

AIDS Update
WPKN www.wpkn.org

Friday 8–9pm Eastern. Weekly summary of the week's news on the battle against AIDS, from both scientific and social perspectives.

human interest features

288

AWARE–Health Talk Radio

Nationally syndicated program dealing with issues of HIV infection. WLUW (**www.wluw.org**) airs it Tuesday 9–9:30am Central.

Spirituality and Metaphysics

Alan Watts
KGNU **www.kgnu.org**

Tuesday 9–9:30am Mountain. These talks by Watts, recorded by his son in the 1970s, used to be broadcast on many stations, and you can still find them here and there. Watts is discursive to the point of rambling, but always brings back something well worth the ramble.

New Dimensions Radio
www.newdimensions.org

New Dimensions discusses alternative approaches to life. This might sometimes involve an interview with an author of a book on voluntary simplicity, sometimes a talk with people who had mystical visions as a child. You can hear the current program any time on the *New Dimensions* website.

The Next Dimension

www.talkamerica.com
Saturday 9pm–midnight Pacific. Host: Patte Purcell. Purcell says that the goal of her program is "to bring a forum for New Age and metaphysical topics and to promote a non-fear-based shift to the love vibration." Archives at **www.outofthisworld radio.com**.

The Spirit of Things
Australian Broadcasting Corporation Radio National **www.abc.net.au/rn/audio.htm**
Archived for listening any time. Host: Rachael Kohn. *The Spirit of Things*

Rachael Kohn

human interest features

part two

explores contemporary values and beliefs as expressed through ritual, art, music, and sacred texts, focusing on how humans discover, celebrate and make sense of spiritual meaning in their lives, both in established traditions and novel beliefs and practices.

Sports

Only A Game
WBUR **www.wbur.org**

Saturday 7–8am Eastern (and syndicated on 95 other stations). Host: Bill Littlefield. Sports discussion show that attempts to be intelligent.

Sport on Five
BBC Radio Five Live
www.bbc.co.uk/fivelive/sportonfive

In addition to live coverage of athletic events from around the world, Five Live also lets you hear the latest sports news any time from the website.

Auto Racing

human interest features

Formula One
BBC Radio Five Live
www.bbc.co.uk/fivelive/sportonfive

Thursday 2030–2100 Greenwich. Host: Jonathan Legard.

Baseball

Baseball and radio have had a close affinity and long history together, partly because baseball is such an ideal sport for radio, with its discrete actions more easily captured in words than, say, the freely flowing action of soccer or basketball. So it should be no surprise that baseball is the focus of the first major push to turn Internet radio

Jonathan Legard

290

into a paid subscription concern. In 2000, Major League Baseball signed an agreement with RealNetworks which designates RealNetworks as the exclusive outlet for major league games. RealNetworks streams the games only to purchasers of its "GoldPass" service. In addition to English, baseball streams are available in Spanish, French, and Japanese. RealNetworks archives every game for later listening, as well. GoldPass currently costs $9.95 per month, and you must purchase three months in advance. (This price also entitles subscribers to RealPlayer Plus, which costs about the same as three months of GoldPass, so if you're interested in RealPlayer Plus, it makes economic sense to try out GoldPass for three months.)

For those who don't subscribe to GoldPass, two ways remain to hear baseball on Internet radio: the minors and college teams. Many minor league games are still on the radio, and many college stations offer coverage of their college teams.

Horse Racing

2KY Racing Radio   **www.2ky.com.au**
Horse racing from Australia.

Motorcycling

Open Road Radio   **www.talkamerica.com**
Sunday 8–9pm Eastern. Hosts: Gina Woods and Jim Viverito. Includes comprehensive American Motorcycle Association race results and interviews with racers.

Travel

Excess Baggage   BBC Radio 4 **www.bbc.co.uk/radio4**
Sunday 1000–1030 Greenwich. Host: Arthur Smith. Travelers' tales, anecdotes, and conversation.

human interest features

The Savvy Traveler

http://savvytraveler.com

Host: Diana Nyad. In addition to tips on low fare specials and other travel advice, *The Savvy Traveler* airs extended features on the travels of others, such as cellist Yo Yo Ma's exploration of the historical Silk Route, or Barrett Golding's retracing of Lewis and Clark's journey… on bicycle. The program is widely syndicated via PRI. You can hear the current show at the website.

Vintage Radio

Vintage radio Favorites	
Antique Phonograph Music Program	see p.292
Classic Stars Radio	see p.293
Metro Golden Memories	see p.293

Antique Phonograph Music Program

WFMU
www.wfmu.org

Tuesday 7–8pm Eastern. *Antique Phonograph Music Program* is a collection of pop, standard, and ethnic music acoustically recorded on discs and cylinders circa 1895-1925 and played on period machines. Archived on the WFMU website so you can listen any time.

The Big Broadcast

WAMU www.wamu.org

Sunday 7–11pm Eastern. Host: Ed Walker. The four-hour format gives Walker time to play full-length episodes of several classic programs such as *Jack Benny*, *Gunsmoke*, *Fibber McGee and Molly*, *Dragnet*, and *Superman* each week.

Classic Stars Radio   http://www.titanicstreams.com/
Devoted to classic radio dramas of the '30s and '40s.

Metro Golden Memories   WQNA www.wqna.org
Sunday 6–7am Central. Host: Bob Greenburg. You can also listen to archived programs at **www.mgmemories.com**.

Old Radio Theater   KVMR www.kvmr.org
Thursday 7–8pm Pacific. Hosts: David and Linda Breninger.

Old Time Radio Drama   Wisconsin Public Radio www.wpr.org
Sunday 8–11pm Central. Host: Norman Gilliland. Features a wide variety of programming, often returning to *The Great Gildersleeve*, *X Minus 1*, *Burns & Allen*, *Nero Wolfe*, and *Johnny Dollar*.

Old Tyme Radio Network
www.otrsite.com/broadcast/index.html
Archive of rebroadcasts of vintage radio programs, including John and Larry Gassman's *Same Time Same Station* and Tom Heathwood's *Heritage Radio Theatre*.

Sing Something Simple   BBC Radio 2 www.bbc.co.uk/radio2
Sunday 1630–1700 Greenwich. This is vintage radio, but it's still going! Started in 1959, the show has been broadcast at the same time every Sunday since, giving it claim to the title of longest-running continuous music program in the world. The Cliff Adams singers (twelve male, four female) walk through a selection of much-loved songs and invite the audience to sing along.

Vintage Radio Hour   WESS http://www.esu.edu/wess/
9–10am Eastern.

WRVO Playhouse   www.wrvo.fm
Monday–Thursday 7:30pm–midnight Eastern, Friday, Saturday and Sunday 8pm to midnight Eastern. WRVO Playhouse encompasses a variety of material, including Westerns, suspense, comedies and contemporary drama. But the largest dose of all is old-time radio programs: *Johnny Madiero*, *Ozzie and Harriet*, *Valiant Lady*, *Shadow of Fu Manchu*, and countless others. WRVO posts the schedule well in advance at **http://www.wrvo.fm/playhous.html**.

vintage radio

WXVU

www.wvxu.org

Mixed in with local shows on WXVU is an assortment of classic radio shows: *Burns & Allen*, *Fibber McGee and Molly*, *Bob and Ray*, *The Life of Riley*, *Riders Radio Theater*, *The Shadow*, and others.

Comedy

Comedy favorites	
CBC Radio Comedy	see p.294
Prairie Home Companion	see p.295

Capitol Steps

www.capsteps.com

Topical political satire set to music, available any time on the website.

CBC Radio Comedy

CBC Radio One **www.cbc.ca**

Sunday 1:05–2pm Eastern. Host: Al Rae. Classic comedy from the CBC vaults and from around the globe.

Firesign Theatre

www.firesigntheatre.com

For a whole generation, the bent, folded, and mutilated humor of Firesign Theatre will always bring back fond memories of oddly altered nights in some dorm room. Firesign Theatre has continued to create original works no less engaging than those their fans of old will remember. Much of the new work centers around the mythical radio station Radio Now (broadcasting at 666.66 on the VM dial, where "V" stands for "Virtual"). Internet radio has allowed Firesign Theatre to bring Radio Now into existence. The Firesign site is a great example of a whole site devoted to organizing and presenting audio information, with excellent snippets introducing you to the whole range of Radio Now characters – *except that there is no sound.*

The Funny Bone   KCSB www.kcsb.org
Tuesday 7–8pm Pacific. Host: Brent Yarkin. Standup, sketch comedy, and comedy music.

Hello, Olympia   KAOS www.kaosradio.org
Tuesday 8–9pm Pacific. Original independent humor from Olympia, Washington.

The Late Show   URN urn.nott.ac.uk
Tuesday–Saturday 0000–0200 Greenwich. Host: Craig Pilling. Alternative comedy from a student station at the University of Nottingham.

Le Show   KCRW www.kcrw.org
Sunday 10–11am Pacific; rebroadcast Monday 7–8pm. Host: Harry Shearer. If there's a wickeder wit than Shearer's practicing today, you would not want to be subjected to it. Shearer's show is highly topical, putting this week's news, particularly the failings of America's elected leaders, squarely in his sights. Archived at **www.harryshearer.com.**

Madly Off In All Directions   CBC Radio One www.cbc.ca
Sunday 1:05–2pm Eastern. Host: Lorne Elliot. A compendium of Canadian comedians.

Prairie Home Companion   Minnesota Public Radio
www.mpr.org
Saturday 5-7pm Central. Host: Garrison Keillor. It is entirely possible that future anthologies of American literature will select Garrison Keillor to represent the late 20th century. Like Robert Frost's, Keillor's use of folksy diction and materials makes him easy to underestimate. His skill as a storyteller, however, puts him in a class with Mark Twain. Like all who improvise, he is uneven. Unafraid to skirt the edge of bathos, he sometimes falls in, and spends far too long pitying himself in public for having been an unpopular child, next to whom no one wanted to sit on the school bus. But at his best, he expands story structure like a carnival magician blowing up a balloon, and twists it into more shapes than you would think possible. Keillor's long-running radio show, *Prairie Home Companion*, is based around one long story, his "News from Lake

comedy

Wobegon." But *Prairie Home Companion* is a variety program, reviving skit formats you thought went out with the "Golden Age of Radio," faux commercials, musical guests, world-class sound effects, and even the occasional invited poet. Poetry on a popular radio show? Only part of what makes Keillor unique. Archived snippets (no whole shows) on the *Prairie Home Companion* website (**www.prairiehome.org**).

Garrison Keillor

Rewind
KUOW **www.kuow.org**

Sunday 2–2:30pm Pacific, archived for listening any time. Host: Bill Radke. Topical comment on the news, sketch comedy, and repartee between host and guests.

comedy

Children's

Children's favorites

Kinetic City Super Crew   see p.298

Pot O' Gold   see p.298

Daniel Pinkwater

Chinwag Theater   WBUR
www.wbur.org
Sunday 7–7:30pm Eastern. Hosts: Daniel Pinkwater and Scott Simon. "Chinwag Theater tells a story, plays good music and laughs at a joke or two."

Circle Round   KVMR
www.kvmr.org
Tuesday 7–8pm Pacific. Host: Jill Hockwald. Also good is *All Together Now* at the same time Wednesday.

Go4It   BBC Radio 4
www.bbc.co.uk/radio4
Sunday 1915–1945 Greenwich. Fun, games, books, and stories.

children's

Halfway Down the Stairs
KPFK www.kpfk.org

Sunday 8:30–9am Pacific. Host: Uncle Ruthie. Stories and songs.

HB Children
HBC www.hbc.com.np

Saturday 0815–0915 Greenwich. Stories and talk, in English, from Nepal.

Kinetic City Super Crew
WREK www.wrek.org

Saturdays noon–12:30pm Eastern (but available any time on WREK's website). A science drama for kids produced by the American Association for the Advancement of Science. Join the crew and their supercomputer as they use science to solve various mysteries.

Playground
WERS www.wers.org

Saturday and Sunday 5–8pm Eastern.

Pot O' Gold
KVNF www.kvnf.org

Saturday 9–10am Mountain, but you can listen to the archives any time. Hosts Don and Wally look at the view out their window on Main Street in the small Mountain town of Paonia, Colorado, play a sweet song, and then tell a story, often reading a chapter out of a book.

Time Out of Mind
CJSF www.cjsf.bc.ca

Monday 4–5pm Pacific. Children's literature read aloud.

Wake, Rattle, and Roll
KCSN www.kcsn.org

Sunday 6–7am Pacific. Host: Jamie Wisehaupt. Eclectic mix of music and stories, from Pete Seeger to the Care Bears.

The Zucchini Brothers
WAMC www.wamc.org

Weekdays 3:30–4pm Eastern. Made for kids and families, this is modeled on old-time radio, back before there was TV. The three zany Zucchinis serve up jokes, anecdotes, daily chores, facts about science and nature, and lots of sprightly music.

children's

Radio Drama

"I live right inside radio when I listen"

Marshall McLuhan

Radio drama is a genre all its own, as different from stage drama as film is. Before the advent of television, radio drama had a huge popular audience and dominated much of the broadcast schedule. Although TV knocked out this huge audience, radio drama persisted, kept alive by practitioners who love the genre and audiences who find it engrossing. Large American public radio stations often carry about an hour a week of radio drama. Other nations with traditions of public support for the arts have subsidized the continued creation of original work. (If most Americans have heard a radio drama recently, it was probably courtesy of the BBC or CBC.) Small drama groups across the country have continued to do innovative work with little audience other than that provided by a local community radio station, little income other than that which they could scrounge together through mail-order sales of cassettes.

Internet radio has provided a huge boost to radio drama groups. Now the audience for radio drama can find the work of these independent groups. In addition to Webcasts from radio stations, many offer their works from their own websites, available on demand rather than a schedule.

radio drama

Radio drama favorites

Act One
www.kpfa.org

Sunday 8–9pm Pacific. A variety of original radio drama, usually by Bay Area group Pagliacci's Fools, always interesting.

AudioTheater.com
www.audiotheater.com

This site hopes to be a Central clearing house for the art form they call audio theatre. AudioTheater.com is a single access point for the work of 150 drama groups across the country, some associated with radio stations but many not, groups such as The New Hampshire Radio Theatre, Sound Mind Theater, Great Northern Theatre, and particularly the Atlanta Radio Theatre Company.

Audio Theatre Hour
WREK www.wrek.org

Live Saturday 5–6pm Eastern, but available any time. A weekly one-hour showcase of Audio Theatre groups, often featuring the Atlanta Radio Theatre Company.

BBC Radio 3
www.bbc.co.uk/radio3

The BBC offers so many radio dramas that itemizing them is rather like trying to list the music played on a contemporary American station. *The Wire* offers ten new radio dramas each season, along the lines of Mark Ravenhill's "Feed Me," Lavinia Murphy's "Swallow," and Richard Bean's "Unthinkable." This single show probably offers more total minutes of serious radio drama than everything produced this year in the United States. Saturdays, November–January. *The Sunday Play* (Sunday 1930 Greenwich) airs a full play each Sunday. Recent examples include "Autumn Sonata," based on the film by Ingmar Berman, Chekov's "Three Sisters," Jackie Kay's "Every Bit of It," based on the life of blues singer Bessie Smith, and "Are UR," an updating of Karel Capek's 1921 satirical allegory which introduced us to the word "robot."

BBC Radio 4
www.bbc.co.uk/radio4

In addition to *Saturday Play* (1430–1530 Greenwich), Radio 4 also offers

radio drama

numerous short works, and at any given time there is more than one series in progress. On one random day in 2001, there was a new series, *The Little World of Don Camillo* (a dramatization of Giovanni Guareschi's comic novel) broadcast at 1130 Greenwich daily; the afternoon play at 1415 was "Maine Voices" by Ian MacMillan; at 1045 and 1945 was the fifteen-minute short, "Not Either an Experimental Doll," a dramatization of correspondence between an orphaned black schoolgirl and a white educator in 1950s South Africa.

CBC Radio Drama
www.cbc.ca

Canada gives levels of support to the arts that neighbors to the south can only marvel at, and their support of radio drama is no exception. The national treasure CBC Radio produces more than 150 hours of original drama each year in regional centers across the country as well as in CBC's studios in Toronto. They also pick up interesting material from elsewhere, such as Radio New Zealand, the Australian Broadcasting Corporation, and Radio Hong Kong. It's hard for a resident of the United States to imagine the depth of the dramatic schedule; you need to go read the web page for yourself. Shows of particular note:

- Great Plays of the Millennium. Sunday 8:05pm.
- Sunday Showcase. Sunday 10:05pm.
- Monday Playbill. Monday 3:30pm.
- Monday Night Playhouse. Monday 9:05pm.
- The Mystery Project. Friday 3:30pm.

A note on time: CBC has stations nationwide. If you're interested in catching *Sunday Showcase*, you can pick it up at 10:05 in any of four different time zones, from East to West Coast (plus some odd times, usually offset by half an hour, in the Maritimes and Newfoundland).

Imagination Theater
http://www.transmediasf.com/imag.html

A weekly, one-hour mystery playhouse, recorded live before a 500-seat studio audience, with original scripts, live Foley sound effects, and big-name talent such as Harry Anderson, Patty Duke, and Roddy McDowell. The three most recent shows are available on the website.

Mark Trail Radio Theatre
KFAI www.kfai.org

Host: Babs Economon with Kurt Cederquist. A radio comedy-drama based on the adventures of the daily comic strip hero. New episodes are not currently being produced, but the old ones are archived on the KFAI website for listening any time.

radio drama

NPR Playhouse

National Public Radio helps fund and distribute radio drama under the title NPR Playhouse. Each week, NPR distributes four half-hour segments with slightly different emphases:

▶▶ **Playhouse I–Classics**. Classic world literature. Recent examples include *Beowulf*, *Masque of the Red Death*, and *The Phantom of the Opera*.

▶▶ **Playhouse II–American Tales**. American themes and settings, often from American literature. Recent examples are *The Legend of Sleepy Hollow* and *Occurrence at Owl Creek Bridge*.

▶▶ **Playhouse III–Science Fiction, Mystery, Adventure**. Most recently a series of 26 radio plays set in the future, introduced by Harlan Ellison.

▶▶ **Playhouse IV–Open Stage**. Contemporary Dramas, often fresh original work commissioned for the series.

Sources for NPR Playhouse include Independent Radio Drama Productions (**www.irdp.co.uk**), Generations Radio Theater (**www.radiotales.com**), L.A. Theatre Works, and California Artists Radio Theater (**www.otrsite.com/cart**). The most complete coverage can be found on *WRVO Playhouse*, WRVO (**www.wrvo.fm**) Monday–Thursday 7:30–midnight Eastern; Friday, Saturday and Sunday 8pm–midnight. Note that *WRVO Playhouse* carries a full roster of other radio drama as well, high and low, new and old.

Playhouse   www.kcrw.org

Sunday 7–9pm Pacific. Various producers (often L.A. Theatre Works) create high-production-value programs, always well done, though rarely very adventurous. Recent offerings: Carson McCullers' *The Member of the Wedding*, N. Richard Nash's *The Rainmaker*.

Portland Radio Theater   WMPG www.wmpg.org

Many original productions, archived on the WMPG website for listening any time.

Riders Radio Theater   WVXU www.wvxu.org

Tuesday 11–11:30am Eastern. Comedy and melodrama featuring the musical group Riders in the Sky, in all their yodeling splendor. You can hear a few sample episodes on the WVXU website.

Seeing Ear Theatre   www.scifi.com

Several different stories available on this site. For example, Octavia E. Butler's *Kindred*, which stars Alfre Woodard, the story of a contemporary African-

American woman suddenly snapped backwards in time to the pre-Civil War south.

Sound Affects
KFAI **www.kfai.org**

Saturday 3–3:30pm Central. A selection of contemporary audio theater from many of the producers listed in this section.

WCRS Audio Stage
http://members.nbci.com/radiodave1

A dozen short dramas available on the site.

ZBS
www.zbs.org

Independent, not-for-profit foundation that produces inventive original audio drama series, including the adventure series *Jack Flanders*; three-minute episodes of fantasy in *Ruby; Gumshoe*; and *Dinotopia*, the story of a boy and his father rescued by dolphins and taken to an island where dinosaurs teach humans how to live in harmony with nature.

Readings

Being read to can be very pleasant. With the widespread popularity of books on tape, the practice of reading a whole book on the radio on successive days has become less popular. But you can still find stations that read books.

When visitors came home from Castro's Cuba with tales of how different things were there, the free medical care was much admired, the universal literacy was applauded, but the single story that most fired imaginations was the book readers in the cigar factories. While Cubans of all ages and backgrounds sat and

readings

hand-rolled tobacco, a reader chosen from among them was paid to sit and read books aloud. The position held incredible status, enhanced even further by its defining perquisite: the reader, brooking no outside influence, chose what books to read. The most successful radio readings seem to follow a somewhat Cuban system. The reader, usually a long-time volunteer, has a good voice and a love of literature. He or she might try to do different characters' voices, but most simply read through the work.

Caution: radio readings can elbow other activities aside. You might find yourself scheduling social obligations around reading times.

Readings Favorites

A Book at Bedtime	see p.304
Chapter-A-Day	see p.305
Radio Reader	see p.305

Afternoon Reading
BBC Radio 4 **www.bbc.co.uk/radio4**
Weekdays 1530–1545 Greenwich. Usually a complete short story in one reading.

Between the Covers
CBC Radio One **www.cbc.ca**
Weekdays 10:45–11pm Eastern. *Between the Covers* features contemporary novels and short stories read in fifteen-minute installments, favoring Canadian contemporary fiction, with international authors also represented. Readings are by Canadian actors or, infrequently, by the authors.

A Book at Bedtime
BBC Radio 4 **www.bbc.co.uk/radio4**
Weekdays 2245–2300 Greenwich.

Book of the Week
BBC Radio 4 **www.bbc.co.uk/radio4**
Weekdays 0945–1000 Greenwich. (Repeated at 1230.) A non-fiction work is abridged until it can be read aloud in an hour and fifteen minutes, and those minutes are parceled out fifteen per day over the week.

readings

Chapter-A-Day
Wisconsin Public Radio **www.wpr.org**

Ideas Network. Weekdays 12:30–1pm Central and 11pm–11:30pm Central.

New Letters on the Air

Host: Angela Elam. Each week this program presents a contemporary author reading from their work and talking with the host about the craft of writing. *New Letters* is a literary journal produced at the University of Missouri at Kansas City. *New Letters on the Air* is a companion radio program produced by *New Letters* staff at UMKC radio station KCUR. It is distributed free to public radio stations around the country. One is WFHB (**www.wfhb.org**) which airs it Thursday noon–1pm Eastern.

Radio Reader
WQLN **www.wqln.org**

Weekdays 6:30–7pm Eastern. Host: Dick Estell. For millions of Americans, any mention of readings on radio will immediately activate the sound of Dick Estell's voice in their mind's ear. And it is in that voice they will remember the many books they have heard him read. One of the many treasure troves Internet radio offers is the complete Dick Estell archive (on the WQLN website), where you can hear every chapter of every book on your own schedule.

Selected Shorts

Host: Isaiah Sheffer. This weekly, one-hour program featuring actors reading short fiction is recorded live at New York's Symphony Space and syndicated to NPR stations. You can hear it on KPBX (**www.kpbx.org**) Sunday 4–5pm Pacific. The schedule of upcoming programs is at **www.symphonyspace.org**.

Writer's Radio
5UV **www.adelaide.edu.au/5UV**

Monday 0330–0400 Greenwich. Host: Cath Kenneally. *Writer's Radio* presents a reading, usually of short stories or poems, usually read by the (Australian) author, then a discussion of books.

readings

Original Radio Art

The Listening Room

Australian Broadcasting Corporation Classic FM **www.abc.net.au/classic**

Monday 1100–1200 Greenwich. Host: Andrew McLennan. The Listening Room creates original radio art. It's a space for the exploration of radio forms and imaginative program making. There is a core group of *Listening Room* producers and sound engineers who bring in Australian and international artists to create radiophonic works. It's sometimes musical, sometimes dramatic, always interesting.

The Other Side

KCRW
www.kcrw.org

Sunday 11am–noon Pacific, re-broadcast Saturday 7–8pm. Joe Frank is a long-time creator of original spoken-word programming for radio that defies genre. His programs are perhaps best defined as original literature written for radio. Frank's tales twist and morph. There is nothing quite like them. For some ten years beginning in 1986, KCRW in Santa Monica supported his program first

Joe Frank

called *Work in Progress*, then *In the Dark*, *Somewhere Out There,* and now *The Other Side*. Archives of *The Other Side* are available at the KCRW website for listening any time. WFMU has older archives at **www.wfmu.org**.

Word Jazz
WBEZ **www.wbez.org**

Monday (that is, Sunday night) midnight-12:30am Central. Host: Ken Nordine. Just what you would think from the name. Nordine creates improvisational work using the spoken voice. He starts with an incredible instrument, one of the grainiest, most seductive voices you ever heard. Then a hip sensibility and a willingness to go anywhere. If you don't know Ken Nordine, you should not leave this life without listening to him once. "Ken Nordine is the real angel sitting on the wire in the tangled matrix of cobwebs that holds the whole attic together." – Tom Waits.

Overheard

Audio Kitchen
WFMU **www.wfmu.org**

This strange program plays found tapes of all kinds, down to and including cassettes discovered in a bin at the Salvation Army. Motivational tapes of affirmations people have made for themselves, old answering machine messages, audio letters, you name it. It's not all spoken word: home-made music tracks also appear. Archived on the website so you can eavesdrop any time.

Police Scanner
www.policescanner.com

Different people like different things, and some people are interested enough in fires, or aviation chatter, or police work to spend hundreds of dollars for scanner radios for their homes. Thanks to the Internet, such expenditures are no longer necessary. This Yahoo-sponsored page has links to several scanner streams, from the Los Angeles or New York police departments, to the Dallas-Fort Worth Airport.

overheard

Science

Earth and Sky

www.earthsky.com

Hosts: Joel Block and Deborah Byrd. Listeners at a thousand radio stations around the world enjoy Block and Byrd's delightful little snippets of astronomy, cosmology, meteorology, and other physical and life sciences so thoroughly that their skittery intro music can cause conversation to cease for 90 seconds until the program is over. You can hear today's program or any of the archives (and read transcripts) at the *Earth and Sky* website.

Joel Block and Deborah Byrd

Engines of Our Ingenuity
KUHF **www.kuhf.uh.edu**
Host: John H. Lienhard. An engineer's comments on technology. Transcripts and audio archives of all the programs are available on the KUHF website.

Frontiers
BBC Radio 4 **www.bbc.co.uk/radio4**
Wednesday 2100–2130 Greenwich. News and features from the cutting edge of science.

The Green Room
WFMU **www.wfmu.org**
Monday 7–8pm Eastern. Interviews with people from science, technology, mathematics, and occasionally, the arts. Recent guests included the President of the Royal Society and the CEO of Merck. Past episodes archived on the website for listening any time.

Inspire (Earthsounds)
www.spaceweather.com/glossary/inspire.html
Dennis Gallagher, a space physicist at the Marshall Space Flight Center, streams the sounds of a Very Low Frequency (VLF) receiver, so that you can hear the ambient sounds of the atmosphere ("sferics"). Among the most prominent low-frequency sounds is the sound of lightning. Lightning strokes emit a broadband pulse of radio waves, just as they unleash a visible flash of light. VLF signals from nearby lightning, heard through a speaker, sound like the crackling of a fire. More info at **http://science.nasa.gov/headlines/y2001/ast19jan_1.htm**.

The Research File
Radio Nederland **www.rnw.nl**
Available any time from the site's "Sound Library". Hosts: Liesbeth de Bakker, Anne Blair Gould and Laura Durnford. This well-produced program surveys new discoveries, ongoing research, and current events. A recent season included a visit to Chernobyl 15 years after the great nuclear disaster, an in-depth look at depression, and a special on languages and how we learn them. (In English.)

The Material World
BBC Radio 4 **www.bbc.co.uk/radio4**
Thursday 1630–1700 Greenwich (archived for listening any time). Host: John Watkins. From a feature on telescopes to a debate on supercavitation.

Nature
BBC Radio 4 **www.bbc.co.uk/radio4**
Monday 0900–0930 Greenwich (archived for listening any time). Host: Mark

science

Cawardine. Environmental news stories, wildlife spectacles, topical features, and global concerns about the natural world.

Quirks and Quarks
CBC Radio One **www.cbc.ca**

Saturday 12:05–1pm Eastern, and archived on the website. Host: Bob McDonald. Unlike so much superficial and sensationalistic reporting on science, this superbly produced program covers serious topics in a thoughtful way, while always being easy to follow. Recent topics include: autoimmune disease, "Elegant Universe," "We Came From Space," "Return of Thalidomide," "Terraforming Mars," and "Golden Rice."

Science Friday
www.sciencefriday.com

Host: Ira Flatow. Flatow's is that rare science program which does not sacrifice depth and precision while striving for understandability. *Science Friday* does not merely, as so many radio programs do, examine the effect of technology on daily life; it actually tries to explain the *science*. The good news is that Flatow's program is usually *more* understandable than the ones which are watered-down. The program is syndicated widely to public radio stations in the United States. You can hear it on KQED (**www.kqed.org**) Friday 11am–1pm Central.

The Science Show
Australian Broadcasting Corporation Radio
National **www.abc.net.au/rn/audio.htm**

A weekly, hour-long program available on the website for listening any time.

Star Stuff
Australian Broadcasting Corporation NewsRadio **www.abc.net.au/newsradio**

Sunday 1300–1330 Greenwich. Host: Stuart Gary. The latest in astronomy and space exploration.

Today
HBC **www.hbc.com.np**

Daily 0005–0015 Greenwich. Daily information about day, date, lunar phases, planetary positions and stars (in both Nepali and English).

Mind/Brain/Psychology

The Infinite Mind
www.theinfinitemind.com

Host: Fred Goodwin. *The Infinite Mind* is a weekly, hour-long program focusing on the human mind, behavior, and mental health. Each program focuses on a

science

single topic, from how children learn to why adults forget, from character and creativity to schizophrenia and depression. Goodwin is the former director of the National Institute of Mental Health. His guests include leading researchers on the mind and the brain, psychiatrists, psychologists, policy experts, advocates, clinicians, celebrities, authors, musicians, journalists and people who have experienced mental disorders. Each program also includes a short commentary by NPR science reporter John Hockenberry. You can listen to it any time from the website.

Technology

The Buzz

Australian Broadcasting Corporation Radio National
www.abc.net.au/rn/audio.htm

Archived for listening any time. Host: Richard Aedy. This show provides an intelligent look at a wide range of interesting intersections between technology and human life. Recent shows treated robotic surgeons, Bluetooth, "bioinformatics for beginners," and an open-source novel.

The CompuDudes Show

WHYY **www.whyy.org**

Thursday 9–10pm Eastern. Hosts: Peter Cook and Scott Manning. Features invited guests discussing current computer topics, from privacy issues in Windows XP to making digital movies. Also takes calls from computer users with questions. Programs are archived on the WHYY website for listening later.

NetNews

Australian Broadcasting Corporation NewsRadio
www.abc.net.au/newsradio/netnews.htm

This program takes the Internet itself as its subject. *NetNews* is **archived on the website for listening any time**.

TechNation

www.technation.com

Host: Moira Gunn. A weekly program focusing on the impact of technology on daily life. Usually features interviews with authors of recently published science books. Topics range from the aging power grid to the art of design. Archives on the website are broken up so you can listen to just the interview that interests you.

science

Technology Bytes
KPFT **www.kpft.org**

Tuesday 8–10pm Central. Computer call-in show in Houston, TX.

Religious Services

Chagiga
WERS **www.wers.org**

Sunday 8–11am Eastern.

ChicagoLand Radio Mass
WLUW **www.wluw.org**

Sunday 7:30–8:30am Central. Hour-long, live Catholic mass from Holy Family Church in Chicago.

Friday Prayer Congregation
Islamic Republic News Agency (IRNA) Radio **www.irna.com/en/radio**

Archived for listening any time.

Marsh Chapel
WBUR **www.wbur.org**

Sunday 11am–noon Eastern. Protestant services from Boston University.

Sunday Worship
BBC Radio 4 **www.bbc.co.uk/radio4**

Sunday 0805–0845 Greenwich.

Unitarian Services
WERS **www.wers.org**

Sunday 11am–noon Eastern.

religious services

Vatican Radio   **www.vatican.va**
In addition to its live broadcast, Vatican Radio has several programs available on demand, including news and the Sunday Angelus prayer.

WDVR   **www.wdvrfm.org**
Sunday 6–11am Eastern. Services from several churches in the Delaware Valley, including Presbyterian, United Methodist, and South Branch Bible.

Affinity Groups

First Peoples

First Peoples Stations

AIROS   **www.airos.org**
The American Indian Radio on Satellite (AIROS) network is a national distribution system for Native programming to tribal communities and other community radio stations. You can listen to AIROS programs (which include many of those listed below) directly from the AIROS website, which rotates through the entire selection several times per day.

Affinity Groups Favorites	
AIROS	see p.313
GayBC	see p.325
Wings – Women's International News Gathering Service	see p.323

KWE
www.tyendinaga.net/kweradio

Mohawk Nation Radio. Limited bandwidth and scratchy reception at best, but fresh and original programming.

WOJB
www.wojb.org

WOJB is licensed to the Lac Courte Oreilles Band of the Lake Superior Ojibwe in Northwestern Wisconsin. It is a thriving community radio station, full of variety, playing everything from big band music to bluegrass. But music and information of particular interest to Native Americans have a prominent standing in the programming, well-integrated into the mix. For example, the morning news is NPR's *All Things Considered*, but following is locally produced news incorporating *National Native News* at 8:06am Central, as well as a daily Ojibwe language feature. *Saturday Morning's Fire*, 10am–noon, hosted by Paul DeMain and Camille Lacapa, is a public affairs program featuring local, regional, and national Native issues, Native music, and interviews with Native leaders, elders, and youth. WOJB carries *Native America Calling* weekdays noon–1pm. The excellent locally produced music program *Drumsong* airs Tuesday 7pm–midnight.

First Peoples Programs

Aboriginal Messages
5UV **www.adelaide.edu.au/5UV**

Wednesday 0330–0400 Greenwich. Hosts: Kerrynne Liddle, Grace Nelligon. Produced by the Aboriginal Legal Rights Movement in Australia.

Aboriginal Voices
CFRC **www.queensu.ca/cfrc**

Monday 6–8pm Eastern. Canadian program airing the concerns of First Nations peoples.

AlterNativeVoices
KUVO **www.kuvo.org**

7–8am Mountain. Host: Z. Susanne Aikman. Features Native music, interviews, and news. Aikman is Eastern Band Cherokee/Scot. This program is also available on AIROS.

Beyond Beads and Feathers CJSW www.cjsw.com

Thursday 11–11:30am Mountain. Host: Tom Horvath. Aboriginal people discussing current issues. Regular features include panel discussions, and interviews with artists, musicians, and community leaders. From Calgary, Alberta.

California Indian Radio Project www.flickerfeather.org

Hosts: Joseph Orozco, Peggy Berryhill, and Susan Newstead. After an opening montage of traditional music and song, tribal participants narrate several programs about the more than 300 tribes in California. You can hear the program directly from the CIRP website, from one of the many public stations listed on the website, or from AIROS.

Different Drums www.differentdrums.com

Although *Different Drums* covers issues of interest to Native Americans, the emphasis in the weekly, one-hour program is on the music. You can hear it several times a day on AIROS.

Dreamwalk KVMR www.kvmr.org

Thursday 10am–noon Pacific. Host: Skip Alan Smith. Contemporary and traditional Native American music and spoken word.

Earthsongs KNBA www.knba.org

Thursday 10–11am and Saturday noon–1pm Alaska. Host: Gregg McVicar. *Earthsongs*, from the Koahnic Broadcast Corporation, a nonprofit Alaska Native

Gregg McVicar

media center in Anchorage, Alaska, is a weekly, hour-long music program on contemporary music by a wide range of Native artists, from Robbie Robertson to Robert Mirabal. Each program usually features a conversation with a guest. Playlists on the website (**www.earthsongs.net**). You can listen to *Earthsongs* on AIROS.

affinity groups

Indian Time
KUCR www.kucr.org

Thursday 5:30–6:30pm Pacific. Native American music, interviews with artists, political and cultural leaders, news on indigenous issues from around the hemisphere.

Indian Voices
KGNU www.kgnu.org

Sunday 3–4pm Mountain.

National Native News
WOJB www.wojb.org

Weekdays 4:30–4:35pm Central (repeated at 8:06am). Host: Bernadette Chato. News from the native perspective, emphasizing issues such as development, community and urban revitalization, environmental protection, health care, cultural preservation and education.

Native America Calling
www.airos.org

Monday–Friday 1pm Eastern. *Native America Calling* is the flagship program of AIROS, a live call-in program. The website also has archives of some past programs.

Native Sounds–Native Voices
www.airos.org

Host: John Gregg. A music service featuring traditional and contemporary Native American music.

Native Voices
KSUT www.ksut.org

Monday 10pm–midnight Mountain. From KSUT, which broadcasts from the Southern Ute Nation in the Four Corners area.

Notes from the Fourth World
KCSB www.kcsb.org

Wednesday 5–6pm Pacific. An exploration of indigenous issues around the world.

Our Americas
KAOS www.kaosradio.org

Sunday 5–6pm Pacific. Vigorous discussion of indigenous issues.

Oyate Ta Olowan–Songs of the People
KGNU
www.kgnu.org

Friday 12:30–1pm Mountain. Hosts: Jamie and Milt Lee. Native music from across the continent. A list of other stations that carry the program is available at **www.oyate.com/radio.htm**.

affinity groups

Raven Clan's Musical Potlatch
KNBA **www.knba.org**

Saturday 2–3pm Alaska. Host: Ryan Olson. This musical program focuses primarily on younger artists who deliver rap, hip-hop and the urban sounds of contemporary Native American music.

Renegade Radio
CKLN **ckln.sac.ryerson.ca**

Monday 8–10pm Eastern. Host: Brian Wright-McLeod. Music, culture, and politics from Toronto.

Tropical Rhythms
CHKG **www.fm961.com**

Saturday 9–11am Pacific. This music program on a multicultural radio station in Vancouver, B.C. centers on the music of Hawaii and the Pacific, but also includes quite a bit of music of First Nations peoples. In particular it is a good source of Metis and Inuit music.

View from the Shore
KAOS **www.kaosradio.org**

Sunday 6–8pm Pacific. Host: Gary Galbreath. Traditional and contemporary Native music.

Voices from the Circle
WLUW **www.wluw.org**

Sunday 9–10am Central. Hosts: Barbara Jersey (Menominee/Potawatomi) and Jim DeNomie (Bad River Chippewa). *Voices from the Circle* highlights Native news, music, issues, entertainment and storytelling from reservations and urban communities. You can also hear it on AIROS.

Latino/Chicano

¡Ahora Si!
KLCC **www.klcc.org**

Sunday 8:30pm–1am Pacific. *¡Ahora Si!* provides music, news and events information for the Latino community. The program is considered bilingual, but is delivered mostly in Spanish. Musical styles include traditional music of the Americas, African/Caribbean music, new songs, romantic music, and Latin rock.

Aqui Nuestra America
CKLN **ckln.sac.ryerson.ca**

Sunday 10:30–11:30am Eastern. News from Latin America and Spanish-speaking communities in Canada, in Spanish. The program also features region reports from sister radio stations across the Americas.

affinity groups

Chicano Headline News
KUCR **www.kucr.org**

Friday 5:30–6:30pm Pacific. Before twelve hours of music on *Radio Aztlan*, an hour of news about La Raza.

¡Corriente!
KGNU **www.kgnu.org**

Tuesday 7–9pm Mountain. Hosts: Ellen Klaver and T. Valladares. A bilingual program featuring music, news, poetry and features.

La Esquina Latina
WPKN **www.wpkn.org**

Sunday 2–6pm Eastern. Program with a strong social conscience that has aired on WPKN, in Bridgeport, Connecticut, since 1974.

Orgullo Latino
WMSE **www.wmse.org**

Noon–3pm Central, but archives can be listened to at any time.

Latino USA
KUT **www.kut.org**

Friday 3:30–4pm Central. Host: Maria Hinojosa. Half-hour weekly syndicated news, cultural and public affairs journalism show in English. You can also listen to this week's show directly from the *Latino USA* Web page (**www.latinousa.org**).

El Mensaje Del Aire
KAOS **www.kaosradio.org**

Saturday 1–5pm Pacific. All-Spanish language variety show from Olympia, Washington.

Nuestra Palabra
KPFT **www.kpft.org**

Tuesday 9–10pm Central. Latino writers talk.

La Nueva Voz
KUVO **www.kuvo.org**

Sunday 8–9am Mountain. Host: Jack Mudry. This program, which has been on KUVO continually since the station's inception in 1985, combines musica de contenido, commentary, interviews, and historical briefings on various countries in Latin America and the Caribbean, emphasizing issues of human rights, civil rights, and social justice.

Ondas en Español
WKAR **www.wkar.org**

(The AM Webcast, not the FM one.) Saturday and Sunday, sign-on (varies gradually from 6am in high summer to 8am in dead winter) to 9am, and 5:30pm to sign-off (varies from 5:30pm in January to 8pm in June). Host: Tony "Chayo" Cervantes.

affinity groups

Sabados Alegres
KFAI **www.kfai.org**

Saturday 11am–1pm Central. Host: Willie Dominguez. In addition to cultural affairs news for the Latino communities of Minneapolis and St. Paul, this program provides some lively Latino and Tex-Mex music.

¡Tertulia!
WFCR **www.wfcr.org**

Sunday 8pm–midnight Eastern. Host: Luis Meléndez. *¡Tertulia!* is the space where a dialog takes place among Spanish speakers and all those who are interested in Latin American culture and in the music, the arts, the language, and community issues for Latinos in New England.

A View from the Other Side
KNON **www.knon.org**

Monday 8–9am Central. Host: Francis Rizo, a community activist in Dallas.

Guatemalan

Voice of Guatemala
WLUW **www.wluw.org**

Friday 10:30–11am Central.

Puerto Rican

Puerto Rico
WJUL **wjul.cs.uml.edu**

Sunday 1–3pm Eastern.

African-American

African Kaleidoscope
KCSB **www.kcsb.org**

Sunday 5–6pm Pacific. Host: Shery-alle M. Williams. "An attempt to educate and inform the public regarding the false and stereotypical ideas surrounding peoples of Afrikan descent."

Black Introspectives
WPKN **www.wpkn.org**

Sunday 7–10am Eastern. Hosts: Ameni Harris, Leroy Williams, Eric Ford, and Samba. Features music, news, interviews, commentary, and listener call-ins.

affinity groups

Diasporic Music

CKLN **ckln.sac.ryerson.ca**

Thursday 8–10pm Eastern. Hosts: Norman Richmond and Kareen Glynn. The music and concerns of contemporary black culture, including international reports. From Toronto.

In Black America

KUT **www.kut.org**

Sunday 6:30–7pm Central. Host: John Hanson. Interesting stories from interesting guests.

Power Point

WUMB **www.wumb.org**

Sunday 9–10pm Eastern. National call-in program live from Washington, D.C.

RealBlackTalk

WMBR **wmbr.mit.edu**

Thursday 6:30–8pm Eastern. Boston cultural warriors deconstruct white supremacy and provide a forum for guest voices. See also the website (**www.realblacktalk.com**).

WLIB

www.wlib.com

Since its founding in 1972 by former Manhattan Borough President Percy Sutton, commercial station WLIB has been a forceful and controversial voice for the African-American community of New York. Former mayor David Dinkins hosts a chat show on Wednesday 10–11am Eastern.

Elders

A Touch of Grey

www.atouchofgrey.com

Weekdays 11am–noon Eastern. Host: Carole Marks. This syndicated program bills itself as a "talk show for grownups." Most programs feature an invited guest, and the guests include not only the expected experts on consumer affairs and gerontological health, but also, for example, the president of the Environmental Alliance for Senior Involvement on Earth Day. Available live and archived from the website.

Forever Young

CFUV **cfuv.uvic.ca**

Thursday 2–3pm Pacific.

affinity groups

Over 60/Sunny-Side Up
KVMR www.kvmr.org

Wednesday 1–2pm Pacific. Hosts: Bill and Anita Tuttle. An upbeat show abolishing myths and stereotypes about growing older, which also includes popular music of the 1930s–1950s.

Roundabout
5UV www.adelaide.edu.au/5UV

Weekdays 0400–0630 Greenwich. "Radio for the Third Age" – music, information and guests of interest to older people.

Disabled

Access Unlimited
KPFK www.kpfk.org

Tuesday 2–2:30am Pacific.

Disability Radio Worldwide
KGNU www.kgnu.org

Sunday 5–5:30pm Mountain.

SoundSight
KUT www.kut.org

Sunday 9am–noon Central. Hosts: Elaine Pinckard and Bob Branson. This program for the blind and reading impaired consists primarily of articles from newspapers and magazines read aloud.

Women

Amazon Radio
WPKN www.wpkn.org

First and Third Tuesdays of the month 6:35–10pm Eastern. Host: Pam Smith. Programming from a black lesbian feminist perspective.

At Heart
WCBU http://www.bradley.edu/irt/wcbu/

Mondays 6:30–7pm Central. Host: Suzette Boulais. Interviews with all kinds of women who discuss topics relevant to their work, family, health, career, and personal growth. Guests may be asked to discuss their views on a particular issue or concern, an area of their lives where they've had a change of heart, who they are "at heart" aside from their public persona, "lines they live by" that reflect their philosophy of life, or music that touches their hearts.

affinity groups

The Big Broadcast

CFUV **cfuv.uvic.ca**

Monday 9–10pm Pacific. Show on women and their music from Victoria, British Columbia.

CKUT

CKUT from Montreal streams several women's programs. (All times Eastern.)

▸▸ *Dykes on Mikes* alternating with *Ballades des Furies.* Monday 7–8pm.

▸▸ *XX Files* (a "technogyny" program). Wednesday 11:30am–noon.

▸▸ *Hersay*. Wednesday 6–7pm.

▸▸ *Venus*. Thursday noon–2pm.

Feminist Magazine

KPFK **www.kpfk.org**

Wednesday 7–8pm Pacific.

FemmeFM

KUT **www.kut.org**

Saturday 10pm–midnight Central. Host: Teresa Ferguson. Music show concentrating on music by women.

51%

WAMC **www.wamc.org**

Thursday 8–8:30pm Eastern. Hosts: Jeanne Kammer Neff and Mary Darcy. Features and interviews focusing on issues of particular concern to women, archived on the WAMC website for listening any time.

Girls' Night Out

WUKY **wuky.uky.edu**

Friday 8–9pm Eastern. Host: Anne Deck.

Mom-bo

KFAI **www.kfai.org**

Wednesday 11:30–noon Central, and archived on the Web page. Host: Nancy Oleson. "A mom's show with an attitude."

Morning Mommy Update

WPKN **www.wpkn.org**

Sunday 12:30–1pm Eastern. Host: Janet Golden. An alternative look at parenting from a woman's perspective, featuring interviews, readings, and occasional comments from Golden's kids.

Radio Active Feminism

CKLN **ckln.sac.ryerson.ca**

Sunday 11:30am –1pm Eastern. News, guest interviews, call-in forums, music, newsbytes, monthly features and special programming abound. The last Sunday of the month features the "Unheard Voice of the African Woman," the second Sunday features young women.

affinity groups

Riotgrrrl Hour
KUGS **www.kugs.org**

Sunday 10pm–midnight Pacific.

Sirens
KUGS **www.kugs.org**

Sunday 3–5pm Pacific.

Sister Sound
KAOS **www.kaosradio.org**

Sunday 10:30am–1pm Pacific.

Token Zone
CFUV **cfuv.uvic.ca**

Alternate Mondays 8–9pm Pacific. By and about women of color.

V is for Voice
KUGS **www.kugs.org**

Tuesday 6–8pm Pacific. Herstory lessons, interview and discussions "for and about the everyday goddess."

Wimmin Do This Every Day
KAOS **www.kaosradio.org**

Monday noon–2pm Pacific. "Blues, punk, folk, indigenous, spoken-word, and feminist rants and raves." (Right before KAOS's broadcast of *Wings* – see below.)

Wings – Women's International News Gathering Service
www.wings.org

A wide-ranging half-hour show. Recent programs have been devoted to anti-death penalty activist Sister Helen Prejean, disability rights in El Salvador, harassment and murder of gays in the U.S. military, and Australian aboriginal women's resistance to nuclear power. You can listen to *Wings* at any time directly from the Wings website, which also has a list of stations that carry the programming.

Woman's Hour
BBC Radio 4 **www.bbc.co.uk/radio4**

Monday 2200–2300 Greenwich. Topical interviews and discussion.

Women
United Nations Radio

The UN produces a syndicated show covering issues of women around the world. You can listen to the archives any time (in six different languages) at **www.un.org/av/radio/women**.

affinity groups

Womenfolk
KFAI www.kfai.org

Sunday 1–3pm Central. Host: Catherine Azora-Minda. Usually features interviews as well as the music, which is not just folk music, but anything from country to world beat.

Women Hold Up Half the Sky
KALX kalx.berkeley.edu

Saturday 11am–noon Pacific. Interviews, news, Bay Area calendar, and music.

Women in Music
WERS www.wers.org

Saturday 6–10am Eastern.

Women in Music
WOJB www.wojb.org

Friday 9–10am Central. Host: Laney Goodman.

Women's Music
KLCC www.klcc.org

Monday 9:30–11pm Pacific. Host: Nikki Breece.

Women on the Line
5UV www.adelaide.edu.au/5UV

Thursday 0330–0400 Greenwich. A national women's news and current affairs program from Australia.

Women on Waves
JOY joy.org.au

Monday 1100–1300 Greenwich. Alternative women's music program from a volunteer-operated community gay and lesbian radio station in Melbourne, Australia.

Women's Radio
WMSE www.wmse.org

Sunday 10:30pm–midnight Central – but you can listen to the archives anytime.

A Women's Show
KVMR www.kvmr.org

Monday 8–10pm Pacific.

WomenSpace
WFHB www.wfhb.org

Thursday 9–11pm Eastern. Women's music.

Women Writing for a Change
WVXU www.wvxu.org

Sunday 9–10pm Eastern (archived for listening any time).

affinity groups

Gay and Lesbian

Gay and Lesbian Stations

GayBC
www.gaybc.com

The world's gay and lesbian radio network. A full-time schedule of music, news, health, and conversation.

JOY
joy.org.au

JOY is a volunteer-operated, community gay and lesbian radio station in Melbourne, Australia. Its specialty shows include world music, dance music, soul, and comedy, along with substantial amounts of discussion and public affairs programming to serve the community.

Purple Radio
www.purpleradio.net

The club music of young gay London, live nightly from the city's dance floors.

Gay and Lesbian Programs

Around the Bend
95B **www.95bfm.com**

Sunday 0800–0900 Greenwich. Host: Stephen Oates. From the University of Auckland, in New Zealand.

Girls Night In
CFUV **cfuv.uvic.ca**

Alternate Mondays 8–9pm Pacific. News and issues of interest to queer women.

Homo Sapiens
Radio Campus Lille
www-radio-campus.univ-lille1.fr

Sunday 2000–21000 Greenwich. Program produced by the gay and lesbian magazine *Flamands Roses*. (In French.)

IMRU
KPFK **www.kpfk.org**

Monday 7–8pm Pacific. Gay and lesbian radio magazine.

affinity groups

Lavender Wimmin
WUSB **www.wusb.org**

Thursday 6–7pm Eastern. Hosts: Gail Polivy and Den Amato.

Lesbian and Gay Voices
KPFT **www.kpft.org**

Monday 8–10pm Central. Also try "After Hours" Sunday midnight–3am Central.

Lesbian Power Authority
KFAI **www.kfai.org**

Sunday 9–10:30pm Central.

This Way Out
Nationally syndicated half-hour gay and lesbian audio magazine. You can hear it on WLUW (**www.wluw.org**) Tuesday 9:30–10am Central.

Lambda Weekly
KNON **www.knon.org**

Sunday 1–2pm Central. Host: Dave Taffet. On the air weekly in Dallas since 1983.

Queer FM
CITR **www.ams.ubc.ca/citr**

Sunday 6–8pm Pacific. From Vancouver, British Columbia. Lots of human interest features.

Queerly Canadian
CFUV **cfuv.uvic.ca**

Tuesday 8:30–9pm Pacific.

Queer Radio
KJHK **kjhk.ukans.edu**

Sunday 3–5pm Central. Host: Buck Rowland. KJHK is the student station from the University of Kansas, so don't be surprised when the schedule changes.

Rainbow Radio
KSHU **www.shsu.edu/~rtf_kshu**

Sunday midnight–3am Central. From Huntsville, Texas.

Youth

Global Youth Speak
Trent Radio **www.trentu.ca/trentradio**

Monday 7:30–8pm Eastern. This program gives voice to Canadian youth.

affinity groups

In the Zone
WMBR **wmbr.mit.edu**

Sunday 2–4am Eastern. Teen call-in show, with musical interludes.

Street Soldiers

On many stations, for example WQNA (**www.wqna.org**). Sunday 10pm–midnight Central. Hosts: Joseph Marshall, Margaret Norris. *Street Soldiers* is a weekly call-in show for youth that focuses on the issues of violence, gangs, drugs, and teen pregnancy. The program began when rap performer Hammer approached KMEL with the concept for a show that focuses on social concerns. The show was dubbed *Street Soldiers* after a song on one of Hammer's albums. The first show aired in November, 1991 and was hosted by Hammer. In 1997, the show was syndicated and is now heard on 39 stations. *Street Soldiers* is sponsored by San Francisco's Omega Boys Club, which offers a variety of services for young people.

Ethnic Communities

Programs listed in this section are designed to serve ethnic communities by bringing them news and cultural programs primarily of interest to those communities. There is considerable crossover with two other sections of this book: World Music, which also contains music that can also sometimes be heard on the Ethnic Communities programs, and Foreign Language, which describes programs from the point of view of those primarily interested in language. The difference is that while the programs in this section may play Italian music, and may speak Italian, the programs are primarily designed to inform members of the Italian-American community about news and events of interest to their community, while World Music has programs more of interest for Italian music, and Foreign Language describes streams more useful to those interested in practicing their Italian listening skills.

Assyrian

The Assyrian Canadian Hour
CHRW **www.usc.uwo.ca/chrw**

Saturday 1–2pm Eastern. Host: Lazar Chimon. Music and culture from the Assyrian community.

affinity groups

Bulgarian

Bulgarian

WLUW **www.wluw.org**

Sunday 1–1:30pm Central. News updates and cultural reports from Chicago's Bulgarian community.

Cambodian

Cambodian

KNON **www.knon.org**

Sunday 4–5pm Central.

Somneang Khmer

WBRS **www.wbrs.org**

Saturday 10:30am–12:30pm Eastern.

Chinese

Victoria's Chinese Radio

CFUV **cfuv.uvic.ca**

Monday 11pm–1am Pacific.

Eritrean

Eritrean Community

KFAI **www.kfai.org**

Sunday 6–7pm Central. By, for, and about the Eritrean Community in Minneapolis; archived on the website for listening any time.

Ethiopian

Ethiopia

KNON **www.knon.org**

Sunday 3–4pm Central.

Ethiopian Hour

WLUW **www.wluw.org**

Sunday noon–1pm Central. Weekly coverage of Chicago's Ethiopian community.

affinity groups

Voice of Ethiopia
Sunday 8–9am Pacific.

CFUV **cfuv.uvic.ca**

Voice of Ethiopia
Sunday 4:30–6pm Central.

KFAI **www.kfai.org**

Francophone

C'est la Vie
CBC Radio One **www.cbc.ca**
Friday 11:30am–noon Eastern. Host: Bernard St-Laurent. A program – in English – about what it's like being French-speaking in Canada.

Franco Magazine
CFUV **cfuv.uvic.ca**
Wednesday 9–11pm Pacific; archived on the website. Covering issues of interest to the French-Canadian community, from Victoria, British Columbia.

Jacques-Antoine Jean

Haitian

Haitian WMBR **wmbr.mit.edu**
Sunday 8–10am. Eastern Host: Jacques-Antoine Jean. This is a radio show dedicated to the Haitian community. Featuring music and news from Haiti and community information. Interviews and reports issues related to women, immigration laws, health care, education, politics, and the current situation in Haiti.

affinity groups

Hmong

Hmong
Sunday 8–9am Central.

WMSE **www.wmse.org**

Hmong Wameng
Tuesday 8:30–10:30pm Central. Community news and information, Hmong rock, and traditional music, archived for listening any time.

KFAI **www.kfai.org**

Indonesian

Indonesia
Saturday 7–8am Pacific. This is the Indonesian hour on a multicultural station in Vancouver, B.C.

CHKG **www.fm961.com**

Italian

Italian
Sunday 11am–noon Pacific.

CFUV **cfuv.uvic.ca**

Jamaican

Jamaican
Sunday 10pm–midnight Eastern. Music and information of interest to Toronto's Jamaican community.

Fairchild Radio Toronto **www.fairchildradio.com**

Jewish

Arutz Sheva
News and views, often contentious, from Israel, in English, Hebrew, Russian, and French.

www.israelnationalnews.com

Jewish Moments in the Morning
Weekdays 6–9am Eastern. Host: Nachum Segal. Three hours of music, talk

WFMU **www.wfmu.org**

affinity groups

and information geared toward the Jewish community of New York and New Jersey. Archived on the website so you can listen any time.

Radio Judaïca   www.judaica.be
All-Judaica station from Belgium. (The website and most of the programming is in French.)

Khmer

Khmers in Minnesota   KFAI www.kfai.org
Monday 9:30–10:30pm Central. Archived on the website for listening any time.

Korean

Korean   Fairchild Radio Toronto www.fairchildradio.com
Weekdays 8–9am Eastern. Music and information of interest to Toronto's Korean community, in Korean.

Laotian

Laotian   KNON www.knon.org
Sunday 5–6pm Central.

Polish

Polish   CFUV cfuv.uvic.ca
Sunday 10–11am Pacific.

Portuguese

Portuguese   WRTC www.wrtcfm.com
Saturday and Sunday 9–11:30am Central.

affinity groups

Postal Portuguës
CFUV **cfuv.uvic.ca**

Saturday 8–9:30am Pacific. Hosts: Paulo Eusébio and Paulo Garrido. Music and news from the Portuguese-speaking world.

Russian

Polyot Chizha
WBRS **www.wbrs.org**

Friday 5–7pm Eastern. "The only Russian radio show in Boston."

Somali

Somali Voices
KFAI **www.kfai.org**

Sunday 4–6pm Central.

Thai

KNON
KNON **www.knon.org**

Sunday noon–1pm Central.

Yugoslavian

Yugoslavian
CFUV **cfuv.uvic.ca**

Sunday 9–10am Pacific.

affinity groups

Mega-Sites

Live365

Live365 is an amazing place. There are over *37,500* streams there. Some are the streams of actual radio stations, which found this economical means to get their sounds onto the Internet, and a few are put there by artists, record labels, or others with something to promote, but the vast majority are the work of individuals, who simply want to share their music. It's like the world's largest college station, only even more open. There's no program director, no application process, no format restrictions. So, unless it's patently obscene, libelous, or violating copyright laws, you can find it on Live365.

The site is categorized by genre. Click on the area of your interest, and you'll be presented with scores of streams to try. Because the site is wide open to all contributors, you might think the quality would be extremely uneven, but it's actually quite the opposite. For starters, everything sounds technically good. Unlike the complicated mixing board of a radio station, which can make even experienced veterans sound ham-fisted, the Live365 software is easy to operate and produces a quality sound. Most of the streams have only music, with no announcer, so another main source of unprofessionalism (the host droning on about what they ate for breakfast) is eliminated. While the stream is playing, you can see a playlist of what you're hearing. This is a great feature. Every radio station should have it.

The first time you try to listen to a Live365 stream, Live365 wants to know about your bandwidth, and then gives you an opportunity to download a Live365 player. Your alternative is to use RealPlayer. There's no reason not to just use the RealPlayer you already have. Note that Live365 is supported by advertising, so it will pop up ad windows at you.

Another useful feature of the Live365 site is ratings. When you look at the list of programs available, you can see how other listeners have rated the programs. There is also a listenership rating, which lets you see how many people have listened to the program. While the highest rated and most listened to shows may not be what interest you most, they're not a bad place to start.

ORANG Open Radio   www.orang.orang.org

ORANG is an open-access audio archive run by Berlin's Radio Internationale Stadt. As of press time it had 900 hours of contributed audio material. Its list of genres includes radio documentaries, "new music by and for the unusual," field recordings, and radio plays, in addition to numerous music streams covering everything from klezmer to dark ambient. With an open access policy the quality obviously varies greatly, but the site is particularly strong on experimental music, with contributions from the likes of Pan Sonic's Mika Vainio, Carsten Nicolai, V/VM, and labels like Mego and trente oiseaux.

Shoutcast   www.shoutcast.com

Shoutcast is Nullsoft's WinAmp-based streaming media site. (That is to say, its streams are based on the MP3 format.) Thousands of streams are available on the site, and you can search through them based on genre or other qualifications. However, note that, while the list of genres is longer than Live365's, just because a genre is in the list doesn't mean there are any streams to play. If you choose, say Opera/Vocal, for example, you might well find no programs of that genre to play. Unlike Live365, Shoutcast does not host the streams. What you listen to is coming directly from someone else's Shoutcast server. So it's not unusual to run into bandwidth limitations, drop-outs, etc. There is a wealth of audio material indexed at Shoutcast, and it is definitely worth your time to prowl through it.

Index Sites

There are many more radio stations on the Internet than are in this book. For example, at least half a dozen stations broadcast news from Taiwan, and this book lists only two. If you're interested in exploring further, the index sites listed below are the place to begin. Don't expect much in the way of descriptions, and do expect lots of links to stations you won't be able to receive.

BRS Radio Directory   www.web-radio.com
BRS Media is an e-commerce company targeting Internet radio. Their directory site is well organized and unusually thorough. Particularly useful is the international section, arranged by country.

ComFM   www.comfm.com
Over 4000 stations, broken down by country or genre. ComFM also has its own "1000%" channels: "1000% Blues," "1000% Dance," etc.

Internet Radio List   www.internetradiolist.com
Features a "station of the day" that is always worth a listen.

Live Radio   www.live-radio.net
Conveniently breaks out stations country by country around the world.

Radio Locator   www.radio-locator.com
This is a search engine from MIT. You choose search parameters from drop down lists (for example, genres or countries), and the search engine returns a list of stations that match.

Radio Now   www.radionow.co.uk
A guide to radio stations in the United Kingdom.

Radio-Stations.net   www.radio-stations.net
The world broken down first by region, then further by region or by format.

RealGuide   realguide.real.com/tuner
RealNetworks' guide containing 2500 stations, all in RealAudio format, naturally.

Rough Guides   www.roughguides.com/internet/
                                        directory/radio.html
Has an index of indexes, and a nice list of multi-stream sites.

index sites

Sunset Radio

www.sunsetradio.com

Heavily commercial site that breaks streams down into genres; useful for finding foreign stations. One drawback is that they want you to use Sunset Radio as your tuner, and so make it difficult for you to find the URL of the streams to which they point.

TV Radio World

www.tvradioworld.com

This site is really designed more as a guide to broadcasters. TV is more prominent than radio, shortwave is huge, and most of the stations displayed are not on the Net. It takes lots of clicks to get anywhere, but you can end up in some interesting places.

Windows Media Guide

www.windowsmedia.com/ mediaguide/default.asp

The Microsoft-maintained site indexing radio streams in the Windows Media format.

part three

becoming a
broadcaster

Becoming a Broadcaster

One great promise of the World Wide Web was that it would diminish the distinction between intellectual producers and consumers, between publishers and readers, between broadcasters and audience. By reducing the barriers to entry, the Web would let *everyone* be both reader and writer. Any prediction that a given technology will overturn deeply entrenched power relationships is probably naïve, and after a brief flurry of anarchy on the Web, well-capitalized organizations moved in to establish dominance. Half the page hits on the entire Web now go to a few commercial sites. But still, if the Web has not utterly overturned producer/consumer relationships, it has made it much easier for individuals to get a message out, and for small groups of people with common interests to find each other and share information, without the mediation of huge corporate gatekeepers. The Internet can do the same for radio. In most communities it requires millions of dollars to acquire a broadcast license. (The FCC and Congress recently rejected a proposal to allow many low-power community stations.) But it takes very little to start putting out your own Internet radio show.

The Easy Way to Get Started

Creating an Internet radio show does not necessarily require *hosting* an Internet radio stream yourself. If you wanted to put your own home page up on the Web, the straightforward way would be to install Web server software on a computer at your house, keep that computer connected to the Internet at all times, design your Web page, and write the code to implement it. Most people don't do this. Instead they let their Internet Service Provider (or some specialized service such as Geocities) host the site, and they employ some templates provided by the ISP that make putting together a Web page easier. Similarly, with Internet radio, to create your own Internet radio station requires a computer system connected to the Internet, and some audio server software, described below. But you don't have to set up your own station. Instead, you can employ the easy-to-use tools at some third-party sites to create your program, and leave it to them to stream your program for you. This is definitely the way to get started; to experiment without a major investment of time or money. Getting a program up on these sites can be a matter of minutes.

Live365

www.live365.com

Live365 is probably the easiest way for an individual to get a radio stream onto the Internet, which is why so many people do it. There are over 37,000 streams on Live365 right now. It is a great way to experiment. Before you undertake any of the more complex and difficult forms of Internet radio, you should try creating a Live365 show first. Doing so is free of charge.

Start by surveying the site. Listen to a bit of what is there. See what the headings are. Hear what other people have done. When you are ready to think about putting together a program, go to the Broadcasting section of Live365's site. There you will see detailed instructions. Live365 has two kinds of streams you can broadcast: Basic, a canned program you prepare in advance, and Live, streaming live from your own server. Obviously, the place to start is with a Basic stream. To create one, you will perform these steps:

❶ Sign up as a Live365 user, and get a name and password.

❷ If your music is not already in MP3 format, you need to convert it to MP3 format. Live365 has pointers to the tools with which to accomplish this. The easiest is probably MusicMatch Jukebox, available from **www.musicmatch.com.**

❸ Upload your MP3 files to Live365 using Live365 tools.

❹ Enter basic broadcast information: name your stream, pick your genres, etc.

❺ Enter playlist information. When listening to Live365, you can see on the screen the artist and song title information. Typing in this information is probably the most time-consuming part of the process, but it makes a huge difference to your listener.

❻ Review the rules.

❼ Hit Play. Congratulations, you're on the air!

It is worthwhile, particularly if you have questions, to take a look at the message boards where experienced Live365 participants give advice and answer technical questions.

To repeat, this is far and away the easiest way to get started. Who knows, it may very well satisfy your requirements and mean that you don't ever have to do anything more complicated.

the easy way to get started

Hosting an Internet Radio Stream

If you want to go beyond what Live365 offers, and have your own radio station on the Internet, you still do not need to host it yourself. You can contact a professional hosting service (the same ones that will host your website for a fee, or specialized radio hosting sites), and they'll do all the heavy lifting for you. They will, however, charge you money. Hosting your own signal from your home or office, on the other hand, can be essentially free, at least until you develop a significant audience.

System and bandwidth requirements

Server

A server is differentiated from a desktop computer by being beefier, having more memory, more storage, and a larger power supply. Specific requirements are detailed below, in the sections on the various streaming servers. At a minimum, assume 256 megabytes of memory. You will definitely need a server operating system: that is, Linux, Unix, Windows NT, but not Windows 98 or Millennium Edition.

You do not need a dedicated server for your audio stream. That is, you can continue to use the same machine for word processing, playing games, etc. There are, however, some caveats. First, the machine has to stay up all the time. It's rude to your users to reboot right in the middle of a song, and if you have a popular radio program, someone will always be right in the middle of a song. Think about how many times your favorite word processing program gets hung up, and you can see why you might not want to run it on your server machine. Similarly, if you're surfing the Web at the same time you're streaming, you can fight yourself for bandwidth, again being discourteous to your listeners.

Web Server

Any of the widely used Web servers will work with most audio streaming servers. Of course, if you use Microsoft's Windows Media Services, you need Microsoft's Internet Information Server.

Bandwidth

Even if you're just playing around for fun, don't try to host a streaming server on a dial-up line. It can be done, but you don't want to. At least a DSL-class connection to the Internet is required. The different servers have different requirements, but one good rule of thumb is that FM quality sound requires 44 Kbps per user. So 20 users would require 880 Kbps. Bare minimum sound quality can be provided using 20 Kbps per user. RealAudio will use up to 88 Kbps.

Note: you might want to check with your ISP to see the billing rate on your bandwidth. You may be paying $20 a month for bandwidth today, but only because you're not using very much. Open up 20 audio streams 24 hours a day, and you might have an unpleasant surprise when you get next month's bill.

Storage

Audio files can be big. Different formats create different file sizes, but if you estimate that six minutes of audio will equal one megabyte on your disk, you'll be in the ballpark.

hosting an internet radio stream

Shoutcast

www.shoutcast.com

Shoutcast makes it pretty easy for you to create and stream your own radio program, and then includes your stream in an index on their site.

The advantages of Shoutcast over RealSystem Server and Windows Media Services are several. Shoutcast is based on open standards, while the other two are proprietary. Most of all, Shoutcast is free. One disadvantage of Shoutcast is that it's not particularly easy to set up. If you are interested, check the Shoutcast website for details. It is more involved than setting up either Microsoft or RealNetworks' products. The other disadvantage of Shoutcast is that it traps you in somewhat of a radio ghetto. Most radio stations stream in Real or Windows formats, most users listen via RealPlayer or Windows Media Player, and streaming MP3 limits you and marks you as marginal. (Of course, that may be what you want.)

RealSystem Server

www.realnetworks.com

RealSystem Server Basic 8.0 Server is currently free for one year, for up to 25 simultaneous users. RealSystem Server Plus, which will handle more users, starts at $1995, and gets progressively more expensive as you add users. RealNetworks has other products designed to help you deploy streaming media as well, particularly RealProducer, used to create your programming.

RealSystem Server's strength is its cross-platform support. You can bring up RealSystem Server on: Linux, other Unixes (Solaris, AIX, HP-UX, FreeBSD, etc.), and Windows NT (2000, XP, etc.). However, note the curious omission of Macintosh.

The tutorials at **www.realnetworks.com/getstarted**, as well as the more technical ones at **www.realnetworks.com/devzone/tutorials**, will introduce you to the issues you need to think about.

Windows Media Services

www.microsoft.com/windows/windowsmedia

Microsoft Windows Media Services (current version 4.1) will, of course, work only on Microsoft operating systems. As this book goes to press, the oldest supported software is NT 4.0 with Service Pack 6 or later. With the release of Windows XP, Microsoft is expected to drop support for NT 4.0 and require at least Windows 2000. Note that on Windows 2000, Server or Advanced Server is required. That is, you can't install Windows Media Services on Windows 2000 Professional Workstation. If you do not already have a Windows 2000 Server license, you should look at the license fees before making plans to stream any audio. The server license fees are substantial. On the other hand, if you already own Windows 2000 Server, you already own the Media Services. After you have paid the license fees for Windows Server, there are no per-stream fees such as RealNetworks charges. This means that, while getting started is more expensive with Microsoft, for a sufficiently big installation Microsoft may be less expensive.

To install Windows Media Services on Windows 2000 Server, open the Control Panel, click on Add/Remove Programs, Select Add/Remove Windows Components, then click the Windows Media Services checkbox. (To install Windows Media Services on Windows NT 4.0, download the software from the website.)

Deploying Windows Media Services can present some complex configuration issues. One way to prepare for these is to watch the online training seminars available on the website.

hosting an internet radio stream

This seminar recommends memory of at least 256–512 MB, and more for on-demand content. There is a Windows Media Load Simulator you can use to test your system.

QuickTime Streaming Server and Darwin Streaming Server

Very high quality, completely free Internet radio servers are available from Apple: **www.apple.com/quicktime**. The QuickTime Streaming Server is the commercial software product from Apple for Macintosh. The Darwin Streaming Server is open source software for Mac, FreeBSD, Linux, Solaris, and Windows NT. These are the highest-quality servers; however, the fact that QuickTime is not used by many radio stations may push your choice in the direction of something that is.

Creating a Radio Show

A radio program can be just a collection of songs you like, arranged so that there are thematic or musical transitions from one to the next, forming a progression that makes sense and seems to lead the listener somewhere. While you're putting your program together, pay particular attention to the end of one song and the beginning of the next. Play the last few seconds of one song, then the first few seconds of the next, and check what they sound like where they meet.

The single technical characteristic that can make your program most quickly sound unprofessional is uneven sound levels. The worst thing to do is to make listeners turn up the volume to hear a quiet song you're playing too quietly, and then blast them with a loud song played too loudly. And it's hard to tell that you're doing it. The technology you use to put together your program, whether it's Live365, RealProducer, or whatever, will attempt to help you with this, and to save you from the most egregious unevenness. But you should still listen carefully to your own stream before sending it out to users, checking to be sure that the sound levels are even.

Now that listeners can see title and artist information for songs you're playing live on their screen, there is less need for you to come on and announce them. In the beginning, you will probably not want to try to announce at all. Announcing makes everything much more complicated and difficult. But adding a voice personalizes your show, and gives the listener someone to feel on the other end of the line. And radio can serve so many other purposes than just music.

Presenting your voice on radio requires some additional equipment, but it need not be a lot. Douglas Rowlett runs a poetry radio station (swc2.hccs.cc.tx.us/iradio/) out of his office in the English department at Southwest Houston Community College. He says it was fast and easy to get the station online. "This whole thing cost about $500 to put together," he says. "We have a $79 Radio Shack mixer and a $100 microphone."

When you get ready to begin announcing, you should practice with your microphone first. Record yourself. Play it back. It is extremely easy to sound like you're in a bathtub. It is easy to sound like you're spitting, or as though your consonants are exploding. Don't subject listeners to it until you get it right. Practice reading into the mike, telling a story, having an imaginary conversation. You will quickly observe that it is

347

creating a radio show

unnatural for humans to keep their heads in a stationary position while talking. When talking into a microphone, you do need to keep your head in a stationary position. Moving from left to right, up or down, or closer or further away from the microphone will have dramatic effects on your sound. You'll fade, boom, and sound terrible.

In addition to practicing microphone technique, you should also time yourself. What seems to you like a short, funny digression when you're delivering it can go on for an incredible length of time for your listeners. A stopwatch in front of you can help you detect when you're rambling. It is a natural human tendency, when you realize you're talking too much, to talk more, thinking you need to somehow climb out of the hole you have dug. Instead, when you find yourself in a hole, *stop digging*.

These issues should be manageable because you need not work live on Internet radio. Preparing a canned show, you can employ as many takes as it requires to get it right. The main way to improve your radio programming is to listen to it. Listen to it and re-cut it until you like it.

Attracting Listeners

If you are interested in attracting listeners (and be sure that you really want them before you invite them), the first thing to do is to tell them you're online. Email is a very effective way to do this. Do not spam anyone you don't know, who has not given you permission to email them. But anyone with whom you exchange email should be interested in the fact that you now have a radio program available. Then you should list your program with all of the index sites mentioned in the guide section of this book.

Search engines can also deliver listeners. Note that text on a website is easier for search engines to index than an audio stream. If you are broadcasting a stream of audio information on the topic of, say, Project Echelon, no search engine will detect it. If, however, you create a page of static text (no dynamic content), linking to your radio stream, with the term "Project Echelon" prominently displayed in the text, search engines will find you.

Links to your site are the single most effective way to show up in the huge noise of cyberspace. Spend some time looking for other websites that might be interested in your program. Email the webmasters of those sites and volunteer to exchange links.

Above all, consider your audience when creating your program. If all you want to do is hear the sound of your own voice, there is nothing wrong with that. But if you want to attract listeners, think more about your listeners' interests than your own. If you are truly interested in establishing yourself on the Net, the most reliable way to success is to establish yourself in a small niche. The wider the potential audience, the harder it is for a beginning individual to connect with it. Paradoxically, you can get more listeners by appealing to a narrower range of interests. It is unlikely that you can get much notice, for example, with yet another jazz stream. If you put together a truly excellent stream devoted to the work and influence of Charles Mingus, however, the many fans of Charles Mingus will find you.

How to Stay Legal

If you are in the United States of America, the law of the land is The Digital Millennium Copyright Act of 1998. The full text of this law is available at **http://lcweb.loc.gov/copyright/ legislation/hr2281.pdf**. Even with the massive amounts of campaign contributions America's elected representatives accept, it is hard to imagine how this legislation ever got passed. It's an insane mishmash of wacky regulations, seemingly intended to avoid the creation of free digital jukeboxes on the Web. Here are the basics:

❶ If you take requests, you must impose a *one-hour* wait before satisfying each request.

❷ In any three-hour period, play no more than *three* cuts from the same recording, and no more than *four* cuts by the same artist.

❸ Do not continually loop a program shorter than three hours in length.

❹ Do not publish your playlists in advance. Never say what you are *going* to play, only what you *have* played.

❺ Don't play any bootleg material, or material cleared for broadcast only in the U.S.

❻ Do not disable or remove any identifying information in the music you play.

While these rules might seem desirable to a record executive trying to make sure that Internet radio never becomes a substitute for purchasing the product, they were obviously not drafted by anyone who has ever worked in radio. Every radio station in America has violated these rules. Before the copyright police come to arrest you for playing four Bach pieces in the same hour of your Bach program, they'll have to bust a lot of other people first. Nevertheless, those are the rules.

If you play music on your radio program, you may also owe royalties to the organizations that license music. The courts in the United States are busy with arguments over what royalties Internet radio stations must pay record companies. The most recent rounds of this fight have been victories for the record companies, and some radio stations have even stopped streaming their signal until the economic impact becomes clear.

If you are in Canada, you may be bound by regulations of the Canadian Radio Television and Telecommunications Commission (C.R.T.C.) The main regulations prohibit:

» any abusive comment that, when taken in context, tends or is likely to expose an individual or group or class to hatred or contempt on the basis of race, national or ethnic origin, colour, religion, sex, age, or mental or physical disability;

» any obscene or profane language;

» any false or misleading news;

» any telephone interview or conversations, or any part thereof, with any person unless the person's oral or written consent to the interview or conversation being broadcast was obtained prior to the broadcast, or the person telephoned the station for the purpose of participating in a broadcast.

If you are in the United Kingdom, playing music on the Internet may subject you to claims from three bodies. The British Phonographic Industry (www.bpi.co.uk) claims that "If you don't hold the copyright to a sound recording you can't reproduce the work (or any clips and samples from it) or distribute it without permission. This means that you can't copy it on to a server, download it, upload it, stream it or play it over the Internet." The Performing Rights Society (www.prs.co.uk) says that "virtually all music-using sites operating from the UK should be licensed by PRS." The Mechanical Copyright Protection Society (www.mcps.co.uk) is also concerned.

index

index

355

index

index

d

index

index

index

k

index

index

index

index

q

r

index

index

index

U

V

W

index

index

index

Around the World

Alaska ★ Algarve ★ Amsterdam ★ Andalucía ★ Antigua & Barbuda ★ Argentina ★ Auckland Restaurants ★ Australia ★ Austria ★ Bahamas ★ Bali & Lombok ★ Bangkok ★ Barbados ★ Barcelona ★ Beijing ★ Belgium & Luxembourg ★ Belize ★ Berlin ★ Big Island of Hawaii ★ Bolivia ★ Boston ★ Brazil ★ Britain ★ Brittany & Normandy ★ Bruges & Ghent ★ Brussels ★ Budapest ★ Bulgaria ★ California ★ Cambodia ★ Canada ★ Cape Town ★ Caribbean Islands ★ Central America ★ Chile ★ China ★ Copenhagen ★ Corsica ★ Costa Brava ★ Costa Rica ★ Crete ★ Croatia ★ Cuba ★ Cyprus ★ Czech & Slovak Republics ★ Devon & Cornwall ★ Dodecanese & East Aegean ★ Dominican Republic ★ The Dordogne & the Lot ★ Dublin ★ Ecuador ★ Edinburgh ★ Egypt ★ England ★ Europe ★ First-time Asia ★ First-time Europe ★ Florence ★ Florida ★ France ★ French Hotels & Restaurants ★ Gay & Lesbian Australia ★ Germany ★ Goa ★ Greece ★ Greek Islands ★ Guatemala ★ Hawaii ★ Holland ★ Hong Kong & Macau ★ Honolulu ★ Hungary ★ Ibiza & Formentera ★ Iceland ★ India ★ Indonesia ★ Ionian Islands ★ Ireland ★ Israel & the Palestinian Territories ★ Italy ★ Jamaica ★ Japan ★ Jerusalem ★ Jordan ★ Kenya ★ The Lake District ★ Languedoc & Roussillon ★ Laos ★ Las Vegas ★ Lisbon ★ London ★

in Twenty Years

also lookout for our
phrasebooks, music guides
and reference books

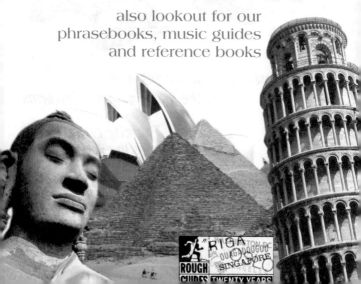

THE ROUGH GUIDE TO
Videogaming
2002

Informed, independent advice
on the major gaming platforms

Punchy reviews
of the top games in every genre

Hints, tips and cheats
to crack each game

Directories
of the best Web sites and gaming resources